AF539846

LABOUR MIGRATION IN AGRICULTURE SECTOR

A SOCIO-ECONOMIC ANALYSIS

LABOUR MIGRATION IN AGRICULTURE SECTOR

A SOCIO-ECONOMIC ANALYSIS

By

Dr. Anil Kumar Verma *Ph.D.*
Associate Professor
Deptt. of Economics
Govt. Brijindra College
Faridkot

DISCOVERY PUBLISHING HOUSE PVT. LTD.
NEW DELHI-110 002

Published by:
Tilak Wasan

DISCOVERY PUBLISHING HOUSE PVT. LTD.
4831/24, Ansari Road, Prahlad Street
Darya Ganj, New Delhi-110002 (India)
Phone: +91-11-23279245, 43764432
Fax: +91-11-23253475
E-mail: parul.wasan@gmail.com
discoverypublishinghouse@gmail.com
info@discoverypublishinggroup.com
web: www.discoverypublishinggroup.com

***First Edition:* 2011**
ISBN: 978-81-8356-793-0

Labour Migration in Agriculture Sector
A Socio-economic Analysis

Printed at:
Shree Balaji Art Press
Delhi

Preface

Economy in the present world—be it developed nations or developing ones—is in a state of uncertainty and depression. It has disturbed international relations, corporate world, trade, industry, agriculture and socio-political organisations over the world. In the present era of urbanisation, globalisation and liberalisation, the study of migration of human beings has become a complex phenomenon. It has brought about structural transformation in the economic set up of both the developed and developing countries. The process of migration needs to be analysed in a broader perspective because it involves the movement of the human labour of a country within and across national and international boundaries.

India is a developing nation with an object to join the category of developed countries in the near future. All the states of India are contributing to the national development. Punjab is one of the prosperous states of India; it is popularly known as "the food basket and granary of India. The development of Punjab economy is mainly based on its agriculture. The Green Revolution in the late 1960s brought general prosperity and increased household incomes. The age-old methods and implements of farming gave way to mechanisation. The adoption of mechanised farming and introduction of high yielding varieties (HYV) necessitated timely sowing and harvesting operations; thus creating a new demand for more labour. This compelled the Punjabi farmers to look for migratory labourers from across the other states. Thus, the increased demand for labour in agricultural sector strengthened the process of labour migration in the state. Over time, migrant labour became institutionalised in Punjab. Now, a significant proportion of Punjab's agricultural labour force consists of migrant labour from Bihar and Uttar Pradesh. Migrant labourers have not only become an important part of Punjab's' economy, but an important constituent of our society.

The migrants have made a significant contribution in Punjab but their migration has created some problems too. The influx of the migrants in Punjab and their settlement here, the over dependence of Punjabis on them and the sore relationship between the Punjabi labour and migrants have led to many socio-economic and cultural problems. All efforts have been made to present a socio-economic analysis of labour migration in the agricultural sector of Punjab in this book.

This book deals with the socio-economic perspective of the agricultural labour migration, causes of migration, impact of agricultural labour migration on wages and employment, income and savings and changes experienced by the migrant agricultural labour in their consumption, social and cultural behaviour. It also analyses the cultural, social, economic interaction and the degree of homogeneity and heterogeneity between the migrant and the local agricultural labourers.

The locale of the study is the state of Punjab. The four stage random sampling technique has been used to select the sample for the study. These four stages are: District, block, village, the respondents (migrant agricultural labourers, local agricultural labourers and the farmers). The field work for the research work was conducted in three districts i.e. Ludhiana—the district having maximum concentration of migrants, Hoshiarpur—the district having less concentration of migrants and Faridkot, having least concentration. All data and information were collected from the selected respondents on the specially structured pre-tested schedule through personal interview method.

The book offers new findings regarding the migratory agricultural labourers. It points out that the socio-economic background of the migrant agricultural labourers have made an impact on the labour supply curve, labour productivity status and assimilation with locals. The state-wise classification of migrant agricultural labourers shows that majority of the migrant agricultural labourers *i.e.* 60.80 per cent belonged to Bihar, followed by 18.52 per cent from U.P. The obvious reason for migration is poverty and lack of employment opportunities in their native states. 74.07 per cent of these labourers belong to the age group of 15-35 years. Out of this, 47.53 per cent of them fall in the age of schooling *i.e.* 15-20 years. The average age of the migrant agricultural labourers in Punjab was found to be 18.60 years. About three-fourths (72.53 per cent) of these labourers are illiterate. 68.21 per cent of them are married and 82.35 per cent of them have wives living in their native places. The majority of these labourers *i.e.* 58.66 per cent belonged to scheduled castes whereas in Punjab 94.05 per cent are from scheduled castes. About 55 per cent of the migrant agricultural labourer's were under debt. About 41.36 per cent migrant agricultural labourers came to Punjab at the instance of their friends, followed by 25.93 per cent at the instance of their relatives. About 96 per cent of the migratory labourers use train as a means of transport.

The book also comes out with the findings on wage pattern, working hours of these labourers and a comparative analysis has been made with the working conditions and wage pattern of the locals.

The book also presents the point of view of the local agricultural labourers about the migrant agricultural labourers. A feeling of bitterness and uneasiness persists among them. The migrant agricultural labourers suffer ill-treatment and step-motherly treatment at the dispensaries and hospitals and other public places. However they have accepted socio-cultural way of Punjabi life, adopted the convenient names, local food habits and Punjabi language. 76.23 per cent of these labourers reported their relations with locals as 'good', whereas 54.65 per cent of the local agricultural labourers have reported their relations with migrant agricultural labourers as 'good'.

Since the migrant agricultural labourers have become a necessity for Punjab, certain steps have been suggested to ameliorate their condition by providing them various facilities for better living. The Government should try to eradicate poverty and institute a separate cell for migratory labourers at the secretariat level to solve any dispute, grievances and problems concerning these labourers.

It has been my humble endeavour to highlight the socio-economic implications of labour migration in the agricultural sector of Punjab. It will certainly open new avenues of research. It will move the Punjab Government to take suitable steps and pass legislations to keep up the pace of agricultural development.

It is my proud privilege to place on record my deep sense of gratitude, invaluable help, kind patronage and able guidance given to me by my learned mentor and guide Dr. Gian Singh, Professor, Department of Economics, Punjabi University, Patiala. He has been the guiding spirit and has expertly shepherded the work with his immense talent, creativity and personal interest to help me to accomplish this mammoth task. I feel unable to adequately express in words the sense of gratitude I feel towards my co-supervisor Dr. Balwinder Singh, Professor, Department of Economics,

Punjabi University, Patiala for his constant encouragement, inspiration, help, able guidance and counselling during the course of completion of this work. I acknowledge my heartiest thanks to Dr. O.P. Miglani, Dr. Surinder Singh, Dr. J.R. Gupta. Dr. Vishwa Mittar, Dr. Gurbachan Kaur Bhatia and Dr. Ramesh Kumar Bansal for the keen interest they have shown in this study.

I can never repay for the understanding, love and care showered on me by my better half Mrs. Sudha Raj. My children Mr. Ankit Verma and Subah Verma helped me in processing the raw data. My heartfelt gratitude goes to my father whose blessings helped me to complete this project.

Anil Kumar Verma

Contents

Introduction

THE SETTING

Migration of human beings is a complex phenomenon. Ever since the dawn of human civilisation, the growing uneven and imbalanced pattern of economic, social, political and cultural development of various parts and regions of the earth has initiated the migration of people from one place to another. In the present era of globalisation and liberalisation, the study of migration has become one of the most dynamic aspects of human beings. It has brought about structural transformations in the economic set-up of both the developed and the developing countries. Now-a-days, the process of human migration is analysed in a broader perspective. It is not only confined to shifting of rural poor families to urban areas but also from one region to another. In a broader framework, the process of migration involves the movement of the whole of the population of a country within and across national and international boundaries.

Economists, sociologists, geographers, demographers and social-psychologists have attempted to discuss and analyse the concept of migration in detail. Although their approach of discussing and analysing the concept differs significantly, yet at the final stage of scientific research, they nodded their heads together affirmatively. Scholars of various streams are of the opinion that the population of a region or area is largely influenced by economic, social, psychological, demographic and geographical factors, so it becomes impossible to understand the phenomena of migration without their cross examination. The migration phenomenon cannot be understood without analysing the dynamics and interplay of economic, demographic, social, socio-psychological and many other factors (Tarver, 1961).

The study of population is a multi-dimensional. As compared to other attributes of population, migration has attracted maximum shades of meaning. In this context, Jones (1981) has indicated that of the three components of population change, migration is the most difficult to conceptualise and measure. The difficulties in conceptualising and measuring the phenomenon of migration arise because, unlike fertility and mortality, migration is not just an unequivocal biological event but a physical and social transaction (Zelinsky, 1971).

The term 'migration' generally refers to the movement of people, especially of whole groups from one place, region or country to another, particularly with the intention of making permanent settlement in a new location. The geographers have emphasised the time and space element for the construction of the theory of migration. In this context, Smith (1960) has explained that the term 'migration' generally refers to all movements of population in physical space with the assumption, more or less implicit, that a change of residence or domicile is involved, excluding the movements of '*nomads*' and those of the migratory labourers who do not stay for longer periods. Hence, all types of spatial mobility of population can't be regarded as migration. Lee (1966) defined migration as a change of residence, permanent or semi-permanent, involving an origin, a destination and an intervening set of obstacles, which always include distance. This broad connotation of the term 'migration' poses some problems while examining the various types of cyclical migration. For example, intra-urban residential mobility or intra-village residential mobility cannot be considered as migration. Thus, migration cannot be considered as a mere shift of people from one place of residence to another (Gosal, 1961). For this, the term 'migration' has been differentiated from commuting and transhumance. The term 'commuting' refers to the movement of people from place of residence to place of work and back either daily or weekly; transhumance refers to the seasonal movement of the people up and down the hills along with their herds; the term 'migration' refers to only those changes of residence that involve a complete change and readjustment of the individual at another place. Perhaps due to the above cited reason that Mangalam (1968) wrote, "Migration is a relatively permanent moving away of a collectivity, called migrants, from one geographical location to another preceded by decision-making on the part of the migrants on the basis of hierarchically ordered set of valued ends and resulting in changes in the interactional systems of the migrants".

The phenomenon of migration has also been widely discussed and analysed, both by economists and sociologists. In the economic sense, a person migrates only if he/she is relatively benefited by migration from one region to another (Kamble, 1983). Economists, primarily place migration in a resource allocation framework because it treats migration as a means of promoting efficient resource allocation and because migration is an activity which requires resources. Migration which involves costs as well as benefits is treated as an investment, increasing the productivity of human resources (Sjaastad, 1962). Migration will take place only if the perceived benefits of the migrants are weighing more than the costs of migration. In a sociological study of Jewish community, Eisenstades (1954) has explained migration as physical transition of an individual or a group from one society to another. This transition usually involves abandoning one social setting and entering another and permanent one. But these views of Eisenstades failed to explain the psychology of individuals or groups formulating plans for a physical transition back to the destination or donor society. His definition does not consider establishing social relationship between the place or society of origin and destination of the migrants (Sinha, 1980). In psychological terms, migration primarily means movement of people from one place or location to another, which is not of a casual nature, as a visit or a tour. Migration is necessarily a pre-emptive move; it is the survival instinct that drives humans to seek better prospects (Sundari, 2005). Thus, migration is an independent human activity which will thrive through cross fertilisation of geographic, demographic, economic, social and psychological and many other factors.

Migration involves a large spectrum of movement from commuting or temporary absence of home location for a couple of days to seasonal migration or permanent relocation (Afsar, 2004). But the term 'migration' should be clearly distinguished from commuting, transhumance and mobility. Mobility represents movements within boundaries; in migration people move across boundaries. Migration expresses multidirectional functional relationship between pre-emptive move of human beings and space, distance, time and motivation. Gould and Prothero (1975) consider space and time as the essential dimensions of population migration. The classification of population migration may be charted on next page.

On the basis of space element, migration may be broadly classified as internal and external (international) migration. India has experienced both, though at a smaller scale as compared to other countries of the world. The movement of population that takes place within the territorial jurisdiction of a country is termed as internal migration, whereas the movement of population from one country to another, across the international borders, is called external (international) migration. Internal migration comprises both intra-state and

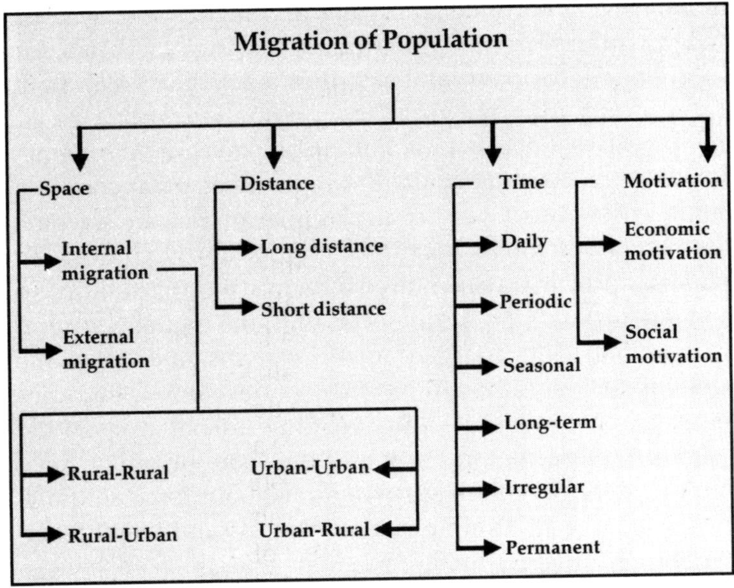

inter-state movement of the people. Indian population has been considered as one of the least mobile population of the world. Zachariah (1964) has supported this view point in his study of inter-state migration in India between 1902 and 1931. Amin (1974) has classified internal migration of labour into: rural-to-rural, rural-to-urban, urban-to-urban and urban-to-rural migration. Rural-to-urban migration among labour is more pronounced in the developing countries. In developing countries, the migratory tendencies among the people are generated by the push and pull factors. In the 'push and pull' hypothesis, there are certain factors which are supposed to push persons away from the area of destination (Thomas, 1941). High density of population in rural areas acts as a push-factor of the rural areas and urban industrial development acts as a pull-factor for urban areas. In rural areas, appalling poverty, unbearable unemployment, low and uncertain wages, uneconomic holdings, poor facilities for education, health, recreation and other services work as the push factors. By comparison, the pull of urban areas may include better employment opportunities; regular and higher wages, fixed working hours, better amenities of living, facilities for education and socio-cultural activities (Chandna, 1986). Both poor and rich from the rural areas migrate to urban areas. Poor migrate out of economic compulsion to earn their living, while the rich migrate for the desire to create great comforts in their life. In brief, rural to urban migration is an outcome of inter-play of forces hostile to comfortable living in the villages and of the availability of lucrative opportunities in urban areas (Raju, 1989). However, with the unplanned rural to urban migration, a large number of slums emerged in the industrial towns. Although big cities in developing countries are turning into industrial hubs, yet these are not in a position to support a sizeable proportion of the share of labour force from the vast reservoir of surplus rural labour force. In India, where the large cities are the recipients of rural migrants on a large scale, a large number of slums emerge in such cities (Gosal and Krishan, 1975). Slums of such cities are unable to provide the basic amenities of life to the migrants. It is the pull of better employment opportunities and wage rate that induces them to live in such sub-standard urban slums. Poor economic condition of the rural people pushes them to live in these worst conditions.

Migration from rural to rural areas takes place among the people who are primarily engaged in agricultural activities, mining and construction work etc. Normally, rural-to-rural migration originates from crowded areas of low productivity to sparsely populated areas experiencing large scale development activities. Such a migration may be for longer distances and may be of permanent nature. An outstanding feature of rural to rural migration is that it is predominated by female migration. Studies of Zachariah (1964), Agarwal (1968), Premi (1978), and Kumar and Sharma (1979) have clearly explained that the pre-dominance of female migrants is due to the prevalence of patrilocal residence after marriage.

Inter-urban migration is more common in the most developed countries of the world today. In developed countries where most of the population already lives in urban areas, the high rates of inter-urban migration of skilled and professional persons are mostly governed by the economic factors; with a view to further improve their economic conditions. Intra-urban migration is also operative in less developed countries but of a smaller magnitude. The big industrial urban centers attract migrants from small towns and cities to absorb them in industries. The vacuum caused in small urban areas is filled by the immigrants from the nearby rural areas. Thus, in developing countries, this migration forms a part of what is commonly known as 'Step-migration' (Chandna, 1986).

Urban to rural migration is relatively less common as compared to other types of migrations discussed above. Over-congestion, high cost of living, and developed and efficient network of transport and communication have led to this type of migration, which is usually of short distance. This type of migration has led to rural-urban-rural migration. Sinha (1980) has supported the idea that a large number of rural urban migrants try to maintain some links with their villages of origin. These people are often considered as 'urban residents, loyal to rural home'.

External or international migration refers to the movement of the population from one country to another across the international borders. International migration may be voluntary or involuntary. The involuntary international migration or refuge contains two main elements: (i) persons who have left their own nation; and (ii) people fleeing from one part of a national state to another, finding protection in national legal norms. This also includes displaced persons, expelled persons and escapees. The problems of refugees are mostly politically motivated and have been taking place since ancient times, although floods and other natural disasters also force people to move (Sinha, 1980). The partition of India and Pakistan in 1947 was accompanied by a large scale involuntary migration of population from India to Pakistan and vice versa.

The 'brain-drain' or the outflow of highly qualified professional labourers is the migration of a particular group of people only. However, sometimes the more intelligent people succeed at home and the less intelligent people seek their future elsewhere; on the other hand, the more intelligent may respond first to any stimulus to migrate; while the duller remain behind (Peterson, 1968). In most advanced countries which have experienced economic growth are facing shortages of qualified and skilled labourers which can't be met overnight. Hence, the demand for qualified labourers exceeds the supply, which raises the level of remuneration in these occupations and attracts immigrants with scarce qualifications. This is even more apparent when better working conditions, research facilities etc. are also provided. This has given rise to the so-called, 'brain-drain' from developing countries to developed areas (Beijer, 1967). Highly educated and skilled professionals from India have migrated to developed countries such as U.S.A., U.K., Canada, Australia and some other countries leading to serious brain-drain problem.

In India, most of the immigration has taken place from neighbouring countries, mainly from Nepal and Bangladesh. The immigrants are mostly settled in Assam and Uttar Pradesh. Immigration in India is mainly from Asian countries followed by Europeans, Africans, Americans and Australians.

The process of human migration is a complex phenomenon and the factors associated with it are difficult to trace. The factors affecting migration vary from area to area, and from person to person. Scholars studying migration have attributed 'economic and non-economic' reasons for migration. But virtually all movements of human beings are oriented for economic purposes. Economics is concerned with the production and allocation of something called wealth, which is socially defined as having a measure of utility and a measure of scarcity (Bartle, 1971). The flow of migration is influenced not only by geographical distance but is affected also by the availability of opportunities at the point of destination, intervening opportunities and the influence of competing migrants (Stouffer, 1960). The factors associated with the process of migration have been broadly classified by Lee (1966) as: factors connected with the place of origin; factors connected with the place of destination; intervening obstacles and personal factors.

Factors associated with the place of origin and those associated with the place of destination differ significantly from each other. Bogue (1959) made an exhaustive list of 25 migration stimulating situations, 15 factors for choosing a destination and 10 socio-economic conditions which can stimulate or retard mobility among population. Factors for choosing a destination include cost of moving, presence of relatives or friends, living with them, employment offers, physical attractiveness of community, physical environment, amenities, population composition, social employment facilities, special assistance, subsidies, information reputation and lack of alternative destinations (Sinha, 1980). Besides the factors associated with the area of origin and those associated with the area of destination, there are personal factors which include age, sex, marital status, level of education, income, land holdings, occupation, previous exposure to urban areas and such behavioural variables as attitude towards risk, aspiration level, value and belief systems and attachment to rural society (Rhoda, 1979). Migration can therefore, be seen as a system linking origins and destinations, in which not just people but money and goods also flow (Skeldon, 2002).

In every area, there are factors which push individuals away from origin as well as those which pull them towards destination. Push factors are those that operate in the area of out-migration and compel the people to move to other areas. Pull factors are those that operate in the area of in-migration and attract the people to these areas (Chandna, 1986). In some areas, both push and pull factors operate simultaneously. It is because of this that sometimes it becomes difficult to differentiate between push and pull factors. On the basis of these push and pull factors people leave their origin and choose new destinations. There are several factors in an area that attract more people to it and there are innumerable factors that repel the people from it. Lee (1970) designates the former category of factors as positive factors and the latter category as negative factors. The depressed economic conditions in an area generate tendencies for out-migration whereas the conditions reflecting economic prosperity offer greater employment potential and attract in-migrants (Chandna, 1986). Among the economic factors which stimulate the process of migration all over the world are the development activities both in industrial and agricultural sector which generate employment opportunities at the place of destination. While distinguishing economic factors, Gosal and Krishan (1975), Premi (1976) and Mehta (1971) have also emphasised that people move for more gains and better living from the areas of less economic opportunities towards fast developing areas. Zachariah (1969) and Gupta and Laishly (1975) have identified poverty as the motivating factor for migration. Further, emphasising the role of economic conditions in migration, Sovani (1966) and Saxena (1977) have opined that both rich and poor were almost equally prone to migration; the rich for better comfortable life, while the poor due to economic hardships. Then it can be asserted that migration is essentially an economic phenomenon (Gill, 1984).

Apart from economic factors, social and demographic factors are equally important. Migratory movements today are no longer expression of a trend towards equalisation of economic density (Kulischer and Price, 1963). Manpower today goes where not only economic but also social opportunities are better. Social customs, religion, caste, culture and traditions generate migration. As a social custom, females move from the place of origin to the place of destination (in-laws) at the time of their marriage. The desire for social upliftment, cultural contact, government policies and socio-economic factors are important in shaping the direction and magnitude of migration. Socio-economic conditions affecting mobility are major capital investments, major business recessions or fluctuations, technological changes, changes in economic organisations, provisions for social welfare, migration propaganda facilities, regulations affecting migration, living conditions and levels, tolerance of minorities of all types and migration policy (Sinha, 1980). For the vertical migration to raise their social status, people belonging to poor socio-economic status are more mobile. In a society like the nineteenth century Britain, the people having lower social status were the most mobile (Pooley, 1979). However in the modern world, people having better economic status, education and technical know-how have the greater propensity to migrate, so as to secure not only their own future but also that of their next generation. Ladinsky (1967), however, showed that not all higher status groups have high rate of spatial mobility. Doctors, lawyers, engineers and architects who require appreciable investments and several years to build contacts with their clients, do not move easily. Information network is another factor which widens the scope of human mobility. Thus, migration generates further migration signifying the role of information network and spatial interaction in stimulating more of migration (Chandna, 1986). Skeldon (2002) emphasised that migrants are among the more innovative, better-educated and dynamic members of any community.

Regional disparities, population pressure, age and sex are some of the determinant demographic factors which also play a decisive role in the propensity to migrate. The mobility of population is related to the age group of the people. It has been observed that teenaged population and people in early 30s are more mobile than the older people. In fact, the studies relating to both developed and the developing countries have uniformly corroborated the young age of the migrants (Kaur, 1999). Zachariah (1964) observed an excess adolescents and adults among the migrants as compared to the general population. Similar were the views of Hamsaleelavathy (1970) and Caldwell (1968) who found that the age at the time of initial migration to the towns (in Ghana) was between 15 and 25 years. The age characteristics of migrants have also been analysed by Oberai and Singh (1981) in their ILO studies of migration to Ludhiana.

It has also been observed that sex and marital status are also important determinants of migration. This fact was supported by Kothari (1980) and Zachariah (1974). The increasing migration participation of women has been closely associated to the increase in education and with the rapid development of urban-based services (Skeldon,). As migration is almost entirely a youth phenomenon, majority of the migrants at the time of first migration used to be unmarried. The marital status of the migrants was unmarried (Rahman, 1999). This view was supported by Nair (1986) in his study conducted during the late 1970s in Kerala and concluded that migrants of less than 25 years of age were almost entirely unmarried.

As regards the distance between the place of origin and place of destination, Zachariah (1964) pointed out that in most of the developing countries; short distance migration was common, while western countries specialised in long distance migration. In this context, Skeldon (1977) held that long distance migration was characterised mainly by urban to urban moves, whereas rural to rural migration was dominated by short distance.

Laws are like lamp-posts which help to shed light on the basis of which certain theoretical models can be put into shape. As human beings are of diverse nature, so is the diversity in the process of migration. Human beings are highly dynamic and change their spatial and temporal dimensions with unusual rapidness, so it becomes difficult, rather impossible, to build a concrete law/model which may streamline the process of migration. Broadly classifying, models may be of two types: deterministic models and probabilistic models. The deterministic models establish the functional relationship between the problem (migration) and its explanatory variables, whereas the probabilistic models have been specifically designed to forecast migration flows. Economists, sociologists, demographers and geographers have tried to explain both types of models of migration flow.

Specifically, the laws of human migration are governed by economic growth and social development. The first theoretical attempt to formulate the laws of migration was made by Ravenstein (1889). He conducted an empirical study into the extent and mode of migration in the United Kingdom, using the census data of 1871 and 1881 and translated it into the first ever format of the laws of migration. The basic conclusion derived from the investigation by Singh (1990) was "Migration means life and progress, a sedentary population, stagnation". Ravenstein suggested that economic motives, of all other motives of human mobility have the primacy in governing the magnitude of migration. The choice of destination is governed by the distance-decay function and the long distance migration generally goes by the preference to the great centers of commerce and industry. The author further observed that the natives of towns are less migratory than those of the rural parts of the country. The author also advocated that human migration steps with technological advancements resulting in the means of transport and communication and is positively correlated with the growth of manufacture and industry. Apart from the desire to better themselves materially, "Oppressive laws, heavy taxation, unattractive climate and uncongenial social surroundings" etc. are the other causes that dominate the currents of migration.

The laws of migration forwarded by Ravenstein were of considerable simplicity and stood the test of time. Pryor (1969), in his study about Malaysia and other countries, found these laws to be largely valid. Zipf (1946), regarded migration as the function of distance. The greater distance required greater effort to overcome the hurdles and hence reduces the tendency of migration. Foot and Milne (1984) stressed that the comprehensive analysis of migration depends not only on the distance alone, but in their gravity model they opined that migration also depends on other variables such as real wage rate and unemployment rates. Similarly, Stouffer (1940) in his 'Intervening Opportunity Model' suggested that apart from distance, the opportunities such as employment, environment, housing, wage rates are the real source of attraction of the migrants.

Lewis (1954) in his article titled, "Economic Development with Unlimited Supplies of Labour" linked the process of migration to the level of economic growth. Later on, his views were modified, formalised and extended by Fei and Ranis (1963). According to Lewis, the developing economies are dualistic in nature, comprising a 'Capitalistic Sector' and a 'Subsistence Sector'. Output per head is lower in the subsistence sector than in the capitalistic sector. In the subsistence sector of the economy, "the marginal productivity of labour is negligible, zero or even negative". The supply price of labour is a wage at the subsistence level. But the wage level in the capitalistic sector of the economy is higher, which is because of the higher cost of living in it and because of the psychological cost of transferring from an easy going way of life of the subsistence sector to the more regimented and urbanised environment of the capitalistic sector. In this dualistic economic set-up, the process of migration begins from the low productivity subsistence sector to the high productivity capitalistic sector and continues till the unlimited supply of labour at the subsistence wage rate exceeds the demand at this price.

Sjaastad (1962) developed the cost benefit analysis of human migration, which involves costs as well as benefits. Migration took place only if the perceived benefits arising out of it weigh more than the costs involved in the process. He has also suggested that 'age' is an important variable influencing migration and must be taken into account. Further to examine the impact of migration on income differentials, gross migration is a relevant concept.

Lee (1966) formulated a broad based theory of migration. Although the author is conscious of the fact that the exact set of factors which impel or prohibit migration can't be specified easily, yet identified the four types of factors which influence the decision to migrate and the process of migration. These four factors are connected with the origin, destination, intervening obstacles and personal factors. He termed 'distance' as the intervening obstacle in the process of migration. The personal factors include, "age, sex, marital status, level of education, income, landholdings, occupation, previous exposure to urban areas and such behavioural variables as attitude towards risk, aspiration level, value and belief systems and attachment to rural society". These sets of factors and obstacles will be subjective in nature and will vary according to life cycle, socio-economic and personality characteristics of individuals. Lee conceptualised a number of hypotheses about the volume of migration, the development of stream and counter stream and the characteristics of migrants. The author concluded with a note of caution that "many expectations will be found, since migration is a complex phenomenon.

Wolpert (1975) proposed a behaviouristic model of human migration in which he suggested that for migration models, the focus should be on the behaviour of individuals rather than on the distance and the economic motives of human beings.

Todaro (1969) presented his model of labour migration in the research article titled, "A Model of Labour Migration and Urban Unemployment in Less Developed Countries", to explain the apparently paradoxical relationship of accelerated rural-urban migration in the context of rising urban unemployment. The author considered migration as a selective process and is influenced by economic and non-economic factors which are varied and complex. However, Todaro suggests that migration is primarily an economic phenomenon and postulates that a potential migrant will proceed in response to expected income rather than actual income. The fundamental premise is that migrants consider the various labour market opportunities available to them in the rural and urban sectors and choose the one that maximises their expected gains from migration.

To sum up, Todaro migration model has four basic characteristics: (i) Migration is stimulated by rational economic considerations of relative benefits and costs, mostly financial but also psychological; (ii) The decision to migrate depends on expected rather than actual urban-rural real wage differentials where the expected differential is determined by the interaction of two variables, the actual urban-rural wage differential and probability of successfully obtaining employment in the urban sector; (iii) The probability of obtaining an urban job is directly related to the urban employment rate and thus inversely related to urban unemployment rate; and (iv) Migration rates in excess of urban job opportunity growth rates are not only possible but also rational and even likely in the face of wide urban-rural expected income differentials. Higher rates of urban unemployment are therefore inevitable outcomes of the serious imbalance of economic opportunities between urban and rural areas of most of underdeveloped countries. (Todaro and Smith, 2004).

Rogers (1966), Compton (1969), Joseph (1975), have designed probabilistic models of migration, which have been designed for forecasting migration flows. They asserted that with the help of these probabilistic models, the future patterns of migration may be predicted. Gould and Prothero (1975) have also made their contributions in the field of model building with regard to migration. They visualised that the economic opportunities in relatively developed areas provide an incentive for migration, only if the conditions prevailing in the areas of destinations are unsatisfactory. Caldwell and Okenjo (1968) also analysed the factors influencing rural-urban migration both in donor and host societies of the tropical Africa. Zelinsky (1971) also studied the process of migration and for this the author applied the principle of spatial diffusion and innovations of the transaction mobility.

The above laws/models of migration lead us to conclude that migration, either internal or international, is influenced by economic, social, demographic, environmental, political and even psychological and religious factors. The laws of migration scrutinised above are too general in nature.

SIGNIFICANCE OF THE STUDY

Punjab is one of the prosperous states of India which has earned a name of "Food basket of the country and granary of India". The development of Punjab economy is mainly based on its agriculture. In the wake of 'Green Revolution' in Punjab in the late 1960s, the introduction of high yielding varieties (HYV) necessitated timely sowing and harvesting operations. The Green Revolution brought general prosperity and increased household incomes. The Punjabi farmer no longer had to labour on his own hands, was able to raise the level of mechanisation and hire labour. The new agriculture created a new demand for labour, for that the farmers have to become dependent on the migratory labourers from across the other states. Thus, the increased demand for labour in agricultural sector strengthened the process of labour migration in the state. Over time, migrant labour became institutionalised in Punjab; and regular long-term relationships between job providers and migrant labourers were established. Now, a significant proportion of Punjab's agricultural labour force consists of migrant labour from Bihar and Uttar Pradesh. In fact, one-third of the agricultural labour in Punjab is made up of migrants from other parts of India. Migrant labourers have not only become an integral part of Punjab's economy, but also an important constituent of our society. Migrant labourers are now replacing the local labourers who may have worked as attached or permanent labour with the farmers. Thus, the migrants have started playing a vital role in the agricultural sector of Punjab. Their participation has become imperative in farm operations like transplanting, harvesting and threshing of paddy and wheat.

The process of labour migration is a significant factor for achieving economic development. The pressure of population on land increases in undeveloped or underdeveloped areas, thereby keeping the marginal productivity of labour either zero or very close to zero. The migration process tends to shift such labour force from these areas to the areas where it contributes to labour productivity. So, the labour migration helps to redistribute the labour power by relieving some areas of the surplus labour power and helping areas where there is shortage of labour. The remittance of money by the migrants to their native areas helps to sustain their families on one hand and promotes the native village economy on the other.

The fact that the migrants repeatedly come to Punjab reveals that work and living conditions are a great deal better than the conditions at their native states. They are generally attracted by high wage rate, labour contract systems and by the cordial relations with their employers in Punjab.

The Punjab peasantry when faced with labour problems prefers migratory labour for the following reasons: scarcity of agricultural labour during peak season, threat by local agricultural labourers to stop work during peak season unless wages are increased, higher wage rates demanded by the local labourers, greater assertiveness of local labour force, perception of migrant labour as honest, docile and obedient, reliable, simple and unaware of their rights.

In this context, for all the aspects and contributions made by migrants in the agricultural sector of Punjab, the significance of the study lies in examining the socio-economic implications of labour migration.

OBJECTIVES OF THE STUDY

The migrants appear to have made a significant contribution in Punjab but their migration has created some problems too. Under such circumstances, any study on labour migration should outline the socio-economic characteristics and status of both the migrants and local labourers, causes of migration, impact of migration on wages and employment, income and savings and changes experienced by the migrants in their consumption, social and cultural behaviour. It is from this perspective that an attempt has been made to analyse the following aspects of migratory labour:

1. To study the impact of migration on the consumption (durable and non-durable) pattern of the migrants;
2. To examine whether the migrants have adjusted themselves to their new place of residence, and their assimilation in the general stream of life (social, political, economic, cultural, language, taste, habits etc.);
3. To access the cultural, social and economic interaction among the migrants and the locals;
4. To analyse the degree of homogeneity and heterogeneity among the locals and the migrants;
5. To examine the nature of dichotomy of wages among the locals and the migrants;
6. To examine the factors affecting the morbidity rate of the migrants.

An endeavour has been made to analyse the socio-economic implications of inflow of labour migration in the agricultural sector of Punjab. So, the attempt is to examine the pros and cons of the phenomenon and its impact on the various interrelated socio-economic aspects.

REFERENCES

Afsar, Rita (2004), "Dynamics of Poverty, Development and Population Mobility: The Bangladesh Case", *Asia Pacific Population Journal*, Vol. 19, No. 2, June, pp. 69-87.

Agarwal, S.N. (1968), "Socio-economic and Demographic Characteristics of Rural Migrants", *Journal of Institute of Economic Research*, Vol. 3 No. 2, July, pp. 39-45.

Amin, S. (1974), *Modern Migration in Western Africa*, Oxford University Press, London, p. 03.

Bartle, P.F.W. (1971), African *Rural-Urban Migration: A Decision Making Perspective*, Master Thesis, University of Columbia.

Beijer, G., (1967), "The Brain-drain from the Developing Countries", *International Migration*, Vol. 5, Nos. 3 & 4, pp. 228-36.

Bogue, D.J. (1959), "Internal Migration" in O.D. Duncan and P. Houser (eds.), *The Study of Population: An Inventory and Appraisal*, The University of Chicago Press, Chicago, pp. 486-560.

Caldwell, John C. (1968), "Determinants of Rural-Urban Migration in Ghana", *Population Studies*, Canberra, Vol. 2, pp. 361-76.

Caldwell, J.C. and Okenjo, C. (1968), "The Population of Tropical Africa", *Longman*, London, pp. 116-30.

Chandna, R.C. (1986), *A Geography of Population*, Kalyani Publishers, New Delhi, pp. 103-29.

Compton, P. (1969), "Internal Migration and Population Change in Hungary Between 1959 and 1965", *Transactions of the Institute of British Geographers*, Vol. 47, pp. 111-30.

Eisenstadt, S.N. (1954), *The Absorption of Immigrants: A Comparative Study Based Mainly on the Jewish Community in Palestine and the State of Israel*, London.

Fei, J.C.H.; and Ranis, G. (1953), "Innovation, Capital Accumulation and Economic Development", *American Economic Review*, Vol. 53, pp. 283-312.

Foot, D.K.; and Milne W.J. (1984), "Net Migration Estimation in an Extended Multiregional Gravity Model", *Journal of Regional Science*, pp. 119-34.

Gill, Indermit, (1984), "Migrant Labour: A Mirror Survey of Jullundur and East Champaran", *Economic and Political Weekly*, June, pp. 961-64.

Gosal, G.S. (1961), "International Migration in India—A Regional Analysis", The *Indian Geographical Journal* Vol. 36, No. 3, July-September, pp. 106-21.

Gosal, G.S. and Krishan, G. (1975), "Patterns of Internal Migration in India", *in L.A. Kosinski and R.M. Prothero (eds.), People on the Move*, Methuen and Co. Ltd., London, pp. 193-206.

Gould, W.T.S. and Prothero, R.M. (1975), "Space and Time in African Population Mobility" in *People on the Move*, Methuen and Co. Ltd., London, pp. 39-50.

Gupta, B. Das and Laishly R. (1975), "Migration from Villages: An Indian Case Study", *Economic and Political Weekly*, Annual Number, pp. 23-34.

Hamsaleelavathy, V. (1970), Migration *Differentials in the Metropolitan Cities in India*, Ph.D. Thesis, University of Bombay, pp. 21-30.

Jones, H.R. (1981), A *Geography of Population*, Harper and Row Publishers, London, pp. 201-55.

Joseph, G. (1975), "A Markov Analysis of Age/Sex Differences in Inter-Regional Migration in Great Britain", *Regional Studies*, Vol. 9, pp. 69-78.

Kamble, N.D. (1983), *Labour Migration in Indian States*, Ashish Publishing House, New Delhi, pp. 1-2.

Kaur, Gurinderjit (1999), Migratory *Labour in Punjab Agriculture*, Ph.D. Thesis, Department of Economics, Punjabi University, Patiala, p. 45.

Kothari, D.K., (1980), *Patterns of Rural-Urban Migration—A Case Study of Four Villages in Rajasthan, (India)*, Australian National University, Canberra, Ph.D. Thesis, p. 41.

Kulischer, E.M.; and Price, D.O. (1963), "Migration", Encyclopaedia Britannica, p. 463.

Kumar, A and N. Sharma, (1979), "Bihar's Population on Move: Issues on Inter-district Migration", in Sinha, V.N.P. and Mandal R.B. (eds.), *Dimensions in Geography*, Associated Book Agency, Patna.

Ladinsky, J. (1967), "The Geographical Mobility of Professional and Technical Manpower", *Journal of Human Resources*, Vo1. 2, pp. 475-94.

Lee, Everett S. (1966), "A Theory of Migration", *Demography*, Vol. 3, No. 1, pp. 47-57 & 288-97.

Lee, Everett S. (1970), "A Theory of Migration", *in Population Geography—A Reader*, ed. by G.J. Demko and Others, McGraw-Hill Book Co., New York, p. 290.

Lewis, W.A. (1954), *Economic Development with Unlimited Supplies of Labour*, The Manchester School of Economics and Social Studies, Vol. 22, pp. 139-91.

Mangalam, J.J (1968), *Human Migration", A Guide to Migration Literature in English*, 1955-1962, Lexington, University of Kentucky Press.

Mehta, S. (1971), "Patterns of Migration in the Bist-Doab, 1951-61", Panjab *University Research Bulletin (Arts)*, Panjab University, Chandigarh, pp. 17-33.

Nair, P.R.G. (1986), India, in Godfrey Gunatilleke (ed.), Migration of Asian Labourers to the Arab World, Tokyo, The UN University, p. 74.

Oberoi, A.S.; and Singh, H.K. Manmohan (1981), "Migration, Employment and Urban Labour Market—A Case Study of Ludhiana in the Indian Punjab", Population and Labour Policies Programme, Working Paper No. 113, Geneva, ILO, pp. 509-10.

Peterson, W. (1968), "Migration; Social Aspects", *International Encyclopaedia of Social Sciences*, p. 10.

Pooley, C. (1979), "Residential Mobility in Victorian City", Institute *of British Geographers*, Vol. 4, pp. 255-77.

Premi, M.K. (1976), Out-Migration Towns: A Study into the Nature, Causes and Consequences of Out-Migration, Report sponsored by *ICSSR*, New Delhi, pp. 1-10.

Pryor, R.J. (1969), "Laws of Migration: The Experience of Malaysia and Other Countries", *Goegraphica,* University of Malaysia Vol. 5 pp. 65-75.

Raju, B.R.K. (1989), *Developmental Migration: A Proecessual Analysis of Inter-State Rural-to Rural Migration,* Concept Publishing Co., N. Delhi.

Ravenstein, E.G. (1889), "The Laws of Migration", *Journal of the Royal Statistical Society,* Vol. 52, pp. 198-99 & 240-305.

Rahman, Anisur (1999), "Indian Labour Migration to West Asia", *Manpower Journal,* Vol. XXXV No. 2, July-September, pp. 87-99.

Rhoda, Richard E. (1979), *Development Activities and Rural-Urban Migration: Is it Possible to Keep them Down on the Farm?* Agency for International Development, Washington, p. 15.

Rogers, A. (1966), "A Markovian Policy Model of Inter-regional Migration", *Papers of Regional Science Association,* Vol. 17, pp. 205-24.

Saxena, D.P. (1977), *Rural-Urban Migration in India,* Popular Prakashan, Bombay, pp. 50-54.

Singh, Kamaljit (1991), *Internal Migration in a Developing Economy,* National Book Organisation, New Delhi, p. 13.

Sinha, V.N.P. (1980), "Migration: An Interdisciplinary Topic", *Geographical Review of India,* Vol. 42, No. 2, June, pp. 103-19.

Sjaastad, Larry A (1960), "The Costs and Returns of Human Migration", *Journal of Political Economy,* Vol. LXX, No. 5, pp. 80-93.

Skeldon, R. (1977), "The Evolution of Migration Patterns During Urbanisation in Peru", *Geographical Review,* Vol. 67, No. 4, pp. 396-411.

Skeldon, R. (2002), "Migration and Poverty", *Asia-Pacific Population Journal,* December, Vol. 17, No. 4, pp. 67-82.

Smith, T.Lynn (1960), *Fundamentals of Population Study,* Lippincott Co., New York, pp. 417-19.

Sovani, N.V. (1966), *Urbanisation and Urban India,* Asia Publishing House, New York, p. 7.

Stouffer, S. (1960), "Intervening Opportunities and Competing Migrants", *Journal of Regional Sciences,* Vol. 2, pp. 1-26.

Stouffer, S. (1940), "Intervening Opportunities: A Theory Relating to Mobility and Distance", *American Sociological Review*, Vol. 5, pp. 845-67.

Sundari, S. (2005), "Migration as a Livelihood Strategy", *Economic and Political Weekly*, May-June, pp. 2295-2303.

Tarver, J.D. (1961), "Predicting Migration", *Social Forces*, Vol. 39, pp. 207-14.

Thomas, D.S. (1941), *Social and Economic Aspects of Swedish Population Movements*, McGraw-Hill Book Co. New York, p. 52.

Todaro, M.P. (1969), "A Model of Labour Migration and Urban Unemployment in Less Developed Countries", *American Economic Review*, Vol. 59, No. 1, March, pp. 138-48.

Todaro, M.P.; and Smith, S.C. (2004), *Economic Development*, Pearson Education (Singapore) Pvt. Ltd. India, Delhi, pp. 338-42.

Wolpert, J. (1975), "Behavioural Aspects of the Decision to Migrate" in Emrys Jones (ed.), *Readings in Social Geography*, Oxford University Press, Oxford, pp. 191-99.

Zachariah, K.C. (1964), *A Historical Study of Internal Migration in the Indian Sub-continent, 1901-31*, Asia Publishing House, Mumbai, pp. 1-30 & 369-70.

Zachariah, K.C. (1969), "Bombay Migration Study – A Pilot Analysis of Migration of an Asian Metropolis", in G. Greese (ed.), *The City in Newly Developed Countries*, Prince Town University, pp. 367-70.

Zachariah, K.C. (1974), "A Note on Internal Migration in India, in Rural-Urban Differences in Southern Asia, Some Aspects and Methods of Analysis", UNESCO Research Centre, on Social and Economic Development in Southern India, Delhi, pp. 70-76.

Zelinsky, Wilbur (1971), "The Hypothesis of the Mobility Transition", *Geographical Review*, Vol. 61, No. 2, pp. 219-50.

Zipf, G.K. (1946), "The P_1, P_2/D Hypothesis: On the Intercity Movement of Persons", *American Sociological Review*, Vol. 11, No. 6, pp. 677-85.

Review of Literature

A large number of scholars from different streams have touched the various aspects of human migration. Most of the migration studies deal with its impact on poverty, employment, remittances, income generation etc. Very few studies have tried to analyse the morbidity rate among the migrants and their adjustment to the new place of residence (destination) and assimilation in the general stream of life.

The studies available on labour migration have been classified into three broad categories, *viz.* International Level, National Level and State Level. The literature on the subject has been analysed in a chronological order.

STUDIES OF INTERNATIONAL SCENE

The research studies covering various aspects of labour migration at the international level have been reviewed closely in the following paragraphs.

Castles and Kosak (1973) conducted a study of migrant labourers and their class structure in Western Europe. The authors found that the migrants generally belong to the poor and illiterate sections of the society. The migratory labourers are mainly engaged in semi-skilled and unskilled activities. They analysed that the availability of migrant labourers has created a ditch in the working class of Western-Europe into two groups, *i.e.* the local labourers and the migrants. The employers have benefited from the division of the labourers and they exploit the economical and legally weaker position of the migrants. The migrants are even ready to work at low wage rates and in uncongenial atmosphere. As a result of that, the authors observed that migrants have become an integral part of production in Western Europe.

Ward (1975) found that immigrant labour is docile and cheap, low paid and unorganised working class in Europe. Mostly immigrants are not skilled, so they do only those jobs which require physical strength. They mostly work in mining, automobiles and assembling services. The author has termed the immigrants as the 'reserve army' of cheap labour for the strengthening and stability of capitalism in Europe.

Moore (1977) in his study on migrant labour in Western Europe made some observations about the class structure of the migrants. The author in his analysis highlighted that the sustainability of the capitalistic system in Western Europe is the result of the presence of migrants, who are ready to work at the low wage rate. The clash of interest among the locals and migrants has benefited the capitalistic class. The author observed that owing to the poor economic position and weak bargaining power, the migrants are not well organised in any sort of union to protect their economic and social rights.

Ballard (1983) in his study stated that emigration means different things to different communities. While studying emigration from Indian Punjab and Pakistan Punjab, the author noted that migrants from Jalandhar in the Indian Punjab and from Mirpur in Pakistan to U.K. follow basically the same pattern of migration, but the remittances sent by migrants to Jalandhar are used in a fruitful manner. As a result of that, the area enjoys new development opportunities which subsequently enable the people of the lower castes to move out of agriculture and to migrate to urban areas, whereas the remittances at Mirpur in Pakistan have led to stagnation and increased degree of dependency on migration.

Odaman (1988) investigated the participation of migrants of Nigeria in the rural community development projects and observed rural out-migration to be instrumental for rural households to combat rural poverty. The study brings out that community development projects have had a high participation of rural out migrants. The author has suggested that the removal of unwanted and unnecessary constraints by the governments will form a major package for encouraging migrants' contribution to compensate for the ever limited public expenditure on rural development.

Azam (1991) has also noticed the characteristics of migratory labour to middle-east countries and the impact of migration at the local and household level. Azam observed that migrants are not from poor families rather they are from middle income groups. Although migration has raised the level of income and consumption, yet these gains are temporary in nature. As a result of that, no substantial investment has been made both in industry and agriculture which may boost production and generate more employment.

The study undertaken by ***Mahmood*** (1991) examined the impact of emigration on the wages of both skilled and unskilled labourers. On the basis of his study, the author analyzed that emigration of either skilled or unskilled labourers in the long run would raise the wage level both in nominal and real terms but returns on capital would be depressed. For this the author reasoned that when emigration takes place, it raises the price of labour intensive activity, which in turn raises the wages of both skilled and unskilled labourers. In brief, the author observed that emigration of any kind of labourers would turn income distribution in favour of labour class and against capital and capital class.

Rodrigo (1992) pointed out two major trends of economic migration, an earlier one comprising of highly skilled professionals who migrated to developed countries and a later one comprising of semi-skilled/unskilled manpower to Middle Eastern Countries such as Kuwait and Saudi Arabia. An interesting impact of migration is that the flow to the Middle-Eastern countries had a bias towards females. This was conducive to an aggravation of tensions and frustrations among the male youth. The author noted that the remittances by the migrants have accounted for up to 5.5 per cent of the GDP in the mid 80s and currently remittances rank second only to tea and garments as a source of forex (16 per cent). The study also brought out that these inflows helped the country to maintain the viability of external payments and avoid falling into severe external debt trap. They also helped to sustain the country's liberalized trade and exchange system of the post- 1977 era.

Although contribution to domestic output and employment generation seems to be limited, yet a positive impact is noted on the consumption and income distribution since the migrants came mainly from low income households. The impact on labour market is considered a mixture of positive and negative effects. The largest group of migrants belonged to unskilled category which is in surplus. Migration has, therefore, increased opportunities for these people. The author noted that in case of professional sectors such as doctors and engineers, there is a serious brain-drain as these people are not in excess. The author also noted adverse social repercussions in the form of neglected children, weakened marital bonds and even broken families. Some migrants found their remitted hard money dissipated on wasteful consumption by the spouse and families left behind. New values acquired abroad have also in some cases created problems of adjustment to family and social environment on return.

Shah (1994) in his paper attempted to outline some of the major determinants of migration flaws for Bangladesh, India and Pakistan. The author noted that in the post-1970s era, most of the migration has been towards the Middle East countries in response to the oil boom. The most important determinants at the national level are labour market conditions, in both sending and the host countries. The author suggested that networks facilitate movement and, in due course become a cause of migration. Aggressive policy in Sri Lanka and Bangladesh has also helped migrants to move. The study noticed that wage differentials are the major contributors in the decision to migrate at the family level. The author also discussed the impact of migration on sending countries both at family as well as national levels. The study suggests that foreign employment alleviated the unemployment situation in India, especially in Kerala. The major reason being that to protect the pride, the return migrants did not prefer to join low paid jobs. Emigration has been considered a safety valve to supply pressure generated by population growth. No evidence of brain-drain has been noticed.

Premi and Mathur (1995) while explaining the collective nature of the decision-making process, suggested that though neo-classical theory may be relevant to the extent of wage differentials, yet it could not explain migration in its totality. The authors in their study explained that large-scale migration from India began in the mid-70s, following the oil boom in the Middle-East. It was noted that about 36% of the migrants were unemployed prior to migration. The author pointed out that on the remittances side, a large amount was received which was mainly used to finance land acquisition, improvement in housing quality and ownership of consumer durables in migrant households.

Rahman (1999) in his study of labour migration analysed that Indian labour migrated to West Asia, especially to the oil exporting countries of the Gulf on a large scale in the mid-

70s. The new trend in Indian labour migration was triggered by oil boom in the Gulf countries. The author has lauded the circulatory nature of the migratory labour which has brought out more positive changes than the negative ones. The migrants to Gulf countries are generally less educated, relatively young and unmarried. They normally come from rural and comparatively poor economic background. Although the working and the living conditions in the host countries are not much satisfactory, yet the economic gains by the migrants outweigh all these, which pull the maximum number of migrants to Gulf countries. Rehman emphasised that Gulf remittances earned by the migrants are generally beneficial to add foreign exchange reserves on one hand and to their families on the other as well as increased flow of remittances, the expenditure on education and health of migrant families improved which is a positive sign for human capital development. The author has also noticed social and psychological consequences of migration. There is a positive development trend towards social equality and justice.

Haan (2000) in his paper also indicated that in recent times, migration among the labour force is taking place primarily in search of livelihoods.

Skeldon (2002) in his study about migration and poverty, revealed that though 'push factor' because of abject poverty is the major factor of migration, yet the desire to better oneself is perhaps the root cause of most migration. The author attempted to draw clear relationship between poverty and migration and vice-versa. Further, the author stressed that migrants in itself are among the most innovative and dynamic factors for future migration, thus being both the creator and the product of poverty. The circular nature of migration is supportive to the communities of the migrants at the origin. Skeldon has explained that remittances used either for consumption or for investment, directly or indirectly, help to alleviate poverty. Thus migration, either internal or international, is an integral part of the process of economic development.

Siddiqui (2003) in his paper identified the numbers and profile of international immigrants, examined labour market conditions and remittance flows, and analysed the government policies and programmes for managing migration. The study indicated that during 2002-03, the migration declined due to substantial increase in the cost of migration. Flow of remittances into Bangladesh has grown at around 10 per cent per year during the last 25 years. The author indicated that cost benefit analysis suggests that the amount of remittances sent by migrants is nearly three times higher than the cost of migration. In recent years, the author observed, the migrants move because of their individual contacts and social network.

Afsar (2004) in her study on poverty, development and population mobility, emphasised that though pull factor dominates the process of migration from rural to urban areas, yet social networks both at the origin and destination are to be considered as an integral part in the whole process of migration decision making which minimises the cost of migration and ensures quick and better material returns. Contrary to conventional studies, Afsar in her analysis has revealed that migration, instead of being a hindrance to rural development, has actually been a boon for the expansion of rural land and labour markets by making more rural land available for tenancy. Further, the contribution of remittances to household income has increased significantly. Rural households adopt emigration as a livelihood strategy. In a way, rural-urban migration is an important mean of diversifying rural economics.

A number of studies at the level of international migration have been undertaken and analysed to find out the motivational factors behind migration. Although number of factors such as economic, social, demographic and cultural have been observed, yet it has been noted that most of the studies of the social scientists have emphasised the significance of economic factors in the process of migration.

STUDIES OF INDIAN SCENE

Migration is an independent human activity, which is largely influenced by economic, social, cultural and demographic aspects. In recent times, the trend of migration is mainly the result of the increase in opportunities for economic well-being. Therefore, migration is considered to be a good indicator of socio-economic change in a country like India comprising different castes, cultures and languages.

A large number of scholars of economics, demography, sociology and geography have studied and analysed the process of migration in India. Some of the important and relevant studies have been analysed as follows:

Davis (1974) in his study has provided a detailed account of different types of migration in India, *viz*, short-term migration, marriage migration and rural-urban migration. ***Gosal*** (1961) assessed the regional pattern and magnitude of internal migration in India during the period 1931-51, whereas ***Zachariah*** (1968) in his study explained the guidelines for the analysis of migration to urban centers and discussed the problems of migrants of the large cities of India. Inter-state and Intra-state movements of different types of migration, according to rural-urban composition were explained by ***Bose*** (1965).

Kamble (1983) has clearly elucidated that various qualitative and quantitative economic opportunities have influenced migration. It was observed that distance is a crucial factor in determining the volume and composition of migration. The author clearly explained that it is not the high population density of Kerala that motivated large scale out-migration, but the cultural and social background of Kerala's population was also responsible for out-migration. It was observed that population of the state was more dynamic, courageous and of adjustable nature. The excess flow of money, from other states and foreign countries, has shown its effects in the form of fast rising prices of agricultural lands and houses.

While discussing the sociological aspect of migration of agricultural labourers, ***Gupta et al.*** (1988) have explained that the abundant inflow of migratory labour has not only affected the employment opportunities of the local labourers but also has adverse effect on the wage rate of the local labourers.

Sharma (1989) in his research paper has analysed the process and patterns of in-migration in Madhya Pradesh. The state of Madhya Pradesh has been attracting comparatively large segments of migrants. The study witnessed that in 1981, one-third of the total population was constituted of the migrants. The excess in-migration in the state is directly related with industrialisation, urbanisation and development of service industries. The powerful pull-factor operating the mechanism of in-migration in the state has been the potential of employment. The author highlighted the fact that the availability of job opportunities and modern amenities in the towns and cities have been the major pull force for migrants.

Yadava (1996) in his study about rural-urban migration has identified that in the process of migration, 'poverty and hunting for job', were the main push factors, while job opportunities, friends and relatives who had already migrated act as pull factors. The propensity to move from rural households is positively related to education, social and economic status and larger land-holdings. Landless households and households belonging to the lower strata of economic status were most likely to migrate than those belonging to the middle strata.

Choudhri (1998) in his study about the seasonal migrants observed that seasonal migration by the agricultural labourers has proved to be a blessing for them. Instead of starving at home, these poor labourers migrate seasonally to agriculture sector and work for higher wages. These migrant labourers earn a reasonable amount of cash and spend on a few luxuries which add a little spice to their life. They also learn new and better techniques of cultivation and try to introduce such techniques at the place of their origin. The author noticed that migrants have also become aware of their rights and are motivated to use this knowledge for collective bargaining. In this sense, migration has given them a new meaning of life for their self-preservation. The author also observed the negative aspect of seasonal migration. The continuous move from origin to destination during the year has proved to be a hindrance for the education of their children. The constant movement has also hindered adoption of any long-term employment and development schemes for the betterment of their life style.

Subramanian and Balasubramaniam (2000) have focussed their attention on trends, patterns, characteristics, reasons and effects of migration. The study correlated the inter-state migration with economic development as migration has played an important role in the development and urbanization of Tamil Nadu. The single predominant reason for male migration is employment; whereas marriage as a reason for migration is the single most important factor for female migration. The authors observed that migration has mitigated caste, religious and linguistic barriers. The authors concluded that the migrant population has a positive impact on the local population as it adds to the economically active, educationally qualified and occupationally skilled population and therefore, it is a blessing and not a burden provided that resources are harnessed properly.

Sivakumar (2001) in his study has stressed that both migration and development are positively interrelated. The author observed that most of the rural migrants belong to better occupational status and higher income group than rural non-migrants. They belong to large land holding families, yet the better life opportunities in the urban areas operate as a strong pull factor in case of rural migrants. It was also noticed that rural migrants being significantly better educated than rural non-migrants, get married at a later age and have smaller size of their families. In a nutshell, it has been clarified by the author that the rural migrants are much better off than the rural non-migrants in all aspects of life.

While explaining the phenomenon of distress migration, ***Mukherjee*** (2001) has explained that majority of the migrants are illiterate or semi-illiterate peasants and labourers who are virtually compelled to move from stagnant villages or countryside and crowd into Indian mega cities. The study analysed that the migrants are forced to leave their villages because of lack of employment opportunities, but mega cities also failed to provide them jobs because of limited job opportunities. It is indicated that out-migration of labourers is occurring from comparatively neglected and backward states where poverty is rampant and investment for rural development is negligible. It is a state of poverty-induced migration from rural to urban areas. Based on the sample survey of 443 districts of India, the author analyzed that the high volume of out-migration occurs from those districts where services and constructions were less and where general literacy and agricultural investment were also low (canonical correlation 0.53) whereas in-migration occurs in those districts where more economic development-cum-urbanization and greater investment, particularly in agriculture prevail (canonical correlation 0.74).

It is also noted that globalisation, liberalisation and privatisation policies are adversely affecting the poor and rural people's lives and their economy because of cheap imports. The lives and livelihoods of poor peasants, farmers, agricultural labourers, artisans and village operatives are badly affected. Although such socio-economic factors of underdevelopment and poverty were prevalent since independence and much before, which continued uninterrupted even during planning era, yet these negative forces are now strengthening these factors which in turn are inducing distress migration.

Rogaly et al. (2001) conducted ethnographic research of seasonal migration from West Bengal based on the information gathered from 141 gans of migrant labourers. The study revealed that the temporary migratory labourers are not properly unionized and are often unprotected by effective legislation against travel and workplace risks. The methodological approach of this study examined social, political and technological conditions which led to the causes and consequences of migration. The authors found that migrants have been excluded from the welfare schemes initiated by the Government. Health and education facilities to the migrants and their families are not available. The study also revealed that migrants could make more of their remittances, if health and education facilities are actually free and of high quality.

Chatterjee and Kundu (2001) in their study have emphasised that tenets of globalisation and free trade have encompassed the agricultural sector of the country. In order to marshal the benefits of remunerative prices in the world market, the importance of productivity enhancing factors has gone up tremendously. This has affected the landlord's choice between local and migrant labourers. The paper with the help of consumption efficiency hypothesis has shown that employment of migrant labour should not always be welcomed by the landlord in spite of their availability in the poor working and living conditions and readiness to work for longer hours. It is observed that as the agriculture sector is exposed to the forces of globalization, the landlords adopt 'Green Revolution' technique in agricultural production. So the landlords, instead of labour hours give more importance to labour power. To control labour power, to remove the uncertainty about the supply of labour in the peak season, the landlord binds the labourers into a nutrition based interlinked contract through offering consumption loan in the form of kind against committed labour service in the agricultural peak season. The local labourer, to check the uncertainty of getting job in the peak season also binds himself in such type of piece rate contract. On the basis of the hypothesis, it was noticed that landlords always prefer local labourers after binding them into nutrition based interlinked contract.

The work of ***Gupta and Mitra*** (2002) examines the links between duration of migration, distance of migration, occupation and incidence of poverty. The study was conducted on 150 slum households (1996) from several parts of Delhi. The study evidenced that majority of the migrants are from the rural areas of different states. It was noticed that the employment structure of the migrant slum dwellers in Delhi is by and large dominated by the informal tertiary activities. It is also observed that with a rise in the period of stay and experience, the migrants are more likely to move from low income and casual jobs to high income and regular jobs and are able to improve their standard of living.

Zachariah et al. (2003) have analysed the contribution of the transformation of Kerala from its basic status of non-migrating state in 1940s to that of a remittance-oriented economy in the impressive achievements of the state in social and human development spheres. The 20th century witnessed the migration prevalence rate (MPR) of Kerala to rise to 50-60 per cent. International migration among the Keralites has gradually out placed internal migration in the recent times. Although the authors emphasised the pull and push factors in determining migration, yet they studied the phenomenon based on push factors. Demographic and economic factors were found crucial in determining migration. Every facet of life in Kerala, *viz.* economic, social, demographic, political and religious had been influenced by migration. The major structural impacts of migration include decrease in the population growth rate, evolution of a unique sex ratio (favouring females) and a reduction in the working age of population. There had also been reduction in the unemployment rate of the state. The study also provided evidence supporting the enhancement of the status of migrant households in terms of health and sanitation, education of children and qualitative shifts in the nature of household requirements. Migration has also led to increased family responsibilities for the women which could also be seen as advancement in terms of financial empowerment and spatial mobility beyond the traditional family boundaries.

Mehta (2003) explored the low economic base of hill economy of Uttranchal. Increasing population pressure, heavy dependence on low productive agriculture, industrial backwardness, lack of social services, inadequate infrastructure and harsh geographical features are the major push factors which led to out-migration from hill areas in search of livelihood and employment. The migrants had been supporting their families back home through remittance; the author has termed this phenomenon as 'money-order economy'. The study clearly brought out the fact that out-migration of able-bodied men entailed heavy burden on women. The study also revealed that higher literacy rate accentuated the process of out-migration. This drain of educated youth was primarily due to the low productive base of the economy.

Factors affecting migration and spatial and temporal variations in them have been studied by ***Khairkar*** (2003). The study analysed the various socio-economic factors affecting the volume of rural-urban migration. The study revealed that people migrate from one place to another because of some problems in sending region (push) and due to attraction (pull) of urban areas. Better educational facilities, better job opportunities in the industrial sector and low level of crime influenced the volume of migration to Pune city. The study maintained that the level of urbanization and the proportion of area under irrigation are two significant factors which influence the volume of migration from other states to Pune city. The author concluded that non-agricultural labourers, urbanisation, population density, literacy, educational facilities, proportion of active population, occurrences of natural calamities, ratio between employer and employee have positive and significant relationship with migration. Agricultural labourers, backward and minority communities, sex ratio and proportion of labourers affect the volume of migration negatively.

The economic contributions made by the immigrants have been highlighted by ***Gupta and Sharma*** (2003) in their study. The basic reason for this is that about three-fourth of population of in-migrants is of youth age and mature people. The authors observed· that the level of education of in-migrants is better and they are dedicated to economic pursuits. The industrial and urban development has opened the possibilities of in-migration to big cities. The authors also noticed that migrants being outsiders have to face many social problems. In spite of all these, the economic contributions made by in-migrants for the strong economic base of the city are commendable.

Radhakrishna et al. (2004) have discussed the process of out-migration from Bihar and identified that the main push factors were: stagnation in agriculture, corruption, crime, caste dominance, social, economic and cultural exploitation etc. In the wake of poverty and exploitation by the rich peasants and landlords, the agricultural labourers and poor peasants from northern part of the state made heavy out-migration. It was observed that the increased migration of labour from the state has contributed its own share in changing the rural labour markets and social structure. The remittances from migration have contributed significantly to the household income which not only helped the migrants and their families in meeting their current consumption needs but also raised the wage level, particularly in most parts of north Bihar.

The socio-economic factors influencing migration of labour have been analyzed by ***Namasivayam and Kumar*** (2004) based on a survey of 250 labourers. The study revealed that caste and size of family has no relationship with the migration of labour. Migration of labour is primarily motivated by age, education, occupation, income and seasonal employment. It was witnessed that agricultural labourers belonging to middle and upper age groups preferred to migrate. The study indicated a greater degree of tendency of migration among the labourers belonging to forward community because of literacy and relation with friends and relatives at the destination. Duration of seasonal employment and level of income are other important factors affecting the volume of migration.

Joshi and Verma (2004) have conducted a comprehensive and analytical interdisciplinary study of labour migration based on the empirical data covering 1498 households from 100 sample villages. The study analyses the quantum, nature and direction of seasonal migration from Chhatisgarh, together with its effects on the society in general and the family of the migrants in particular. The study revealed that the labour migration of this area cannot be categorised as the development migration based on the maximum of profit, but it is a part of household survival strategy of migrant farmers/ landless labourers who are unable to find work locally.

Mahesh (2004) in his study has visualised that the structure of labour force in Kerala has changed since 1970, as a result of reduced new entry into the agricultural sector. Forced with the limited employment opportunities in the village and uncertainty in getting local employment, a large number of rural labourers change their occupations and place of work or both. On the basis of primary data collected from 300 households, it was found that dislike for agricultural work, eagerness to obtain cash and worsening of economic situation were the most frequent push factors for the migration of labour. Apart from this, the study explained that the expansion of transport and communication facilities in rural areas have also widened the scope for rural to urban and urban to rural migration of the labourers. It was also observed that migration of labourers depends not only on economic motivations and conditions but also on family circumstances, social institutions and psychological factors. The analysis of data indicated that apart from other things, age, sex, educational level and occupation of the labourers were the major factors contributing to the migration process of the labourers. Young, male and educated labourers had greater tendency to migrate.

Chand (2005) made an attempt to look into the dynamics of trends and patterns of internal migration in India and analysed the extent and direction of the migration. Based on the data of National Sample Survey 55th round, the author indicated that the share of the migrants in the total population is higher in urban areas than in rural areas. Although females migrate due to marriage, yet mostly the males migrate for economic reasons. The lack of employment opportunities in the rural areas and better employment prospects and infrastructure amenities in the urban areas are the basic motivating forces behind migration to urban areas. The study also brought out that the excessive migration to urban areas has serious consequences for urban infrastructure, civic amenities, environment etc.

Sharma (2005) in his article on socio-economic change in Bihar has highlighted the increasing in-state migration among the rural people of Bihar. The author concluded that the developed districts of the state generally experience long-term migration, whereas seasonal migration is a feature of backward districts of the state. Both upper-class people and lower caste people migrate to escape from the caste boundaries. It was noticed that majority of the migrants were males; only a few females migrate. Nearly 40 per cent of households report at least one migrant and the remittances received constitute about one-third of the total household income. These remittances helped their families left behind to sustain food security, have a *pucca* house and meet expenses for farm inputs and social obligations.

Paris et al. (2005) in their article studied labour out-migration of rice farming households of Eastern Uttar Pradesh and examined the incidence, patterns and impact of labour out-migration on the livelihood of rice farmers and their women-folk left behind. The incidence of out-migration is higher among the landless than the farming households due to push factors such as small and marginal size of land holdings, lack of regular off farm and non-farm employment facilities in the villages and pull factors such as available employment opportunities in the cities and industrial places as well as strong social networks of migrants with relatives and friends. The study also revealed that migrants send remittances on a lump sum basis to their relatives and these remittances comprise a significant share of total household income. These remittances help their families left behind to sustain food security, have a *pucca* house and meet expenses for farm inputs and social obligations. The study emphasised that though rural to urban migration may be beneficial to the farm households through migrants' remittances, yet it had a negative impact on food production and for women, it translated into a marked increase in agricultural work, a heavier workload and lesser time for domestic work and child care.

Deshingkar (2006) conducted a study to evaluate the impact of internal migration on poverty and development in Asia. He stated that the potential benefits of internal migration are not being fully realized because of an inadequate understanding of migration patterns. The author also recognised the importance of migration for poverty reduction and development.

STUDIES OF PUNJAB SCENE

The studies analysed on the migratory labour in Punjab have been mainly confined to the agricultural sector of the state.

Mehta (1973) conducted a study to highlight the pattern of migration in the Bist-Doab region of Punjab during the period 1951-61. The out-migration and emigration were induced mainly by small and declining size of land holdings and inadequate opportunities in the non-agricultural sectors. The development of new agricultural lands in other parts of Punjab and also in adjoining states was instrumental in stimulating migration of agricultural population. The study also highlighted that Sikhs who are more rural and agricultural than Hindus, migrated in larger number than the latter. It was also noticed in the study that the major factor behind emigration was the tradition of emigrating in the past through which the people of the region had become aware of the great benefits of migration to other countries. Emigration has made a significant impact on the life and economy of the region as emigrants regularly remit money to their family members. As a result of this, the standard of living, level of education and enterprising nature has improved considerably.

Arora and Kumar, Balbir (1980) in their sociological study about rural to rural migration have identified the socio-economic characteristics of the migrants, the method of their recruitment, wage payment, the changing nature of the farmer-labour relationship and the social causes of migration in Punjab. The authors based their study on the field work carried out in four villages of Hoshiarpur. 50 migrants, 39 employers and 39 local labourers contributed to the information gathered. Owing to a network of traders, who brought labourers from outside the state and supplied them to farmers, this district was purposely chosen. The study revealed that majority of the migrants was young having mean age of 23.3 years and having some knowledge of farming. About 88 per cent migrants come from Bihar and the remaining from Orissa, West Bengal and U.P. Nearly half of them were Hindus and the remaining Christians. Majority of the migrants belonged to Scheduled Castes or Scheduled Tribes. About 54 per cent of the migrants were coming to

Punjab for the first time; others came through relatives and fellow villagers and some through Punjabis working in Ranchi. The study also analysed the migration stimulants in terms of pull and push factors. Regular employment opportunities at higher wage rates in the destination area were the pull factors, whereas poverty, low wage rate, small size of holdings, indebtedness, low productivity of land, floods and droughts and strained family relations were the push factors. The process of acculturation of the migrants was neither smooth nor very visible. They found the local environment inhospitable and discriminatory as they had to work longer hours in comparison to the local labourers without any extra payment., Employers-farmers were also often inconsiderate. The study emphasised that a positive gain accruing from migration is that the migrants acquired new status applicable to modern technological inputs in agriculture.

Gill (1980) in his study has analyzed that the basic cause of migration from Bihar and U.P. is the unequal level of development. These migratory labourers mainly belong to the lower strata of the society in the areas of their origin. Moreover they have not been able to spread their roots in Punjab.

Sharma (1982) in his study has explained the factors associated with internal migration and their impact on the employment opportunities and wage rate of the local labour. The migratory labour mainly from Bihar and U.P. working in the rural areas of Punjab was discriminated in the case of wage rates. Further, it was indicated in the study that migratory labour being docile, non-assertive has weakened the strength of the local labour. This has a negative effect on the wage level and employment level of these labourers. The local agricultural labourers were full of resentment, indignation and hatred towards the migrants.

Gill (1982) made an attempt to study the role of migratory labour in the agricultural sector of the state. The author opined that agriculture sector being labour intensive, so during the busy season there is higher demand of labour. The local labour demands higher wages. In this busy season the migratory labour comes to the rescue of farmers by doing labour in the fields at lower wages.

An ILO study on the causes and consequences of internal labour migration in Punjab was prepared by ***Oberoi and Singh*** (1983). The field work for the project was completed during 1977, comprising 2124 households in 26 villages of Ludhiana district. The study was mainly focussed on the determinants of migration and the interaction between internal migration and socio-economic change. The effects of migration on technological change and agricultural productivity, the structure and level of employment, income distribution and consumption, and fertility and population growth were extensively analysed in the research project. It was assessed from the data that all the three flows of migration, *i.e.* in, out and return are on the rise. The data revealed that out-migrants relatively have higher level of education whereas 57.9 per cent in-migrants were illiterate. Majority of the out-migrants were young where the average age of immigrants was about 24 years. The assessment of the data on social composition indicated that in the process of migration, Punjab was gaining more scheduled caste population which has important political and sociological implications. The return migrants constituted only a small proportion of 10.7 per cent of total migrants. The assessment of the data on income and employment revealed that return migrants were doing better than those who had stayed at home. It was estimated that during 1976-77, the net inflow of resources to the rural areas of the district was Rs. 36 million of which 60.8 per cent came from outside the state. The remittances are being received by all income groups and these tend to decline as the level of income rises. The remittances were observed to flow fairly, regularly and the pattern of expenditure of households receiving remittances showed that more than three-fourth of the income received through remittances was spent on food and clothing and a very small proportion on the productive investment such as purchase of land, farm equipments and agricultural inputs. It was also highlighted in the study that migration and urbanisation are the basic factors to reduce fertility as well as the overall rate of the population growth in the economy.

Singh (1983) in his study has provided valuable information on the process of labour mobility. The study emphasised that under conditions of rapid economic development, there is considerable in-migration and out-migration. But the rate of out-migration is higher than the combined rate of in and return migration. The author on the basis of his field studies in Punjab assessed that the poor migrate in and out, in search of work. Those in the middle and upper groups out-migrate to take advantage of better opportunities in occupations such as army, public services, transport and communications, industry, education, medical services etc. From the field survey, it has been observed that most of the in-migrants are those who work to resume farming because of rise in the price of land and educated unemployed who want to grab the increased profitability of agriculture. On the other side, an important segment of out-migrants is the artisan class that cannot find remunerative work because of the disintegration of household industry.

Gill (1983) made an attempt to study the patterns of in-migration and out-migration respectively into Jullundur in Punjab and East Champaran in Bihar. The study traces that the primary abettor of regional migration is the existing and widening differences in the living conditions between these regions. The pull of employment in the agricultural sector of Punjab, along with the push in the home state is the primary determinant of the movement of the labour force from Bihar to Punjab. The typical migrant is marginally literate (Classes 1 to 5), owns little or no land in his home state. The average age of the migratory labourers is 26-28 years for men and

24-26 years for women. Male labourers outnumber females by a large margin. The study noticed that migrants work in a group ranging from 5 to 50 members headed by a *tolidar*. The *tolidars* form the petty contractor system. The *tolidar*, a petty contractor supervises the work and acts as a link between the employer and the migratory labour. In return, he gets his reward in the form of a 'cut' from each labourer's daily wages (ranging from 75 paisa to Rs. 1.50 per labourer, per day).

Mittar (1984) conducted a study about the growth of informal sector in Punjab's urban economy, based on the primary data collected from 300 households in Patiala city and also on the secondary data of 1971 and 1981 census. The analysis of the data showed that a little more than half of the sampled households were engaged in informal sector activities. The analysis of the data revealed that the process of migration is highly selective with regard to age, sex and education. The investigations of the study confirmed that economic factor was the dominant factor in the decision to migrate. Relatives and friends were the most important sources through whom migrants located their first job. Most of the migrants maintained an active link with the places from which they had migrated. The author observed that migrants were generally employed in the informal sector, earning much less than the non-migrant households. Apart from this, the analysis showed that migration brings large benefits to the rural poor besides making cheap labour available to the labour areas and thus contributing to their growth.

Socio-economic characteristics of migrant labourers coming to Punjab have been identified by ***Singh and Singh*** (1984) in their study, based on the sample data of 100 migrant labourers in district Amritsar. It is indicated that majority of the migrants have come from the northern districts of Bihar. About three-fourth of the migrants under sample study were illiterate and those who had gone to school, none of them had crossed the level of middle standard. Caste-wise decomposition revealed that majority of the migrants belong to scheduled caste of which 84 were Hindus and only 16 were Muslims. 78 per cent of the migrant labourers who migrated from Bihar to Punjab were young in the age group of 16 to 30 years. They moved to Punjab for better economic opportunities both for themselves and the family members left at home (Bihar).

The factors associated with migrant agricultural labour in Punjab, the wage and employment structure and the impact of migrant labour on the economic conditions of the local labourers have been studied (worked out) by ***Grewal and Sidhu*** (1984). The study is based on primary survey data collected from 210 migrant labourers, 120 local labourers and 120 farmers. The study highlighted that the major factors causing migration were: extreme poverty, extensive unemployment and low wage rates in the native areas of the migrants. It also confirmed that the migration of labour to Punjab originated from Bihar and U.P. It was estimated on the basis of the primary data that the strength of the migrant labour force in the state is 10 per cent of the total agricultural labour force during the lean period and about 19 per cent during the peak period. Majority of the migrants were young and illiterate. Before migrating to Punjab, all of them except one, were either agricultural labourers or agricultural labourers-cum-cultivators.

The study revealed that the migrants were paid 7.5 to 10 per cent more wages in Punjab as compared to their native places. The authors estimated that the total earnings of migrant labourers during 1983-84 were Rs. 100.82 crore, out of which 44.23 crore were spent in Punjab and rest were remitted to their native places. Two-thirds of the migrants were reported to be under heavy debt. The study also highlighted that local farmers had strong preference for migrant labourers as compared to the local labourers. It was observed during the survey that there is growing tendency of antagonism between the migrant labour and local labour, as the local labourers feel that the migrant labourers are responsible for deteriorating their wage and employment levels. As regards the socio-cultural aspect of the migrants, some changes were observed in their food and dress habits, and also in their language and customs. Although they were better off than their native places, yet they expressed their unwillingness to settle in Punjab.

Gupta (1986) in his study, attempted to identify the socio-economic characteristics of the immigrant farm labourers. The socio-economic composition of the in-migrants revealed that most of them were Hindus. The upper castes in migrants had come to Punjab to earn money by doing low status jobs which they would not do in their native place for fear of losing their social status. The author observed that literacy level has little relationship with migration. The analysis of family background indicated that two-thirds of in-migrants belonged to joint families having large family size. The study manifested that in-migrants hardly experienced any shift in their occupation. Before coming to Punjab, majority of them worked as agricultural labourers in their native villages.

It was indicated in the study that most of the employer-farmers negotiated directly with the in-migrant labourers for their pattern of recruitment and wage structure. It was observed that because of continuous contact of in-migrant labourers with the farming community, the migrants are acquiring a favourable attitude towards family planning. The study also revealed that the overall impact of migration on the socio-economic status of the migrants in their native places was positive as it had enabled them to acquire a better standard of living.

Paul (1989) studied the process of rural-urban migration in Punjab, with the help of primary data collected from 292 rural households of Ludhiana and Sangrur. The author conducted a study on the assumption that migration was a selective process and was the result of the economically rational behaviour of the individuals. The study was an attempt to identify socio-economic characteristics of migrants and non-migrants and to specify the pattern of relationship between propensity to migrate and relevant explanatory variables. The study indicated that the process of migration was highly selective with respect to age, sex, marital status and education. In fact, the decision to migrate is influenced by rural-urban, intra-rural income differentials and expectation of higher incomes in the destination areas and urban contacts. The migrants from the cultivating sector are mainly influenced by the pull factors, whereas those from the non-cultivating areas are mainly influenced by the push factors. It also revealed that migrants from cultivating households are less interested to settle permanently in the urban areas than the migrants from non-cultivating households. It was also observed in the study that migrants with inadequate capital resources and low incomes in the rural areas prefer to stay at destination for a longer time than the others.

Singh (1991) conducted a study on internal migration based on the primary data collected from 200 rural households and 300 urban households. The study analyzed the causes and consequences of migration to trace out the changes which have been induced in the rural and urban sectors of the economy of the state. It was found that majority of the out-migrants had a higher level of education than the in-migrants and return migrants. The study revealed that nearly three-fourth of the in-migrants from the urban areas and two-fifth of the migrants from the rural areas had no land. Both push and pull factors are operating in the rural and urban areas of the state. Landlessness, unequal distribution of land, low agricultural productivity and unemployment and under-employment, low wage rate and rising indebtedness are the major factors which are pushing the people from rural areas, whereas better employment opportunities, education and expectation of higher income are the basic economic factors which are pulling people towards urban areas. Apart from these, abnormal social and political conditions; family tensions and the desire to settle as single unit are some other factors which induce migration. As regards remittances, the study revealed that the level of education has a positive influence on the decision to remit. Similarly, marital status emerges as an important factor in the decision to remit as 91.30 per cent of the married out-migrants sent remittances. Further, the type of household to which the out-migrants belong show that those who are from the non-cultivating households have a greater tendency to remit than those who are from cultivating households. Since high income groups received a significantly larger share of the total amount of remittances, the effect of remittances was to widen the gap between the rich and the poor in absolute terms. Since the remittances are not directly related to any work effort on the part of the households receiving them, the households have a greater propensity to use them for current consumption than for investment. The study also revealed that there was a large transfer of technology and capital resources from urban to rural areas, which was highly beneficial to the rural economy of the state. Migration has brought about phenomenonal changes in the agricultural sector through changes in the size and quality of labour force changes in the volume and periodicity of capital flows and the usefulness of knowledge and information passed on by the migrants.

A study about the socio-economic implications of rural-urban migration was conducted by ***Bhatia*** (1992) based on the primary data collected from 300 households of six villages of Patiala district and also on the secondary data of 1971 and 1981 census. The study analyzed the pattern of migration in Punjab including the socio-economic characteristics of the migrants, the effect of remittances and other related capital flows on the rural economy and the impact of migration on technological change and output in agriculture. It was highlighted in the study that the out-migration from the rural areas in the state was largely dominated by individual rather than family migration which had significant implications for the flow of remittances back to the origin areas. Like other studies, it also reported that the process of migration is selective with respect to sex, age, education and distance. Apart from low level of rural income and rural-urban income differentials, the study brought out that under-employment rather than unemployment was the main cause of migration from the rural areas of the state. It was assessed that the 'pull factors' were comparatively more powerful than the 'push factors'. The author highlighted that the regular flow of remittances depended on distance, education and on the degree of migrants' relationship to those who remained behind. Migration has led to overall economic development as it reinforced the productive forces like human capital and physical capital by the use of modern techniques of production.

Singh (1995) in his study has highlighted some economic aspects of migrant labour. The author analyzed the extent and methods of exploitation of migrant labour in the agricultural sector of Punjab. It was indicated that in almost all the land holdings, the migrant labour was mostly young and belonged to backward castes. The wages of the migrants were found to be lower than those paid to the local labourers. They were compelled to work for more hours. Most of the migrant labourers were under heavy debt. The study indicated that the significant push factors behind the migration of the labour were: the unequal distribution between families, villages and regions and backwardness of agriculture in Bihar. Agriculture being backward in Bihar, served as a potential source of out-migration for Bihari labour and they preferred to settle in Punjab because of developed commercial agricultural sector of the state where they expected to earn better livelihood.

On the basis of a study of a village, ***Abbi and Singh*** (1997) have found that migrant labour has become inseparable part of the village agricultural activities. As *Jat* Sikh cultivators are mostly confining themselves to supervisory work, so most of the agricultural work, both skilled and unskilled, is performed by the migrant labour. The study brought the fact into light that now some of the migrants are working as permanent *siris*, looking after animals, machinery and even delivering grains to the mandis. It is observed that in the emerging scenario of growing unemployment, migrants constitute a situation of potential social conflict. The local labourers blame migrants for deterioration in wages and working conditions and reduction in employment opportunities.

Sidhu et al. (1997) in their study have pointed out that the major factors behind migration to Punjab were: stark poverty, unemployment and low wage rates in the native areas of migrants. The farmers revealed that the migrants were honest, sincere, trustworthy, loyal and humble towards them. The study observed that as a result of working in Punjab, there has been change in the language, food habits, dress, customs etc. of the migrants. Although the inflow of migratory labour had depressed the wage rates and employment opportunities for the local labourers, yet the overall relations between the local and migrant labour and the farmers were cordial. The study also revealed that the habit of smoking *bidis*, chewing *zarda* and betel nuts among the migrants has spread the evil in a big way in the state of Punjab.

Kaur (1999) has made an attempt to examine the overall nature of migration in order to assess its impact on Punjab agriculture. The study reveals that being venturesome and having no social liability, young people are more prone to migration. The main factor which motivated the migratory labourers for farm-labour in Punjab is the economic distress. The low wage-rate and employment only for a short duration at the native places are the push factors which compel them to migrate. Better employment opportunities and relatively high wages in the Punjab agriculture are the pull factors causing the outflow of the migrant labourers. The study also noticed that the local farm labourers do not like the move of the migratory farm labourers. The local labourers consider that the migrants have caused deterioration in the terms and conditions of wage-labour farm-employment in terms of remuneration and duration of work. The amount of remittances is associated to the total labour earnings and the mode of net income after meeting the production and social consumption expenditure. The rural-to-rural migration results in small remittances owing to low earnings of the migratory farm labourers. These remittances of the migratory farm labourers are mostly used for the social and consumption needs and only in a few cases for the productive purposes at the place of origin.

Rangi et al. (2001) have made an attempt to highlight that the post- green revolution period saw an influx of migrant agricultural labour particularly from the states of Bihar and Uttar Pradesh. The farmers of the state had become largely dependent upon migratory labour for various agricultural operations since then. The study showed that the population of the migrant labourers in the lean period comes to about 11 per cent of the total agricultural labour force in the state and about 25 per cent of the landless agricultural labourers, whereas the number of migrant labourers was estimated to be almost double in the peak period of workload which formed about 21 per cent of the total agricultural labour force in the state and about 50 per cent of the landless agricultural labour. The general trend that emerged from the study was that the initial period saw a fast increase in the number of migrant labourers, which later slowed down because the cropping intensity had become almost stagnant. The study also revealed that the influx of the migrant labour in the farm sector has far reaching consequences, both positive and negative. The positive aspect is that migrant labourers improved their economic position, acquired new skills and supply labour in the farm sector. The negative aspect is that the influx of migrant labour depressed the wage rates and reduced the employment opportunities for local agricultural labour which led to their casualisation.

Chand (2002) has made an attempt to analyse the specific socio-economic profile of the migrant labour. Economic hardships such as small size of land holdings, low productivity of land, unusual droughts and floods etc. have pushed these labourers out of their home states. The push factor plays the key role in the migratory process of labour. The study also explored that most of the migrants left their native places in the prime of their youth. The author also witnessed the differences in the caste composition and education level of the local and migrant labourers. A very notable finding of the study is that the perceptions and attitudes of the local and migrant labour are largely identical. It has been highlighted in the study that the mutual relations between migrant and local labour are normal and that there is no hostility among them. Like all other studies it has been observed that the migrants have a depressing effect on the wages in the labour market and labour migration from other states has reduced the employment opportunities for the local labour. The migrant labourers are of a docile and submissive character and give less trouble in doing their duty.

Kaur (2004) in her study observed that the main influx of labour from other states in the rural areas of Punjab started after the initiation of the process of Green Revolution. The motivation for migration to Punjab from other states was mainly for the reason as Punjab has offered employment opportunities for the major part of the year to migrants at higher wage rates as compared to their native areas. The author observed that the state has attracted a large number of rural male migrants and they have constituted more than 15 per cent of the total population. Out of these, 9.45 per cent were involved in rural-rural male migration while 6.27 per cent male migrants were part of urban-rural stream. The author observed that after the advent of green revolution, the farmers of Punjab are doing commercial and intensive agriculture, for which they need large number of labourers. Since the local labour is unable to meet the rising demands of farmers, it attracts a number of migrants from other states, especially from Bihar and U.P. The study also confirms the positive correlation in the volume of migration and the distance travelled. As the distance increased from the state border, the volume of inter-state migrants decreased.

Studies about labour migration reviewed above revealed that in general the major factors behind migration were 'push' and 'pull' factors at the place of origin and at the place of destination. As push and pull factors are the two sides of a same coin, so overpopulation, unemployment and underemployment, insufficient land, meagre sources of income and indebtedness at the place of origin and expected higher earnings and chances of employment at the destination led to migration of human beings. In addition to all this economic development, coupled with various sociological, geographical and physical conditions contribute much to the phenomenon of migration. The authors in their studies also highlighted that the development of means of transport and communication, urbanisation and education facilities also influenced the migration.

The studies at the national and state level in general and the agricultural sector of Punjab indicated that the migrants created slums and majority of them are young and belong to scheduled castes. They remit money to their native places and have strong bonds with their people at the origin. The presence of migrants adversely affected the wage rates and employment opportunities of the local labour. A few studies also revealed that migrants created certain social problems at the place of destination.

REFERENCES

Abbi, B.L.; and Singh Kesar (1997), *Post Green Revolution Rural Punjab: A Profile of Economic and Socio-cultural Change (1965-1995)*, Centre for Research in Rural and Industrial Development, Chandigarh, October, pp. 115-16.

Afsar, Rita (2004), "Dynamics of Poverty, Development and Population Mobility: The Bangladesh Case", *Asia Pacific Population Journal*, Vol. 19 No. 2, June, pp. 69-87.

Arora, D.R. and Kumar Balbir (1980), *Agricultural Development and Rural to Rural Labour Migration*, Department of Economics and Sociology, Punjab Agricultural University, Ludhiana, p. 5.

Azam, F. (1991), "Emigration Dynamics in Pakistan", *Regional Development Dialogue*, Vol. 12 No. 3, pp. 729-62.

Ballard, R. (1983), "The Contexts and Consequences of Migration: Jullunder and Mirpur Compared", *New Community* Vol. 11 No. 1 & 2, pp. 117-36.

Bhatia, Ajit Singh (1992), *Rural Urban Migration*, Deep & Deep Publications, New Delhi, pp. 79-131.

Bose, A. (1965), "Why Do People Migrate to Cities", *Yojana*, Vol. 26, pp. 25-26.

Castles, S.; and Kosak G. (1973), *Immigrant Workers and Class Structure in Western Europe*, Oxford University Press, London, pp. 106-16.

Chand, Himal (2005), "Migration in India—An Overview of Recent Evidences", September, *Man and Development*, Vol. XXVII, No. 3, pp. 51-71.

Chand, Krishan (2002), *Migrant Labour and Trade Union Movement in Punjab*, Centre for Research in Rural and Industrial Development, Chandigarh, July, pp. 162-73.

Chatterjee, B.; and. Kundu, A (2001), "Changing Agrarian Structure and the Choice Between Local Labour and Migrant Labour", *The Indian Journal of Labour Economics*, Vol. 44, No. 4, pp. 873-80.

Choudhri, Anil Kumar (1998), "Seasonal Migration—A Technique for Self-Preservation by the Rural Poor—A Case Study of West Bengal", *Demography India*, Vol. 27. No. 2, pp. 327-36.

Davis, K. (1974), "The Migration of Human Population", *Scientific American*, Vol. 231, No. 3, pp. 92-104.

Deshingkar, Priya (2006), *Internal Migration, Poverty and Development in Asia, Downloaded* from the website www.asia2015conferenceorg/pdhs/Deshingkar.pdf

Gill, Sucha Singh, (1980), Migrant *Labour in Rural Punjab: A Project Report* Punjabi University, Patiala, pp. 116-27.

Gill, Indermit (1983), "Migrant Labour: A Mirror Survey of Jalandhar and East Champaran", *Economic and Political Weekly*, June, pp. 961-64.

Gill, Sucha Singh (1982), "Migratory Labour in Punjab Agriculture: A Study of Its Implications for Agricultural Labour", *Economic Analyst*, Vol., No. 2, December, p. 120.

Gosal, G.S. (1961), "Internal Migration in India—A Regional Analysis", *The Indian Geographical Journal* Vol. 30, No. 3, July-September, pp. 106-21.

Grewal, S.S.; and Sidhu, M.S. (1984) *A Study on Migrant Agricultural Labour in Punjab*, Department of Economics and Sociology, Punjab Agricultural University, Ludhiana, pp. 45-49.

Gupta I.; and Mitra, A. (2002), "Rural Migrants and Labour Segmentation: Micro Level Evidence from Delhi Slums", *Economic and Political Weekly*, January, pp. 163-68.

Gupta, A.K. (1986), *Sociological Implications of Rural to Rural Migration: A Case Study of Rural In-migrants in Punjab*, Ph.D. Thesis, Punjab Agriculture University, Ludhiana, September, pp. 126-36.

Gupta, A.K.; Arora, D.R.; Aggarwal, B.K. (1988), "Sociological Analysis of Migration of Agricultural Labourers from Eastern to North Western Region of India", *Indian Journal of Industrial Relations*, Vol. 23, No. 4, April, pp. 429-45.

Gupta, M.P. and Sharma, S. (2003), "Economic Contributions of In-migrants in Korba City, India", *Annals of the National Association of Geographers*, India, Vol. XXIII, No. 1, June, pp. 46-57.

Haan, Arjen de, (2000) "Livelihoods and Poverty: The Role of Migration — A Critical Review of Migration Literature", *The Journal of Development Studies*, Vol. 36, No. 2, pp.

Joshi, Y.G. and Verma, D.K. (2004), *In Search of Livelihood: Labour Migration from Chattisgarh*, Manak Publications Pvt. Ltd., New Delhi, pp. 137-46.

Kamble, N.D. (1983), *Labour Migration in Indian States*, Ashish Publishing House, New Delhi, pp. 143-53.

Kaur, Gurinder (2004), "Rural-Rural Male Migration in Punjab 1991", *Geographical Review of India* Vol. 66 No. 2, June, pp. 179-93.

Kaur, Gurinderjit (1999), *Migratory Labour in Punjab Agriculture*, Ph.D. Thesis, Department of Economics, Punjabi University, Patiala, July, pp. 190-205.

Khairkar, V.P. (2003), "Factors Affecting Volume of Migration to Pune City", *Geographical Review of India*, Vol. 65, No. 1, March, pp. 23-33.

Mahesh, R (2004), "Labour Mobility and Paradox of Rural Unemployment—Farm Labour Shortage (A Micro Level Study)", *The Indian Journal of Labour Economics*, Vol. 47, No. 1, January-March, pp. 115-33.

Mahmood, Zafar (1991), "Emigration and Wages in an Open Economy: Some Evidence from Pakistan, *The Pakistan Development Review*, Vol. 30, No. 3, pp. 243-62.

Mehta, G.S. (2003), *Non-Farm Economy and Rural Development*, Anmol Publications, New Delhi, pp. 284-85.

Mehta, Swarnjit (1971), "Patterns of Migration in the Bist-Doab, 1951-61", Panjab *University Research Bulletin (Arts)*, Chandigarh, pp. 17-33.

Mittar, Vishwa (1984), Growth of Informal Sector in Punjab's Urban Economy: A Case Study of Patiala District, Ph.D Thesis, Punjabi University, Patiala, pp. 3-10.

Moore, R. (1977), *Migrants and Class Structure of Western Europe*, George Allen and Unwin Ltd., London, pp. 137-49.

Mukherjee, S. (2001), "Low Quality Migration in India: The Phenomenon of Distressed Migration and Acute Urban Decay", 24th IUSSP Conference, Salvador, Brazil, August, Downloaded from the website http//www.iussp.org/brazi/2001/s80/s8004mukherjee;pdf.

Namasivayam, N.; and Kumar, Vijay S. (2004), "Socio-economic Factors Influencing Migration of Labour with Special Reference to Melur Taluk, Tamil Nadu: A Case Study", Downloaded from the website http://www.kli.re.kr./iira2004/pro/ papers/namasivianopdf.

Oberoi, A.S.; and Singh, H.K. Manmohan (1983) *Causes and Consequences of Internal Migration; A Study in the Indian Punjab,* Oxford University Press, New Delhi pp. 399-416.

Odaman, O.M. (1988), "Migration and Rural Development: An Empirical Investigation of Migrants", Participation in Rural Community Development Projects in Nigeria; *Demography India,* Vol. 18, No. 1 & 2, pp. 191-99.

Paris, T. Singh; A. Luis, J.; and Hussain, M. (2005), "Labour Out-Migration, Likelihood of Rice farming Household and Women Left Behind: A Case Study of Eastern Uttar Pradesh", *Economic and Political Weekly,* June 18, pp. 2522-2529.

Paul, R.R. (1989), *Rural-Urban Migration in Punjab,* Himalaya Publishing House, New Delhi, pp. 174-82.

Premi, M.K.; and Mathur, M.D. (1995), "Emigration Dynamics: The Indian Context", *International Migration* Vol. 33, No. 3 & 4, pp. 627-63.

Radhakrishana, R.; Rao, V.M. and Roy, Shoven (2004), "Beyond Quantification of Poverty: Emerging Issues in Poverty Reduction", *Indian Journal of Labour Economics,* Vol. 47, No. 2 April-June, pp. 342-45.

Rangi, P.S.; Sidhu, M.S.; and Singh, Harjit (2001), "Casualisation of Agricultural Labour in Punjab", *The Indian Journal of Labour Economics,* Vol. 44, No. 4, pp. 964-66.

Rehman Anisur (1999), "Indian Labour Migration to West Asia, *Manpower Journal* Vol. XXXV, No. 2, July-September, pp. 87-99.

Rodrigo, C. (1992), "Overseas Migration from Sri Lanka Magnitude, Patterns and Trends", Asian Regional Exchange for New Alternatives, *Asian Exchange* Vol. 8, No. 3 & 4, pp. 41-74.

Rogaly, B.; Biswas, J.; Coppard, D.; Rafique, A.; Rana, K.; and Gupta, S.A. (2001), "Seasonal Migration, Social Change and Migrants' Rights (Lesson from West Bengal)", *Economic and Political Weekly,* December 8, pp. 4547-57.

Shah, N.M. (1994), "An Overview of Present and Future Emigration Dynamics in South Asia", *International Migration* Vol. 32, No. 2, pp. 217-68.

Sharma, S.K. (1989), "Patterns of In-migration in Madhya Pradesh", *Geographical Review of India,* Vo1. 51, No. 3, September, pp. 62-75.

Sharma, A.N. (2005), "Agrarian Relations and Socio-economic Change in Bihar" *Economic and Political Weekly,* March, Vol. XL, No. 10, pp. 967-68.

Sharma, Manmohan (1982), "Impact of Migratory Labour on the Rural Economy of Punjab", *Man and Development*, Vol. IV, No. 3, pp. 66-111.

Siddiquii, T. (2003), "Migration as a Livelihood Strategy for the Poor. The Bangladesh Case", Refugee and Migrating Movements Research Unit (RMMRU), University of Dhaka, Bangladesh, Downloaded from the website: http/www.eldis.org/static/doc 1683.htau.

Sidhu, M.S.; Rangi, P.S. and Singh, K. (1997), "A Study on the Migrant Agricultural Labour in Punjab, Department of Economics and Sociology, Punjab Agriculture University, Ludhiana, pp. 50-53.

Singh, H.K. Manmohan (1983), "Population Pressure and the Labour Absorbability in Agriculture", *Studies in Punjab Economy*, Punjab School of Economics, GNDU, Amritsar, pp. 402-03.

Singh, Kamaljit (1991), *Internal Migration in a Developing Economy*, National Book Organisation, New Delhi, pp. 223-26.

Singh, Manjit (1995), *Uneven Development in Agriculture and Labour Migration: A Case of Bihar and Punjab*, Print Perfect, Mayapuri, Industrial Area, New Delhi, pp. 33-34.

Singh, Parminder; and Singh, Navsharan G. (1984), "Socio-economic Study of Migrant Farm Labour: A Case Study of Amritsar District in Punjab", P.S.E. *Economic Analyst*, Vol. V, Nos. 1 & 2, pp. 43-49.

Sivakumar, M.N. (2001), "Selectivity in Rural-Urban Migration: Evidence from Tamil Nadu", *Man and Development*, March pp. 57-68.

Skeldon, R. (2002), "Migration and Poverty", *Asia-Pacific Population Journal*, December, pp. 57-68.

Subramanian K.P. and C.K. Balasubramaniam (2000), "Migration: Blessing or Burden? A Study of Tamil Nadu and Its Cities", *Urban India*, Vol. XX No. 2, pp. 91-119.

Ward, Antony (1975), "European Capitalism's Reserve Army", *Monthly Review*, Vol. 27, No. 6, November, pp. 30-31.

Yadava, K.N.S. (1996), *Rural-Urban Migration in India*, Independent Publishing Co., Delhi, pp. 113-15.

Zachariah, K.C. (1968), *Migrants in Greater Bombay*, Asia Publishing House, Bombay, pp. 71-76.

Zachariah, K.C.; Mathew, E.T.; and. Rajan, S Irudaya (2003), *Dynamics of Migration in Kerala: Dimensions, Differentials and Consequences*, Orient Longman, New Delhi, pp. 20-25 & 460-70.

Fieldwork Area
Data Base and Methodology

The migrant labourers have been coming to Punjab ever since opportunities in agriculture were created by the state's agricultural leap forward. Soon after the advent of Green Revolution, there have been general prosperity and substantial increase in the incomes of the rural households. In the past few years, agricultural development is being regarded as an active propeller in the era of development of Punjab. This development process led to urbanisation and industrialisation of the state. The labourers from the countryside started moving towards towns and cities in search of work and high wages. The farmers in the rural Punjab have to face the shortage of labour during the peak agricultural season. As a result of imbalance in supply and demand for agricultural labour, the local labourers started demanding high wages. At such a juncture, the migratory labour becomes a source of relief and advantage to the peasantry of Punjab.

Punjab's prosperity has been largely due to the development of agriculture in the state. The major factors that led to the highly productive agricultural system of the state are: fertile soil, extensive irrigation works, suitable climate, hardworking farmers and above all, the advent of green revolution. The state is divided into three Agro-Climatic Zones, *viz.* Sub- mountainous Zone (Zone-I), Central Alluvial Zone (Zone-II) and Southern Dry Zone (Zone-III) (Human Development Report-2004, Punjab). Zone-I comprises of Gurdaspur, Hoshiarpur, Ropar, Fatehgarh Sahib, Patiala and Nawanshahr districts. Zone-II Comprises of Amritsar, Kapurthala, Jalandhar, Ludhiana, parts of Gurdaspur, Hoshiarpur, Fatehgarh Sahib, Patiala and Sangrur districts. Zone-III comprises of Bathinda, Mansa, Moga, Muktsar, Faridkot, Ferozepur and Sangrur districts.

CHARACTERISTICS OF THE STUDY AREA

The state of Punjab* occupies an extremely important place in the country. Although the economy of Punjab witnessed major changes over the years, yet its agrarian sector predominates over all other sectors of the economy. Till date, agriculture is the mainstay of the people of Punjab. Agriculture and livestock contribute more than 40 per cent of the gross state domestic product (Human Development Report-2004, Punjab). Population of the state is rural dominated which accounts for 16.04 millions (66.05 per cent) and urban population accounting for 8.24 millions (33.95 per cent). With this population, the density of population is 482 persons per sq. km. The overall literacy rate in the state at present is 69.95 per cent out of which the share of male population constitutes 75.63 per cent and that of female population 63.55 per cent

---

* The word *'Punjab'* is made up of two Persian words, *'Punj'* meaning five and *'ab'* meaning water (Chib, 1977). Hence, this name was given to this land of five rivers possibly in the era when this region came into close contacts with Persia. In the Vedic period, this region was known as *'Sapta Sindhu'*. Punjab is the fourth smallest state in the Union of India with an area of 50,362 sq. km. and a population of 2,43,58,999 (India,2007). Punjab is bounded on the West by Pakistan, on the North by Jammu and Kashmir, on the North-East by Himachal Pradesh and on the South by Haryana and Rajasthan. It extends between 29.33° and 32.31° North Latitude, and 73.53° and 76.56° East Longitude (Gupta, 2004).

(Census of India-2001). As regards the prosperity of the state; Human Development Index (HDI), which combines three essential elements: longevity, knowledge and per-capita income explains that Punjab stands at 2nd position (Table 3.1).

Table 3.1: Human Development Index for India

States	1981		1991		2001	
	Value	Rank	Value	Rank	Value	Rank
Andhra Pradesh	0.298	9	0.377	9	0.416	10
Assam	0.272	10	0.348	10	0.386	14
Bihar	0.237	15	0.308	15	0.367	15
Gujarat	0.360	4	0.431	6	0.479	6
Haryana	0.360	5	0.443	5	0.509	5
Karnataka	0.346	6	0.412	7	0.478	7
Kerala	0.500	1	0.591	1	0.638	1
M.P.	0.245	14	0.328	13	0.394	12
Maharashtra	0.363	3	0.452	4	0.523	4
Orissa	0.264	11	0.345	12	0.404	11
Punjab	0.411	2	0.475	2	0.537	2
Rajasthan	0.256	12	0.347	11	0.424	9
Tamil Nadu	0.343	7	0.466	3	0.531	3
U.P.	0.255	13	0.314	14	0.388	13
West Bengal	0.305	8	0.404	8	0.472	8
All India	**0.302**	–	**0.381**	–	**0.472**	–

Source: Human Development Report, 2004, p. 5.

RESEARCH METHODOLOGY

In order to achieve the objectives of the study, following research methodology has been used:

Locale of the Study

The locale of the study is the state of Punjab, agriculturally the most developed state of India.

Sampling Design

The four stage random sampling technique was used to select the sample for the study. District was the first stage of the sample while block and village were the second and third stages of the sample respectively. The respondents such as the migrant labourers, the local labourers and the farmers became the fourth and ultimate stage of the sample of the study.

Selection of the Districts from the Study Area

Punjab state is divided into 17 districts. These districts are further divided into tehsils and blocks for the purpose of good governance. To make the study representative of the Punjab state, the field work for the research work was conducted in three districts, *viz.* Ludhiana, Hoshiarpur and Faridkot. The selection of these three districts has been made in the following manner:

(a) Districts having maximum concentration of migrants;

(b) Districts having less concentration of migrants;

(c) Districts having least concentration of migrants.

Table 3.2 shows the concentration of migrants in the various districts of Punjab.

The concentration of migrants in the districts of Punjab has been ranked in the ascending order. District Moga has been ranked at 1, having 12.324 migrants per sq. km. and Ludhiana having the highest concentration of migrants (116.772 migrants per sq. km.). For identifying the maximum, less and the least concentrated districts, the districts have been divided into the following three broad categories:

(i) Districts having concentration of migrants less than 20;

(ii) Districts having concentration of migrants between 20 and 40;

(iii) Districts having concentration of migrants more than 40.

Table 3.2: Concentration of Migrants

S. No.	District	Population of Migrants*	Area** (sq.km.)	No. of Migrants per sq. km. (Concentration)	Rank
1.	Gurdaspur	92,887	3,570	26.019	10
2.	Amritsar	97,620	5,075	19.235	07
3.	Kapurthala	47,400	1,646	28.797	12
4.	Jalandhar	129,150	2,658	48.59	14
5.	Hoshiarpur	94,911	3,310	28.674	11
6.	Nawanshahr	23,718	1,258	18.854	06
7.	Rupnagar	170,932	2,118	80.743	16
8.	Fatehgarh Sahib	40,221	1,180	34.86	13
9.	Ludhiana	437,196	3,144	116.772	17
10.	Moga	20,605	1,672	12.324	01
11.	Ferozepur	106,016	5,865	18.076	04
12.	Muktsar	43,608	2,596	16.381	03
13.	Faridkot	24,113	1,472	25.375	02
14.	Bathinda	85,690	3,377	21.384	09
15.	Mansa	46,489	2,174	18.095	08
16.	Sangrur	90,856	5,021	18.095	05
17.	Patiala	201,304	3,627	55.502	15

Source: * Census of India 2001; D-I Population Classified by Birth and Sex.

** India 2006, Publication Division, Ministry of Information and Broadcasting, G.O.I.

Table 3.3: Classification of Concentration of Migrants District-wise

S. No.	Districts with density* less than 20		S. No.	Districts with density varying from 20 to 40		S. No.	Districts with density greater than 40	
1.	Moga	12.324	1.	Mansa	21.384	1.	Jalandhar	48.590
2.	Faridkot	16.381	2.	Bathinda	25.375	2.	Patiala	55.502
3.	Muktsar	16.798	3.	Gurdaspur	26.019	3.	Rupnagar	80.743
4.	Firozepur	18.076	4.	Hoshiarpur	28.674	4.	Ludhiana	116.772
5.	Sangrur	18.095	5.	Kapurthala	28.797			
6.	Nawanshahr	18.854	6.	Fatehgarh Sahib	34.086			
7.	Amritsar	19.235						

* Density here refers to number of migrants per sq. km.

On the basis of above cited criterion, three districts namely Ludhiana with high concentration of migration, Hoshiarpur with less concentration of migration, and Faridkot with the least concentration of migration were purposively chosen. Moreover, these three districts also represent the agro-climatic zones of Punjab state. Purposive sampling involves selecting items by choice and not by chance. A purposive sample is considered typical of the universe with regard to the characteristics under investigation. The purposive selection of these districts was done because migration has taken place in these districts because of more employment opportunities in the agricultural sector. All these characteristics provide justification for the selection of these districts for the study.

Selection of the Blocks

In order to make the study exhaustive and more representative of the state of Punjab, all the blocks of the selected districts have been taken into account. Ludhiana district is comprised of 12 blocks, Hoshiarpur 10, and Faridkot 2 blocks.

Selection of the Villages

From each block of the three selected districts, a village is selected on the basis of random sampling. Keeping in view the basic requirements of the study, the village was selected very carefully on the following basis:

(a) The village should be large enough so as to be capable of revealing a wide variety of variations suitable to the objectives of the study.

(b) The economy of the village should be pre-dominantly agricultural so that majority of the labourers are engaged in the agricultural sector.

(c) The village should be outside the influence of the nearest town or city.

On the basis of the above criteria, the list of the blocks and villages is presented in the Table 3.4 (*See on next page*).

Selection of the Respondents

Finally, the ultimate respondents of the study, *viz.* the migrant agricultural labourers, the local agricultural labourers and the farmers were randomly selected. As the present study primarily relates to the migrant labourers, so weightage was given to the migrant respondents. From each selected village five per cent of the total strength of migrant agricultural labourers, two per cent of the local agricultural labourers and two per cent of the farmers were taken into account. The total number of respondents and the split of the sampling scheme are given in Table 3.5 (*See on page 70*).

A total sample of 785 respondents was taken in the following scheme. From Ludhiana district, a sample of 436 respondents was taken out of which 206 were the migrant agricultural labourers, 126 the local agricultural labourers and 104 farmers. The sample of 219 respondents from Hoshiarpur district comprises 80 migrant agricultural labourers, 79 local agricultural labourers and 60 farmers. Similarly, the sample of 130 respondents of district Faridkot consists of 38 migrant agricultural labourers, 64 local agricultural labourers and 28 farmers. Thus in all, 324 migrant agricultural labourers, 269 local agricultural labourers and 192 farmers comprised the sample.

Table 3.4: Blocks and Villages Selected from Three Sampled Districts

	Districts		Blocks		Villages
1.	Ludhiana	1.	Ludhiana-I	1.	Jandiali
		2.	Ludhiana-II	2.	Chak Kalan
		3.	Dehlon	3.	Ram Garh Sardaran
		4.	Pakhowal	4.	Gujjarwal
		5.	Doraha	5.	Ghudani Kalan
		6.	Samrala	6.	Mad Pura
		7.	Khanna	7.	Isru
		8.	Machhiwara	8.	Powat
		9.	Jagraon	9.	Malik
		10.	Sudhar	10.	Heran
		11.	Sidhwanbet	11.	Galib Kalan
		12.	Raikot	12.	Nathowal
2.	Hoshiarpur	1.	Hoshiarpur-I	1.	Dhade Fateh Singh
		2.	Hoshiarpur-II	2.	Davida Ahariana
		3.	Bhunga	3.	Ambala Jattan
		4.	Tanda	4.	Jahura
		5.	Dasuya	5.	Changla
		6.	Mukerian	6.	Porika
		7.	Hajipur	7.	Dhamian
		8.	Talwara	8.	Rakri (Datarpur)
		9.	Mahilpur	9.	Maili
		10.	Garhshankar	10.	Possi
3.	Faridkot	1.	Faridkot	1.	Dhudi
		2.	Kotkapura	2.	Panj Grian Kalan

Table 3.5: Sample Scheme

District	Number of Villages	Number of Migrant Labourers	Number of the local Labourers	Number of Farmers	Total
Ludhiana	12	206	126	104	436
Hoshiarpur	10	80	79	60	219
Faridkot	02	38	64	28	130
Total	**24**	**324**	**269**	**192**	**785**

PHYSIOGRAPHY OF THE SELECTED DISTRICTS

Three different districts representing the different degrees of concentration of labour migration were chosen for the study. Ludhiana district represented the Central Zone (Sweet-Water Zone) which was an industrialised area of Punjab having an average literacy rate. The second district was Hoshiarpur which represented the sub-mountainous zone (semi-hilly area) and was having a higher percentage of literate population in the state. The third district was Faridkot which represented the South-Western Zone of the state. The region is prone to water logging; and the ground water quality is saline, not good for irrigation. A synoptic view of the infrastructural variables of the selected districts is given in Table 3.6 (*See on pages 72 to 74*)

Keeping in view the broad objectives of the study, geographical and social variations in the state, numerical strength of the migrants and other relevant variables, a multistage random sampling technique was followed.

DATA COLLECTION

Data on several aspects of respondents, *viz*. the migrant agricultural labourers, the local agricultural labourers and the farmers were collected. Both qualitative and quantitative data were collected from two main sources: primary and secondary. The primary data was solicited from the respondents at the village level through questionnaire survey, group discussions and field observations. Reports, documents, and published books from relevant institutions, were the main source of the secondary data.

The first step in the process of data collection was to review the geographical literature of the area. This was done in order to become acquainted with the respondents so as to collect relevant data for the study. A set of three separate comprehensive schedules was prepared in order to record the observations and behaviour of the respondents from all the three categories, *i.e.* the migrant labour, local labour and farmers. These schedules were initially administered and tested through a pilot survey. The actual field survey was conducted thereafter during the months of April to July 2006, which coincised with the rice cultivating season.

The schedule-cum-questionnaire prepared for the migrant labour was structured and composed of six sections:

1. General information about the migrant labour regarding place of origin, caste, age, family background, marital status, number of family members, family type, nature of work at the place of origin, education level, languages known, house/property, year of migration, etc.
2. Trends and factors associated with migration, mode of migration, selection of the area of destination, mode of journey and hardships faced during the journey, nature of the job and relations with the employer, the local agricultural labour, etc.
3. Consumption and expenditure behaviour of the migrant agricultural labour.
4. Social and cultural particulars of migrant agricultural labourers.
5. Particulars about economic status: wage rate and employment days in Punjab, annual income, expenditure, savings and remittances to their native places.
6. Information about the wife of the migrant agricultural labourer and their children.

Table 3.6: A Synoptic View of the Infrastructural Variables of the Selected Districts

		1 Ludhiana	2 Hoshiarpur	3 Faridkot
1.	Location	It lies between north latitude 30-34° and 31°-01° and east longitude 75°-18° and 76°-20°. It shares common boundaries with Rupnagar and Fatehgarh Sahib districts in east, Moga and Faridkot districts in the west and Sangrur and Fatehgarh Sahib districts in the south and south-east.	It lies in the North-east of Punjab. It is bounded by Nawanshahr, Rupnagar Ludhiana and Kapurthala districts and Una district of Himachal Pradesh.	It touches the boundaries of Ferozepur district in the North-west, Bathinda district in the south, Muktsar district in the west and Moga district in the east.
2.	Geographical Area	3767 sq. kms.	3310 sq. kms.	1476 sq. kms.
3.	No. of Blocks	12	10	02
4.	No. of villages	915	1393	171
	(i) Inhabited	896	1393	163
	(ii) Uninhabited	19	–	8

(Contd...)

			1 Ludhiana		2 Hoshiarpur		3 Faridkot	
5.		Population	30,32,831		14,78,000		5,50,892	
	(i)	Male	16,62,716		7,64,000			
	(ii)	Female	13,70,115		7,14,000			
	(iii)	Density of population population	8051 persons per sq. km.		436 persons per sq. km.		373 persons per sq. km.	
	(iv)	Urban pupulation	55.80		19.66		33.89	
6.		Livelihoods	*1991*	*2001*	*1991*	*2001*	*1991*	*2001*
	(i)	Work participation rate	31.3	37.8	28.6	34.7	32.8	42.4
	(ii)	Female work participation rate	2.6	15.7	4.7	17.3	6.8	23.0
	(iii)	Male work participation rate	55.5	55.9	50.6	51.0	55.7	59.5
	(iv)	Net sown area	325	304	247	218	517	132
	(v)	Cropping intensity (% age)	185	199 (202 in *2003-04*)	160	168 (179 as on *31st March, 2005*)	176	187 (178 in *2005-06*)
	(vi)	Per capita forest area (hect.)	0.004	0.003	0.066	0.074	0.006	0.004

(Contd...)

7.	Literacy rate	67.34	76.54	72.08	81.40	49.97	63.34
(i)	Rural literacy rate	62.28	72.88	70.61	80.09	42.33	58.58
(ii)	Urban literacy rate	71.71	79.42	79.16	86.66	65.45	72.71

Source: 1. Annual Credit Plan 2006-07 District Ludhiana (Punjab), Punjab and Sind Bank, Lead Bank
2. District Credit Plan 2005-06 District Hoshiarpur (Punjab), Punjab National Bank, Lead Bank
3. Annual Credit Plan 2005-06 District Faridkot (Punjab), Punjab and Sind Bank, Lead Bank
4. Human Development Report 2004, Punjab, pp. 214-220.

The schedule-cum-questionnaire for seeking the views of the local labourers was prepared to ascertain their relations with the migrant agricultural labourers, effect of the presence of migrant labourers on the level of employment and wage rate, their addiction to intoxicants because of the presence of migrant agricultural labourers in Punjab and cultural intimacy with the migrants. Information gathered from the local labourers included age, caste, marital status, education level, wages, monthly income, expenditure and savings, types of relations with the migrant agricultural labourers, behaviour of the migrant agricultural labourers, social and economic problems created by the migrant agricultural labourers, dispute among migrants themselves and with local agricultural labourers, etc.

The schedule-cum-questionnaire for ascertaining the opinion of farmers was prepared. Information therein included age, marital status, education level, area of land, crops sown, productivity per acre, kinds of labourers employed, number of local and migrant labourers, reasons for the preference of migrant agricultural labourers over the local agricultural labourers, mode of engaging the migrant agricultural labourers, efficiency of the labourers, problems faced in the agricultural work without the availability of the migrant agricultural labourers, trustworthiness difference between the migrant agricultural labourers and the local agricultural labourers, social and economic problems created by the migrant agricultural labourers, social and cultural intimacy with the migrant agricultural labourers.

Personal interview method was employed to fill the schedules. During the field survey, special care was taken to build a good rapport with all the three categories of respondents so that they may share their genuine perception and attitude with the researcher. The questions from the schedule were read and interpreted into more familiar words of the area. The use of Hindi/Punjabi language and local slangs helped to develop a good working relation with the respondents of all the three categories. A large number of migrant agricultural labourers, the local agricultural labourers and even the farmers were enthusiastic about their participation in the survey because they wanted somebody to listen to their feelings and concerns.

During the field survey, the methodological approach of the study was listening to the relation between the migrant agricultural labourers and the local agricultural labourers, migrant agricultural labourers and farmers, farmers' views about the migrant agricultural labourers and the local agricultural labourers and tried to relate them with regard to the objectives of the study.

STATISTICAL FRAMEWORK

Simple statistical tools like frequencies, percentages, averages as well as advanced statistical techniques like chi-square test, t-test, test of proportions (Z-test), Analysis of Variance (ANOVA), etc. were applied to analyse the data. The results were presented in both tabular and graphical forms.

Chi-Square Test

In order to see the association between two-way classifications of the respondents, chi-square test was applied by using the following formula

$$\chi^2 = \Sigma (O-E)^2/E$$

where,

χ^2 = Chi-square value

Σ^2 = Summation

O = Observed frequency

E = Expected frequency

Student's t-test

In order to compare two mean values, t-test was applied as under:

$$t = \frac{\bar{X}_1 - \bar{X}_2}{SE(\bar{X}_1 - \bar{X}_2)}$$

$$SE = S\sqrt{(1/N_1 + 1/N_2)}$$

$$S = \sqrt{\frac{\sigma_1^{\,2}(N_1 - 1) + \sigma_2^{\,2}(N_2 - 1)}{N_1 + N_2 - 2}}$$

where,

SE = Standard error of mean difference

σ = Standard deviation

S = Common standard deviation

N = Number of observations

Z-test (Test of Proportions)

To compare two proportions of respondents, z – test was applied:

$$Z = \frac{|P_1 - P_2|}{SE(P_1 - P_2)}$$

$$SE = \sqrt{pq(1/N_1 + 1/N_2)}$$

where,

$$p = \frac{n_1 + n_2}{N_1 + N_2}$$

and

q = $1 - p$

n_1 = Specific number in category I

n_2 = Specific number in category II

N_1 = Total number in category I

N_2 = Total number in category II

Analysis of Variance

In order to compare more than two means altogether, analysis of variance (ANOVA) was done through which F-ratio and critical difference were worked out. If the actual difference between any two means to be compared is more than or equal to the critical difference (C.D.), then the difference is significant, otherwise, non-significant.

LIMITATIONS OF THE STUDY

The study which revolves around the social and economic aspects of the respondents is based mainly on the primary data. Although during the field survey, every possible effort was made to obtain accurate information, yet majority of the respondents being illiterate, the possibilities of error in the data due to lack of memory and personal bias could not be ruled out.

At many occasions assurances were given to the migrant agricultural labourers that the information obtained would be used for research work, but some of the migrant agricultural labourers were reluctant to impart the desired information as they feared that giving such information would implicate them in false police cases. However, in certain cases, they readily agreed to give complete information. In certain cases, farmers felt that while talking with their labourers, the researcher was wasting their time. Thus, the employer indirectly refused his employees to give the information. In such situations, a lot of time was wasted to convince the farmers who ultimately agreed not only to provide the required information but also allowed their labourers to provide the desired information. In some of the cases, the farmers preferred that their employees should be interviewed in their presence. In such situations, some of the migrant labourers might be biased while giving the information. The migrant agricultural labourers were not very much against the local labourers and farmers. On the contrary, most of the local labourers were averse to the migrant labourers. But in the presence of migrant labourers, they were reluctant to fully express their views. Under such circumstances, the local labourers were segregated from the migrant labourers so that they may express their views without fear. An attempt was made to gather information about the economic and social offences committed by the migrant agricultural labourers. But neither the migrants themselves nor their employers were ready to share this information.

Socio-economic Background of the Migrant Agricultural Labourers

The socio-economic background of the migrant agricultural labourers bore an important impact on the labour supply curve, labour productivity status and assimilation with the locals. Therefore, it is relevant here to study the socio-economic characteristics of the migratory agricultural labourers in comparison with the local agricultural labourers before elaborating the determinants, trends, factors associated with migration, wage structure, socio-cultural change and assimilation pattern.

The migrants come from a variety of backgrounds and different groups concentrate on specific occupations, migration streams are strongly segmented (de Haan and Rogaly, 1996). They belong to various ethnic groups, castes and are both landless and landowners. The migrants come from a variety of districts, not necessarily the poorest. Some areas have developed a tradition of migration and once certain patterns of migration exist, they do not change easily. Under these circumstances, the socio-economic transformation of the migratory labourers has a special significance. In order to access the relative role of the migratory labourers in the farm sector of Punjab, an evaluation of the socio-economic background of these labourers is required.

The socio-economic background of the migrant agricultural labourers has been viewed on the basis of social and economic parameters. To analyse social parameters of the labour migration, the aspects of native state, caste, family size, family type, marital status and age have been assessed, whereas to examine economic parameters of the agricultural labour migration, education, nature of employment at the native place and housing structure have been analysed.

(A) SOCIAL PARAMETERS

The extent and nature of social parameters of the migratory agricultural labourers have been assessed by the evaluation and analysis of primary empirical information. It covers issues of native state, age, caste, family size, marital status, and number of children of the migratory labourers.

NATIVE STATE

The state-wise classification of the migrant agricultural labourers (*See Table 4.1 on next page*) shows that majority, of the migrant agricultural labourers i.e. 60.80 per cent belonged to Bihar followed by 18.52 per cent from Uttar Pradesh, 11.11 per cent from Jharkhand, 5.86 per cent from Nepal and 1.85 per cent each from West Bengal and other states of India. The reasons of migration to Punjab are reported in detail in the following chapters of the study.

AGE

Although there are a number of factors of migration, yet only migration by age has been found to be more or less similar for developed as well as for developing countries. It is established that adult males are more inclined to migrate than the other people of the community (Rogaria, 1997). Migration differentiated by age has been almost generalised and it is higher for the people aged between 15 and 40 (Yadava, 1988).

Table 4.1: Distribution of Migratory Labourers according to their Native State/Country

State	No. of Migrants	Migration Rate	Rank
Bihar	197	60.80	I
Uttar Pradesh	60	18.52	II
Jharkhand	36	11.11	III
West Bengal	6	1.85	V
Nepal	19	5.86	IV
Others	6	1.85	V
Total	**324**	**100.00**	

Source: Field Survey 2006.

The information contained in Table 4.2 (a) (*See on page 84*) shows that a vast majority of the migratory agricultural labourers, *i.e.* 74.07 per cent belong to the age group of 15-35 years, which is the most labour productive age group. Out of this, 47.53 per cent of them fall in the age group of 15-20 years which is the age of schooling. It is a matter of pity that about 23 per cent of the migratory agricultural labourers were less than 15 years of age. There were only about 2.50 per cent of the migratory agricultural labourers who were above the age of 35 years. This shows that younger migratory labourers attract the labour market more than the older ones due to the level of labour productivity while the older people would be a better option to stay at the native state home to look after the family affairs. The average age of the migratory agricultural labourers in Punjab came to be 18.63 years.

The district-wise analysis also portrayed a similar trend as is clear from the district-wise mean age, *i.e.* 18.40 years in Ludhiana, 19 years in Hoshiarpur and 19.08 years in Faridkot district.

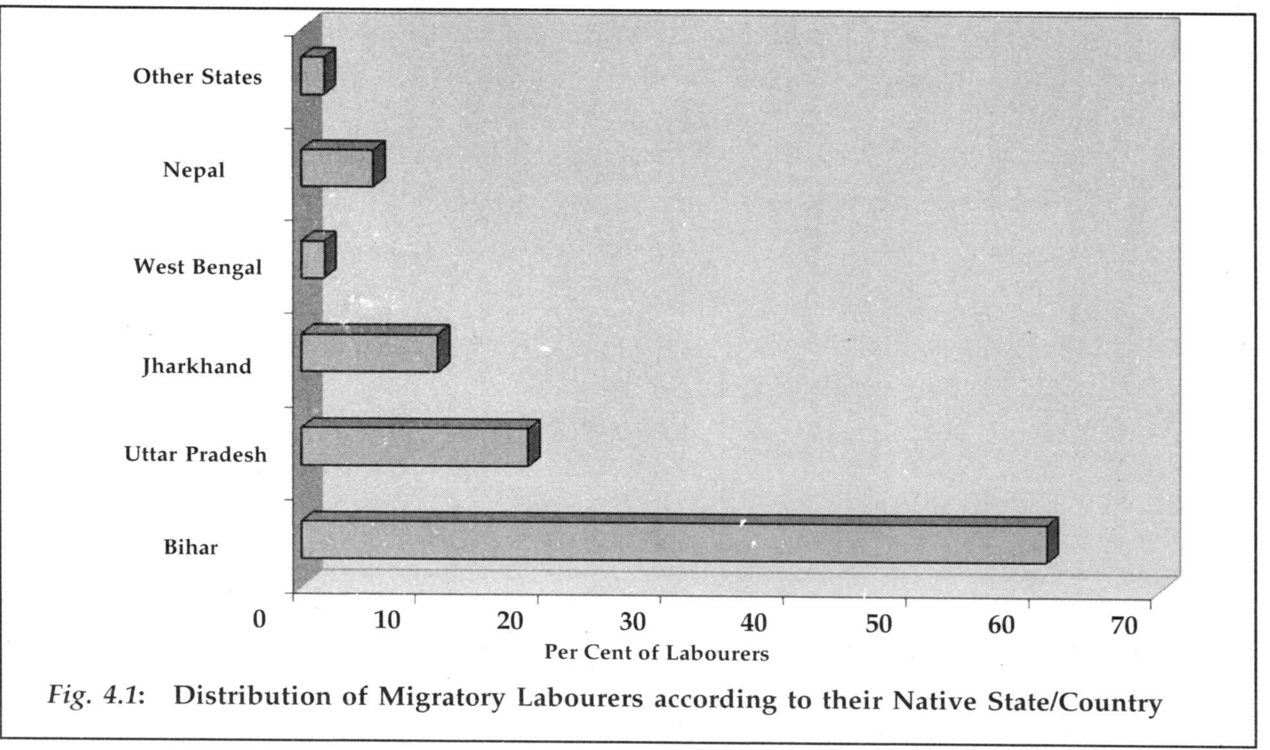

Fig. 4.1: Distribution of Migratory Labourers according to their Native State/Country

Table 4.2 (a): Distribution of Migratory Agricultural Labourers according to Age

District	Age (years)							Mean Age
	<10	10-15	15-20	20-25	25-30	30-35	>35	
Ludhiana	5 (2.43)	49 (23.79)	97 (47.09)	31 (15.05)	12 (5.83)	7 (3.40)	5 (2.43)	18.40
Hoshiarpur	0 (0.00)	13 (16.25)	42 (52.50)	18 (22.50)	4 (5.00)	1 (1.25)	2 (2.50)	19.00
Faridkot	0 (0.00)	9 (23.68)	15 (39.47)	9 (23.68)	4 (10.53)	0 (0.00)	1 (2.63)	19.08
Punjab	5 (1.54)	71 (21.91)	154 (47.53)	58 (17.90)	20 (6.17)	8 (2.47)	8 (2.47)	18.63

Source : Field Survey 2006

Note : The figures given in parentheses represent percentages.

Table 4.2 (b): Distribution of Local Agricultural Labourers according to Age

District	Age (years)								Mean Age
	15-20	20-25	25-30	30-35	35-40	40-45	45-50	>50	
Ludhiana	5 (3.97)	8 (6.35)	7 (5.56)	19 (15.08)	22 (17.46)	22 (17.46)	14 (11.11)	29 (23.02)	39.88
Hoshiarpur	0 (0.00)	3 (3.80)	4 (5.06)	15 (18.99)	14 (17.72)	18 (22.78)	9 (11.39)	16 (20.25)	40.79
Faridkot	3 (4.69)	7 (10.94)	9 (14.06)	12 (18.75)	10 (15.63)	7 (10.94)	6 (9.38)	10 (15.63)	36.41
Punjab	8 (2.97)	18 (6.69)	20 (7.43)	46 (17.10)	46 (17.10)	47 (17.47)	29 (10.78)	55 (20.45)	39.32

Source : Field Survey 2006

Note : The figures given in parentheses represent percentages.

Table 4.2 (c): Migratory Agricultural Labourers *v/s* Local Agricultural Labourers

District	t-value	p-value
Ludhiana	5.54	<0.01
Hoshiarpur	5.18	<0.01
Faridkot	4.09	<0.01
Punjab	5.37	<0.01

In order to make a comparison of age distribution of the migrant agricultural labourers with that of the local agricultural labourers, the age-distribution of the local agricultural labourers is presented in Table 4.2 (b) and t-test is applied to test the significance of differences of mean age as shown in Table 4.2 (c).

Table 4.2 (b) shows that among the local agricultural labourers, none was found to be below the age of 15 years while 20.45 per cent of them were above the age of 50 years. More than 50 per cent of the local agricultural labourers fell in the age group of 30-45 years. The average age of the local agricultural labourers came to be 39.32 years. The district-wise scenario corresponded with the state scenario. The average age of the local agricultural labourers was 39.88, 40.79 and 36.41 years in Ludhiana, Hoshiarpur and Faridkot districts respectively.

Table 4.2 (c) leads us to conclude that there were significant differences in the mean age of the migratory and local agricultural labourers in all the districts under study as well as in Punjab. The mean age of the migratory agricultural labourers was found to be significantly younger than that of the local agricultural labourers. This highlights that the migratory labourers have to do work for their livelihood and to support their families in a much younger age. Instead of books in their hands for study, they have to toil hard in the fields.

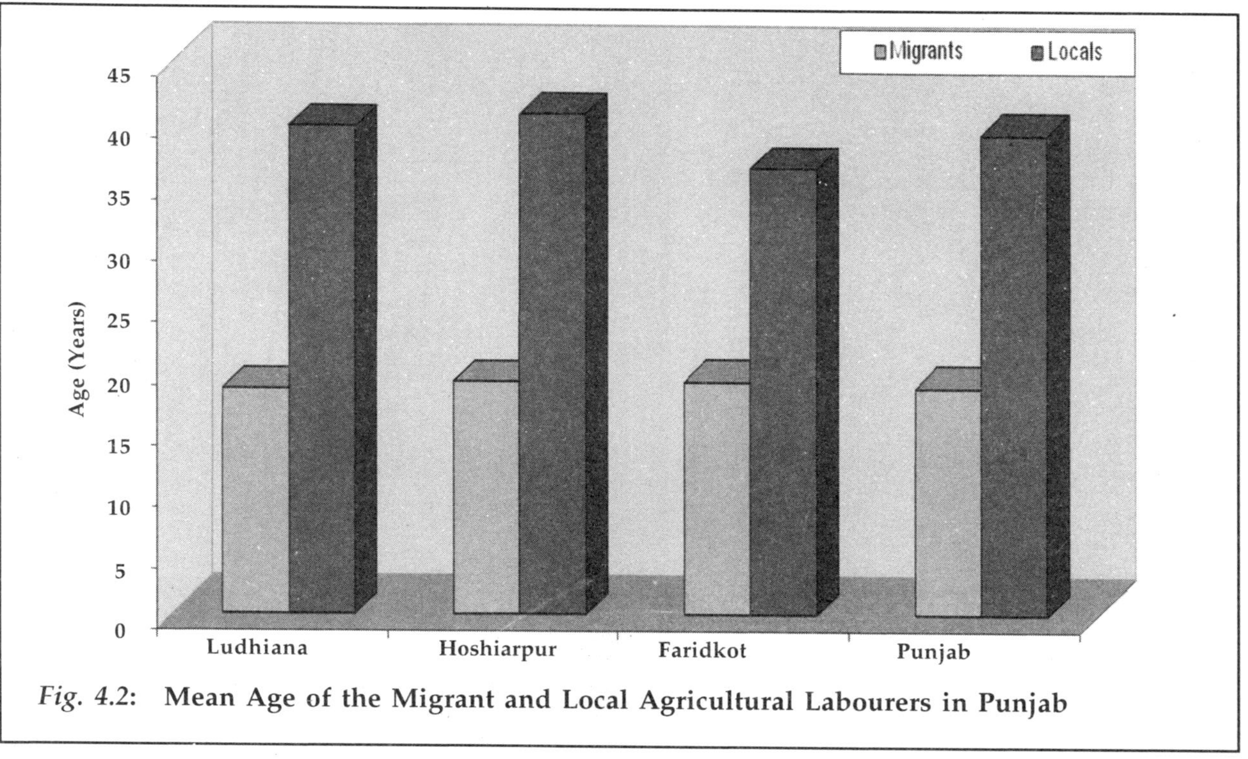

Fig. 4.2: Mean Age of the Migrant and Local Agricultural Labourers in Punjab

CASTE

It is an important and relevant parameter to examine the socio-economic background of the migratory labourers in Punjab.

A perusal of Table 4.3 (a) shows that majority of the migratory agricultural labourers, *i.e.* 58.64 per cent belonged to the scheduled castes followed by 31.17 per cent from the backward classes. It is revealing that as much as 10.19 per cent of the migratory agricultural labourers belonged to the general upper castes in the society. This shows that poverty and unemployment forced all the castes to migrate to Punjab for their livelihood. The trends in different districts followed the same way as was observed in the state as a whole.

Table 4.3 (a): Caste-wise Distribution of Migratory Agricultural Labourers

District	Castes		
	SC	BC	General
Ludhiana	121 (58.74)	64 (31.07)	21 (10.19)
Hoshiarpur	47 (58.75)	25 (31.25)	8 (10.00)
Faridkot	22 (57.90)	12 (31.58)	4 (10.52)
Punjab	190 (58.64)	101 (31.17)	33 (10.19)

Source : Field Survey 2006

Note : The figures given in parentheses represent percentages.

However, the data given in Table 4.3 (b) and analysis shown in Table 4.3 (c) highlighted that none among the local agricultural labourers belonged to the general (upper) castes while a vast majority of the local labourers, *i.e.* 94.05 per cent belonged to the different scheduled castes. The survey revealed that in Punjab, generally, backward castes have adopted parental self-employment pattern such as construction, repairing of farm implements and tools, tailoring and weaving, pottery, etc. Only those among backward castes, who could not survive themselves in these self-employment occupations, were forced to join the rank of the farm labour force.

Table 4.3 (b): Distribution of Local Agricultural Labourers according to Caste

District	Castes		
	SC	BC	General
Ludhiana	118 (93.65)	8 (6.35)	0 (0.00)
Hoshiarpur	73 (92.40)	6 (7.60)	0 (0.00)
Faridkot	62 (96.88)	2 (3.12)	0 (0.00)
Punjab	253 (94.05)	16 (5.95)	0 (0.00)

Source : Field Survey 2006

Note : The figures given in parentheses represent percentages.

Table 4.3 (c): Migratory Agricultural Labourers V/S Local Agricultural Labourers

	SC	BC	General
z-value	9.88	7.68	5.39
p-value	<.01	<.01	<.01

The above discussion brings out the fact that the scheduled castes were significantly higher among the local agricultural labourers as compared to those among the migratory agricultural labourers whereas the proportions of the backward and general castes were found to be significantly higher among the migratory agricultural labourers. The general castes not forming a part of farm labour in Punjab might be due to the socio-cultural factors. The field survey revealed that among the general castes, the landless population prefers either government/private jobs or a business of their own.

PARENTS' STATUS

The parents' status of the migratory agricultural labourers, whether alive or dead, is shown in Table 4.4 (*See on page 92*). A good many of the migratory agricultural labourers, i.e. 46.91 per cent and 38.58 per cent had lost their father and mother respectively. This resulted in a number of problems. This situation may be responsible to push them into seeking work for livelihood at an early age. So, looking after the family members may also be a difficult task for them.

MARITAL STATUS

According to the data given in Table 4.5 (a) (*See on page 93*), 68.21 per cent of the migratory labourers were married. Out of this only 17.65 per cent used to reside with their spouses. The remaining bulk proportion, *i.e.* 82.35 per cent of them could not enjoy the company of their life-partners due to high cost of living in Punjab and had to take care of their children and parents at their respective native villages.

Majority of the migratory labourers' wives residing at native village either had no work opportunity or had to work at very marginal wages in the fields of the feudal landlords. Out of those who used to reside here, about 75 per cent were working as domestic servants. They have to do so to augment their family income as well as to meet the education expenses of their children.

Table 4.5 (b) (*See on page 94*) shows that among the local agricultural labourers as high as 88.48 per cent were married while wives of 71.43 per cent of them were working. They were working mainly as domestic servants (64.12 per cent), followed by field labourers (14.12 per cent).

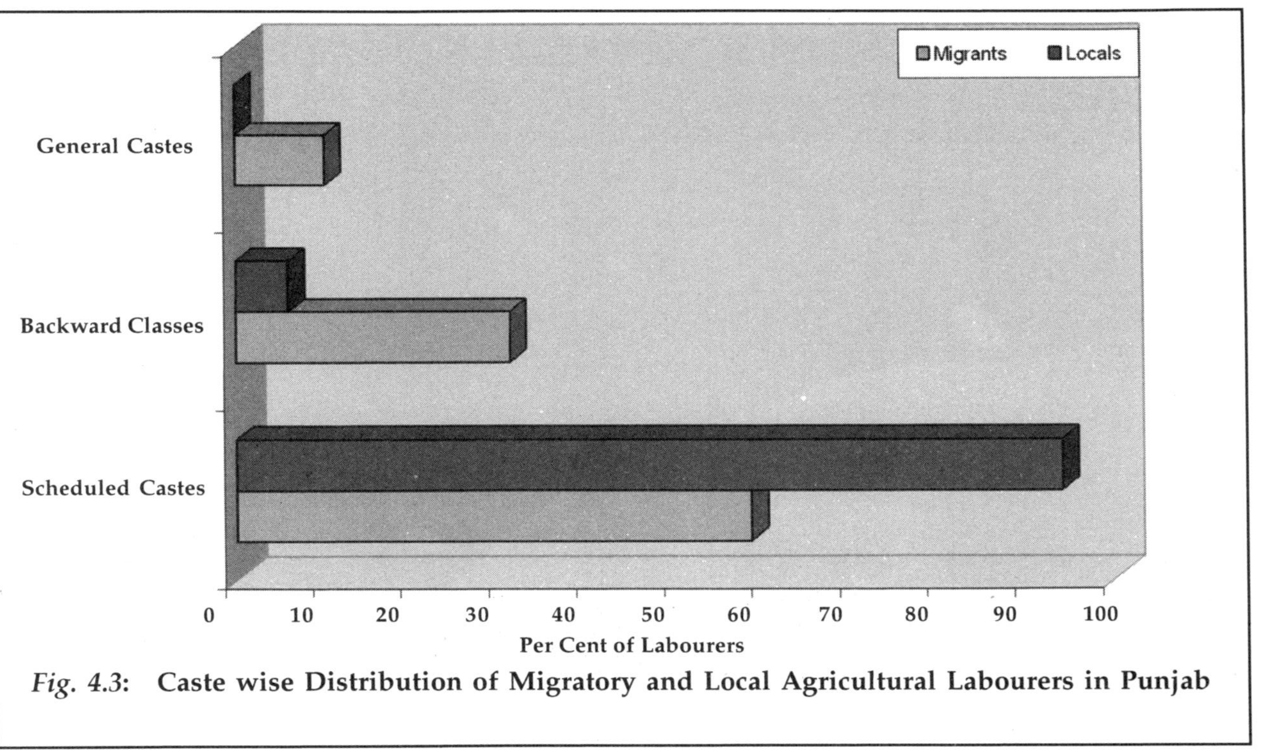

Fig. 4.3: Caste wise Distribution of Migratory and Local Agricultural Labourers in Punjab

Table 4.4: Distribution of Migratory Labourers according to Parents' Status

District	Father		Mother	
	Alive	Dead	Alive	Dead
Ludhiana	112 (54.37)	94 (45.63)	120 (58.25)	86 (41.75)
Hoshiarpur	42 (52.50)	38 (47.50)	53 (66.25)	27 (33.75)
Faridkot	18 (47.37)	20 (52.63)	26 (68.42)	12 (31.58)
Punjab	172 (53.09)	152 (46.91)	199 (61.42)	125 (38.58)

Source : Field Survey 2006

Note : The figures given in parentheses represent percentages.

Table 4.5 (a): Marital Status and Status of Wife

District	Marital Status		Wife living at		Present Place	
			Place	Place		Working
Ludhiana	142 (68.93)	64 (31.07)	114 (80.28)	28 (19.72)	21 (75.00)	7 (25.00)
Hoshiarpur	54 (67.50)	26 (32.50)	45 (83.33)	9 (16.67)	6 (66.67)	3 (33.33)
Faridkot	25 (65.79)	13 (34.21)	23 (92.00)	2 (8.00)	2 (100.00)	0 (0.00)
Punjab	221 (68.21)	103 (31.79)	182 (82.35)	39 (17.65)	29 (74.36)	10 (25.64)

Source: Field Survey 2006

Note : The figures given in parentheses represent percentages.

Table 4.5 (b): Distribution of Local Agricultural Labourers according to the Marital Status and Occupation of their Wives

District	Marital Status		Wife	
	Married	Unmarried	Working	Not Working
Ludhiana	111 (88.10)	15 (11.90)	82 (73.87)	29 (26.13)
Hoshiarpur	72 (91.14)	7 (8.86)	53 (73.61)	19 (26.39)
Faridkot	55 (85.94)	9 (14.06)	35 (63.64)	20 (36.36)
Punjab	238 (88.48)	31 (11.52)	170 (71.43)	68 (28.57)

Source : Field Survey 2006

Note : The figures given in parentheses represent percentages.

This shows that majority of the wives of both the local as well as migratory agricultural labourers used to work as domestic servants residing in Punjab. The study brings out the fact that a vast majority of the wives of the migratory agricultural labourers had to live in separation at their native villages in order to avoid high cost of living in Punjab and to look after their children in the native state.

NUMBER OF CHILDREN

The distribution of the migratory agricultural labourers according to number of children and average number of children are shown in Table 4.6 (a) (*See on next page*). For the comparison of this demographic aspect with the local agricultural labourers, Tables 4.6 (b) and 4.6 (c) (*See on page 96*) have also been incorporated.

Table 4.6 (a) (*See on next page*) shows that majority of the migratory agricultural labourers i.e. 55.20 per cent were having up to 2 children followed by 33.03 per cent having 3-4 children and only 11.77 per cent having 5 or more children.

The average number of children among the married migratory labourers came to be 1.61. District-wise analysis also depicted a similar pattern. The non-significant F-ratio also showed the same.

Table 4.6 (a): Distribution of Migratory Agricultural Labourers according to Number of Children

District	Number of children			Average
	0-2	3-4	>5	
Ludhiana 142	75 (52.82)	46 (32.39)	21 (14.79)	1.73
Hoshiarpur 54	30 (55.55)	20 (37.04)	4 (7.41)	1.45
Faridkot 25	17 (68.00)	7 (28.00)	1 (4.00)	1.32
Punjab 221	122 (55.20)	73 (33.03)	26 (11.77)	1.61
			F-ratio p-value	1.52 >.10ns

Source : Field Survey 2006

Note : The figures given in parentheses represent percentages.

Among the local agricultural labourers 52.94 per cent were having 3-4 children followed by 31.93 per cent having up to 2 children while 15.13 per cent of them were having 5 or more children. The average number of children among the married local agricultural labourers was 3.03.

District to district variation in average number of children was non-significant as indicated by F-ratio.

The comparison made in Table 4.6(c) shows that average number of children was significantly higher among the local agricultural labourers as compared to those among the migratory agricultural labourers in all the districts as well as in the state as a whole.

Table 4.6 (b): Distribution of Local Agricultural Labourers according to Number of Children

District	Number of Children			Average
	0-2	3-4	>5	
Ludhiana 111	42 (37.84)	57 (51.35)	12 (10.81)	2.83
Hoshiarpur 72	17 (23.61)	41 (56.94)	14 (19.45)	3.28
Faridkot 55	17 (30.91)	28 (50.91)	10 (18.18)	3.11
Punjab 238	76 (31.93)	126 (52.94)	36 (15.13)	3.03
			F-ratio p-value	1.87 >.10ns

Source : Field Survey 2006

Note : The figures given in parentheses represent percentages.

The lesser number of children among the migratory labourers seems obviously due to their separation from their wives under the pressure of poverty.

Table 4.6 (c): Migratory Agricultural Labourers *vs.* Local Agricultural Labourers

District	t-value	p-value
Ludhiana	2.54	<0.05
Hoshiarpur	4.56	<0.01
Faridkot	4.46	*<0.01*
Punjab	3.97	<0.01

(B) ECONOMIC PARAMETERS

The economic parameters for migration of the labourers from the poor areas have been evaluated on the basis of education, nature of employment and housing structure.

EDUCATION

The educational level of the migrant agricultural labourers has been presented in Table 4.7 (a) and that of the local agricultural labourers in Table 4.7 (b) (*See on page 99*). Their comparison has been shown in Table 4.7 (c) (*See on page 99*).

Several studies have brought out the fact that the migrant households are socio-economically and educationally better placed than others (Yadava and Yadava, 1996-97), yet the field data shows different dynamics of the study.

It is a matter of pity that about three-fourths (72.54 per cent) of the migratory agricultural labourers were illiterate and only 1.54 per cent of them were matriculates. None was reported to be above matric. The mean score worked out by assigning the weight zero to illiterate, one to primary, two to middle and three to matric, comes out to be only 1.58 for the state as a whole. The mean score of education was 1.41 in Ludhiana, 1.91 in Hoshiarpur and 1.79 in Faridkot district. According to the F-ratio, the level of education of the migratory agricultural labourers was the same in all the districts.

Table 4.7 (a): Distribution of Migrant Agricultural Labourers according to Education

District	Education Level				Mean Score of Education
	Illiterate	Primary	Middle	Matric	
Ludhiana	155 (75.24)	41 (19.90)	7 (3.40)	3 (1.46)	1.41
Hoshiarpur	54 (67.50)	19 (23.75)	6 (7.50)	1 (1.25)	1.91
Faridkot	26 (68.42)	10 (26.32)	1 (2.63)	1 (2.63)	1.79
Punjab	235 (72.54)	70 (21.60)	14 (4.32)	5 (1.54)	1.58
				F-ratio p-value	1.41 >0.10ns

Source : Field Survey 2006

Note : The figures given in parentheses represent percentages.

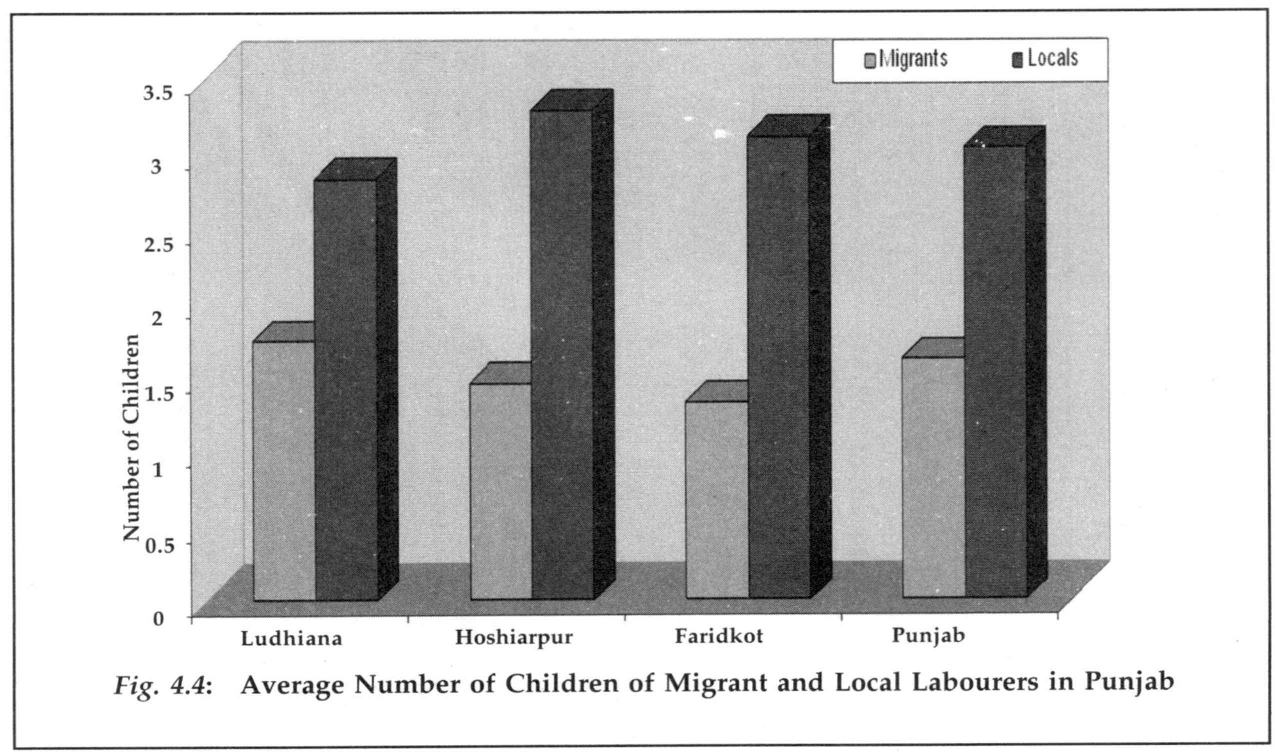

Fig. 4.4: **Average Number of Children of Migrant and Local Labourers in Punjab**

Table 4.7 (b): Distribution of Local Agricultural Labourers according to Education

District	Education Level				Mean Score of Education
	Illiterate	Primary	Middle	Matric	
Ludhiana	61 (48.41)	49 (38.89)	16 (12.70)	0 (0.00)	2.96
Hoshiarpur	52 (65.82)	18 (22.79)	5 (6.33)	4 (5.06)	2.15
Faridkot	35 (54.68)	22 (34.38)	7 (10.94)	0 (0.00)	2.59
Punjab	148 (55.01)	89 (33.09)	28 (10.41)	4 (1.49)	2.64
				F-ratio	2.11
				p-value	>0.10ns

Source : Field Survey 2006

Note : The figures given in parentheses represent percentages.

Table 4.7 (c): Migratory *vs.* Local Agricultural Labourers

District	t-value	p-value
Ludhiana	4.74	<0.01
Hoshiarpur	2.11	<0.05
Faridkot	2.47	<0.05
Punjab	3.01	<0.01

Among the local agricultural labourers, 55.01 per cent were illiterate while 1.49 per cent of them were matriculates. The two extremes show that the local agricultural labourers were somehow more educated than the migratory agricultural labourers as the mean score of education among the local agricultural labourers came to be 2.96, 2.15 and 2.59 in Ludhiana, Hoshiarpur and Faridkot districts respectively while it was 2.64 for the state as a whole. The t-values given in Table 4.7 (c) show that the educational level of the migratory agricultural labourers was significantly lower than that of the local agricultural labourers.

But it is pertinent that labourers, though migratory or local, have to abandon their studies in search of employment amidst poverty.

HOUSING STRUCTURE

It is not feasible for each migratory labourer to live in an independent house or construct his own house for want of surplus income. Therefore, the migratory agricultural labourers, by and large, live jointly in groups in accommodation provided either by the farmers at their tube-well rooms at farm houses or in village community places such as *dharamshala,* temple, etc. *Thus,* the housing conditions of the migratory labourers in Punjab cannot be compared with those of the local agricultural labourers in Punjab because the local agricultural labourers generally own their houses in whatsoever condition may be. Therefore, it is relevant here to compare the housing structure of the migratory labourers in their native village. The housing structures on this pattern have been presented in Tables 4.8 (a), 4.8 (b) (*See on page 102, 103)* and 4.8 (c) (*See on page 103*).

Table 4.8 (a) reveals that about 32 per cent of the migratory agricultural labourers did not have a house of their own in the native village while as high as 51 per cent of them were having only *katcha* house. Only about 5 per cent of the migratory agricultural labourers owned *pucca* house at their native village. The mean score of quality of owning a house came to be 0.90 out of total score of 3 i.e. only 30 per cent score. Districts also depict a similar pattern of quality of owning a house. There is no significant difference in the districts as indicated by the F-ratio.

Among the local agricultural labourers, only 4.46 per cent are living in rented houses while the highest proportion, i.e. 44.61 per cent of them own semi-*pucca* houses. As much as 22.31 per cent of them own *pucca* houses while 28.62 per cent have totally *katcha* houses. The mean score of quality of owning a house comes to be 1.85 of total 3 score, i.e. 61.67 per cent.

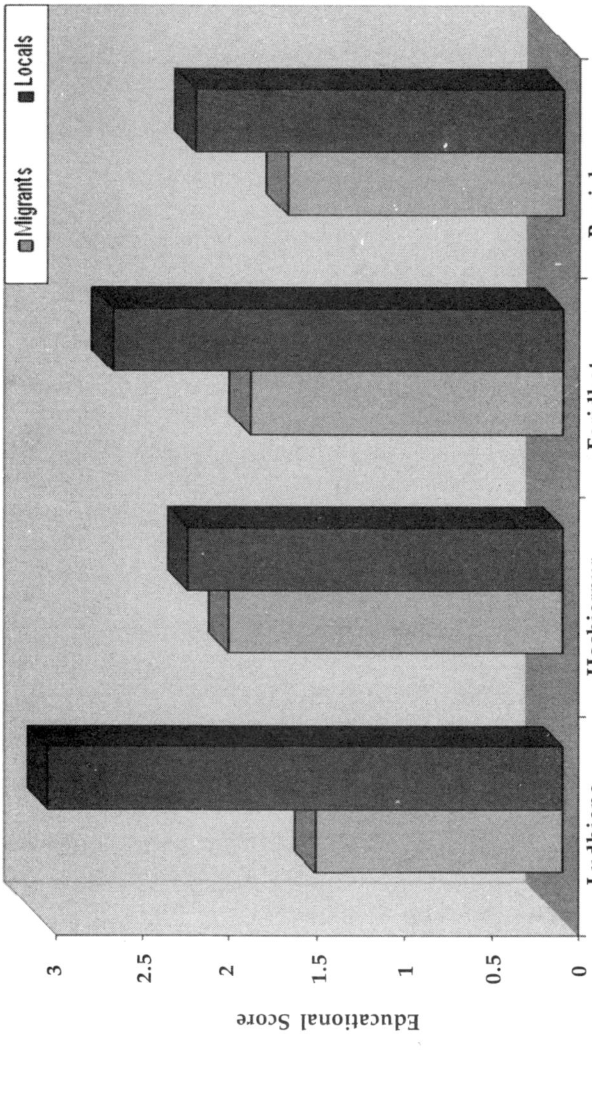

Fig. 4.5: **Mean Score of Education of Migrant and Local Agricultural Labourers in Punjab**

Table 4.8 (a): Housing Structures of Migratory Labourers at their Native Village

District	Condition of the House				Mean Score of Quality of House
	Not Owned (0)	Owned Katcha (1)	Owned Semi-Pucca (2)	Owned Pucca (3)	
Ludhiana	70 (33.98)	92 (44.66)	31 (15.05)	13 (6.31)	0.94
Hoshiarpur	26 (32.50)	47 (58.75)	5 (6.25)	2 (2.50)	0.79
Faridkot	7 (18.42)	26 (68.42)	4 (10.53)	1 (2.63)	0.97
Punjab	103 (31.79)	165 (50.93)	40 (12.34)	16 (4.94)	0.90
				F-ratio p-value	1.13 >.10ns

Source : Field Survey 2006

Note : The figures given in parentheses represent percentages.

The comparison of quality of dwelling house shown in Table 4.8(c) provides that the quality of owning dwelling house is significantly lower in case of the migratory agricultural labourers as compared to the local agricultural labourers. This is true in all the selected districts too. This shows that the family members of the migratory agricultural labourers have to live in more miserable housing conditions as compared to the local agricultural labourers.

OCCUPATION OF THE MIGRANTS

Availability of job opportunities at the place of destination, irrespective of its quality, plays a significant role with regard to the process of migration decision. On the other hand, pre-migration occupation of the people also helps to understand the causes of migration. The migrants' profiles of migrants according to their occupation at the place of origin have been presented in Table 4.9 (*See on page 105*).

Table 4.8 (b): Housing Structures of Local Agricultural Labourers in Punjab

District	Quality of House				Mean Score of Quality of House
	Rented House (0)	Owned Katcha (1)	Owned Semi-Pucca (2)	Owned Pucca (3)	
Ludhiana	3 (2.38)	25 (19.84)	55 (43.65)	43 (34.13)	2.10
Hoshiarpur	3 (3.80)	27 (34.18)	38 (48.10)	11 (13.92)	1.72
Faridkot	6 (9.38)	25 (39.06)	27 (42.19)	6 (9.37)	1.52
Punjab	12 (4.46)	77 (28.62)	120 (44.61)	60 (22.31)	1.85
				F-ratio p-value	1.97 >.10ns

Source: Field Survey 2006

Note : The figures given in parentheses represent percentages.

Table 4.8 (c): Migratory Agricultural Labourers *vs.* Local Agricultural Labourers

District	t-value	p-value
Ludhiana	4.61	<0.01
Hoshiarpur	3.54	<0.01
Faridkot	2.01	<0.05
Punjab	2.89	<0.01

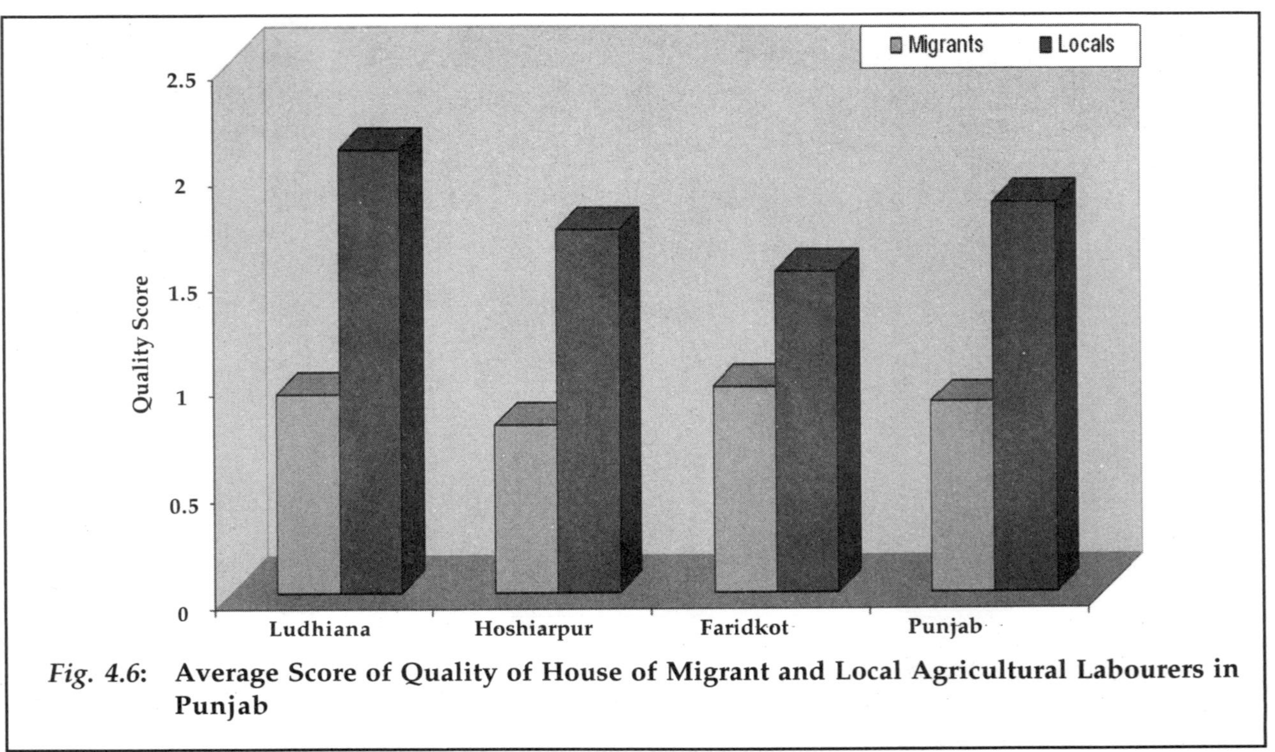

Fig. 4.6: **Average Score of Quality of House of Migrant and Local Agricultural Labourers in Punjab**

Table 4.9: Distribution of Migratory Labourers according to Occupation

District	Occupation						Total
	Labour	Agriculture	Industry	Shop	Service	Any Other	
Ludhiana	144 (69.90)	5 (2.43)	0 (0.00)	19 (9.22)	1 (0.49)	37 (17.96)	206 (100.00)
Hoshiarpur	53 (66.25)	8 (10.00)	0 (0.00)	0 (0.00)	0 (0.00)	19 (23.75)	80 (100.00)
Faridkot	30 (78.94)	3 (7.90)	0 (0.00)	1 (2.63)	0 (0.00)	4 (10.53)	38 (100.00)
Punjab	227 (70.06)	16 (4.94)	0 (0.00)	20 (6.17)	1 (0.31)	60 (18.52)	324 (100.00)

Source : Field Survey 2006

Note : The figures given in parentheses represent percentages.

Table 4.9 reveals that of 324 sampled migrants, 227 (70.06 per cent) were engaged in labour in farm-sector at their native places. Only 4.94 per cent were practicing their own agriculture, followed by 6.17 per cent in shops and only 0.31 per cent in service. Only 18.52 per cent of the sampled migrants were engaged in other subsidiary occupations. Because of poverty, low wages and lesser number of days of employment, the migration rate among the labour class is observed to be the highest.

POSSESSION OF CATTLE/LIVESTOCK AND IMPLEMENTS

Another important economic parameter that reveals the socio-economic background of the migrant agricultural labourers is the possession of cattle/livestock and implements. This aspect is concerned with the possession or no possession of cattle by the migratory households and type of the owned or possessed cattle. The possession of cattle in each case is only one. But, the pattern of ownership of the cattle by the migrant households is somewhat divergent. Out of the different types of livestock, it is mainly the cow (54.17 per cent) that is possessed by the households of the migrants at their native place. But if we examine it on the basis of all sampled migrants, then it comes to 20.06 per cent as indicated in Table 4.10 (*See on next page*). This may be because of the consideration of the use-value of milk. Of the sampled migrants, 10.49 per cent own goat mainly for the use of milk and for selling its meat to earn money. The possession of cattle, especially milch cattle by more than one-third of the migrant households indicate that by the remitted money, they have accumulated enough resources to own cattle.

Of the total sampled migrant agricultural labourers, only 16 migrant households (Table 4.9) possess agricultural land. For all types of farm activities, the possession of farm implements, either traditional or modern, is relevant. Only 5 households out of the 16 who possess land are having some

Table 4.10: Possession of Cattle/Livestock and Implements by Migratory Agricultural Labourers

District	Cattle		Type of Cattle				Implements	Implement Type	
	Zero	One	Buffalo	Cow	Goat	Sheep		Plough	Others
Ludhiana	128 (62.14)	78 (37.86)	16 (7.77)	48 (23.30)	13 (6.31)	1 (0.49)	3 (1.46)	2 (0.97)	1 (0.49)
Hoshiarpur	56 (70.00)	24 (30.00)	0 (0.00)	9 (11.25)	15 (18.75)	0 (0.00)	2 (2.50)	2 (2.50)	0 (0.00)
Faridkot	20 (52.63)	18 (47.37)	3 (7.89)	8 (21.05)	6 (15.79)	1 (2.63)	0 (0.00)	0 (0.00)	0 (0.00)
Punjab	204 (62.96)	120 (37.04)	19 (5.86)	65 (20.06)	34 (10.49)	2 (0.62)	5 (1.54)	4 (1.23)	1 (0.31)

Source : Field survey 2006

Note : The figures given in parentheses represent percentages.

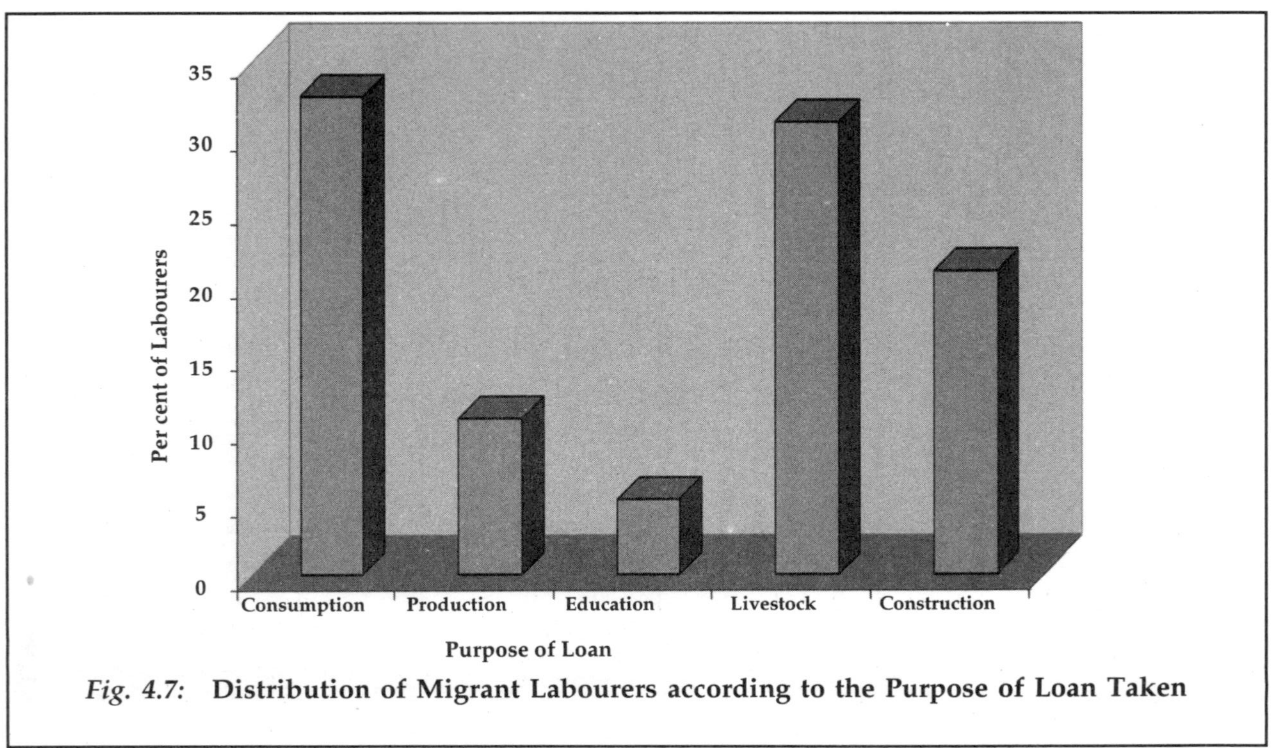

Fig. 4.7: Distribution of Migrant Labourers according to the Purpose of Loan Taken

sort of farm implements and the percentage of families possessing ploughs comes to only 1.23 per cent if we examine it on the basis of all sampled migrants. The main farm implement used by these families is plough. The meagre possession of farm implements on the one hand shows their dependence on others for such implements and on the other, it exposes the poor economic condition of the migratory families, which induce the male members of the poor families to migrate somewhere to prosperous areas to earn their livelihood.

PATTERN OF BASIC PROVISIONS

The provisions relating to housing, entertainment, information technology, conveyance, etc. among the migratory labourers are shown in Table 4.11 (a) (*See on page 110)* and the same among the local labourers in Table 4.11 (b) (*See on page 111)*.

It is disturbing to note that only 28.70 per cent of the migratory agricultural labourers enjoy the facility of electricity against significantly higher proportion, *i.e.* 88.10 per cent of the local agricultural labourers enjoying the facility of free electricity at their residence. There are four different sources of drinking water prevailing in the villages of Punjab. As high as 82.71 per cent of the migratory agricultural labourers depend on hand pumps for drinking water but out of this 35.80 per cent have to use hand pumps of others. On the other hand, 90.33 per cent of the local agricultural labourers use hand pumps for drinking water but 26.02 per cent of them have to go to other houses to use their hand pumps for getting drinking water. The proportion of the migrant agricultural labourers owning hand pumps was found to be significantly lower than the local agricultural labourers. About 10 per cent of the migratory agricultural labourers and 7 per cent of the local labourers get drinking water from community taps. It is again sad to note that 7.41 per cent of the migratory labourers, and 2.60 per cent of the local agricultural labourers are dependent on wells to get drinking water. The drinking water from wells is taken as the most contaminated drinking water which may cause many health hazards.

Table 4.11 (a): Pattern of Provisions with Migratory Agricultural Labourers

District	Electricity	Drinking Water				Other Facilities				
		Owned Hand Pump	Others' Hand Pump	Tap	Well	Fan	Radio/ Tape Recorder	Television	Bicycle	Mobile Phone
Ludhiana	58 (28.16)	103 (50.00)	68 (33.01)	17 (8.25)	18 (8.74)	35 (16.99)	42 (20.39)	18 (8.74)	136 (66.02)	49 (23.79)
Hoshiarpur	22 (27.50)	32 (40.00)	30 (37.50)	12 (15.00)	6 (7.50)	10 (12.50)	12 (15.00)	6 (7.50)	35 (43.75)	17 (21.25)
Faridkot	13 (34.21)	17 (44.74)	18 (47.37)	3 (7.89)	0 (0.00)	4 (10.53)	6 (15.79)	3 (7.89)	18 (47.37)	7 (18.42)
Punjab	93 (28.70)	152 (46.91)	116 (35.80)	32 (9.88)	24 (7.41)	49 (15.12)	60 (18.52)	27 (8.33)	189 (58.33)	73 (22.53)

Source : Field Survey 2006

Note : The figures given in parentheses represent percentages.

Table 11 (b): Pattern of Provision with Local Agricultural Labourers

District	Electricity	Drinking Water				Other Facilities				
		Owned Hand Pump	Others' Hand Pump	Tap	Well	Fan	Radio/ Tape Recorder	T.V.	Bicycle	Mobile
Ludhiana	117 (92.86)	83 (65.87)	28 (22.22)	15 (11.91)	0 (0.00)	116 (92.06)	52 (41.27)	48 (38.10)	117 (92.86)	18 (14.29)
Hoshiarpur	71 (89.87)	42 (53.17)	26 (32.91)	4 (5.06)	7 (8.86)	69 (87.34)	30 (37.97)	29 (36.71)	67 (84.81)	10 (12.66)
Faridkot	49 (76.56)	48 (75.00)	16 (25.00)	0 (0.00)	0 (0.00)	46 (71.88)	26 (40.63)	22 (34.38)	46 (71.88)	7 (10.94)
Punjab	237 (88.10)	173 (64.31)	70 (26.02)	19 (7.06)	7 (2.60)	231 (85.87)	108 (40.15)	99 (36.80)	230 (85.50)	35 (13.01)
Punjab z-value p-value	14.50 <.01	4.24 <.01	2.56 <.05	1.22 >.10 ns	2.62 <.01	17.18 <.01	5.82 <.01	8.44 <.01	7.23 <.01	2.99 <.01

Source : Field Survey 2006

Note : The figures given in parentheses represent percentages.

During the era of ultra modern electrical devices, only 15.12 per cent of the migratory agricultural labourers own electric fans for summer while this proportion among the local agricultural labourers is significantly higher to the order of 85.87 per cent. The entertainment devices such as radio/tape recorders and televisions were also at a significantly higher rate with the local agricultural labourers (40.15 per cent and 36.80 per cent) as compared to the migratory agricultural labourers (18.52 per cent and 8.33 per cent) respectively. This shows that majority of the labourers belonging to both the categories are still deprived of the most common entertainment devices due to their low level of income.

The only mode of conveyance with the agricultural labourers is bicycle. But 41.67 per cent of the migratory agricultural labourers and 14.50 per cent of the local agricultural labourers did not own a bicycle. They have always to move on foot which may be inversely affecting the labour efficiency. In this era of fast communication, and the cost of a mobile phone being in the reach of migratory labourers, they prefer to talk to their families living in their native places on mobile phones. However, the local agricultural labourers do not feel its necessity. Some farmers have provided the local agricultural labourers mobile phones in order to have communication with them at the time of need. That is why, a significantly higher proportion, *i.e.* 22.53 per cent of the migratory agricultural labourers as compared to 13.01 per cent of the local agricultural labourers were having mobile phones with them.

The foregoing discussion leads us to conclude that the labourers in general have insufficient facilities but the migratory agricultural labourers are found with significantly lesser facilities as compared to those availed by the local agricultural labourers.

DEBT POSITION

As majority of the migrants belong to the poor strata of population, so they have to depend on the loans to meet their daily requirements of life.

The data presented in Table 4.12(a) (*See on page 114)* shows that about 55 per cent of the migratory labourers are under debt, and most of them, i.e. 96.63 per cent had taken loans from moneylenders and landlords of their native state. The non-repayment of debt because of less employment opportunities may be one of the major reasons to migrate to Punjab to earn and repay the debt.

A glance at Table 4.12(b) (*See on page 115)* provides that the highest proportion, *i.e.* 32.58 per cent of the indebted labourers had taken loan for daily consumption needs followed by 30.90 per cent for the purchase of livestock and 20.79 per cent for construction of a house. Only 10.67 per cent and 5.06 per cent of them have taken loans for production and educational purposes respectively. District-wise analysis also shows a similar trend as has been observed in the case of Punjab as a whole.

As far as the local agricultural labourers are concerned, 64.31 per cent of them have been found to be under debt. Out of the indebted local agricultural labourers, as high as 71.68 per cent have taken loan from landlords, followed by 24.86 per cent from moneylenders. This shows that the landlords and moneylenders have emerged as the major source of obtaining loan by the migratory as well as local agricultural labourers. By advancing loan at exorbitant rates of interest to the farm labourers, the landlords use this tool for dictating illogical and suppressive terms and conditions on labourers, even up to the extent of bonded labour in some cases. In case of the local agricultural labourers, only 28.90 per cent of the indebted labourers take loan for starting a work project while the remaining vast majority get loan for social and religious ceremonies like marriage, death and other social obligations.

The above discussion leads us to conclude that the loans taken by labourers are mainly used for unproductive purposes. Hence, it becomes difficult or rather impossible to repay the same. Consequently, the labourers are caught in a vicious cycle of debt, poverty and oppression throughout their life.

Table 4.12 (a): Place and Source of Loan Obtained By Migratory Agricultural Labourers

District	Loan Taken	Place of Loan Taken		Source of Loan Taken				
		Origin	Destination	Bank	CCS	Traders	ML	Landlord
Ludhiana	114 (55.34)	109 (95.61)	5 (4.39)	1 (0.88)	0 (0.00)	0 (0.00)	57 (50.00)	56 (49.12)
Hoshiarpur	42 (52.50)	41 (97.62)	1 (2.38)	0 (0.00)	0 (0.00)	0 (0.00)	23 (54.76)	19 (45.24)
Faridkot	22 (57.90)	22 (100.00)	0 (0.00)	0 (0.00)	0 (0.00)	0 (0.00)	14 (63.64)	8 (36.36)
Punjab	178 (54.94)	172 (96.63)	6 (3.37)	1 (0.56)	0 (0.00)	0 (0.00)	94 (52.81)	83 (46.63)

CCS: Co-operative Credit Societies; ML: Moneylenders.

Source : Field Survey 2006

Note : The figures given in parentheses represent percentages.

Table 4.12 (b): Distribution of Migratory Agricultural Labourers according to the Purpose of Loan Taken

District	Loan Taken	Purpose of Loan Taken				
		Consumption	Production	Education	Livestock	Construction
Ludhiana	114 (55.34)	42 (36.84)	12 (10.53)	7 (6.14)	29 (25.44)	24 (21.05)
Hoshiarpur	42 (52.50)	9 (21.43)	4 (9.52)	2 (4.76)	18 (42.86)	9 (21.43)
Faridkot	22 (57.90)	7 (31.82)	3 (13.64)	– (0.00)	8 (36.36)	4 (18.18)
Punjab	178 (54.94)	58 (32.58)	19 (10.67)	9 (5.06)	55 (30.90)	37 (20.79)

Source: Field Survey 2006

Note : The figures given in parentheses represent percentages.

Table 4.12 (c): Distribution of Local Agricultural Labourers Depicting the Particulars about Loan

Particulars	Ludhiana		Hoshiarpur		Faridkot		Punjab	
	No.	%age	No.	%age	No.	%age	No.	%age
A. Loan Taken:								
No	50	39.68	30	37.97	16	25.00	96	35.69
Yes	76	60.32	49	62.03	48	75.00	173	64.31
Z-value	3.28		3.02		5.66		6.64	
p-value	<0.01		<0.01		<0.01		<0.01	
χ^2 value	4.24	p-value	>0.10ns					
B. Source of Loan								
1. Banks	0	0.00	2	4.08	1	2.04	3	1.73
2. Cooperative Societies	1	1.32	4	8.16	2	4.08	7	4.05
3. Moneylenders	16	21.05	9	18.37	18	36.73	43	24.86
4. Landlords	63	82.89	34	69.39	27	55.10	124	71.68
5. Traders	0	0.00	0	0.00	0	0.00	0	0.00
6. Commission Agents	0	0.00	0	0.00	0	0.00	0	0.00
C. Purpose of Loan								
1. Marriage	32	42.11	13	26.53	8	16.33	53	30.64
2. Death	7	9.21	2	4.08	8	16.33	17	9.83
3. Social Obligation	55	72.37	35	71.43	20	40.82	110	63.58
4. Work Project	27	35.53	11	22.45	12	24.49	50	28.90

Source: Field Survey 2006

To sum up, it can be said that majority of the migrant agricultural labourers from Bihar and Uttar Pradesh migrate to Punjab because of poverty and lack of employment opportunities in their native states. The migrants from these states generally move to work in the fields. The agricultural productivity in Punjab being much higher than that of their own states, they earn wage rate which is higher than the wage rate offered in their native states.

The young people are more prone to migration as they are quite venturesome and have no social liability. Moreover, they are preferred by the farmers for handling various farm operations as they are more energetic and have more stamina to do work. The local labourers are comparatively older in age. As a result of migration at an early age, the majority of the migrants are illiterate.

More than two-thirds of the migratory agricultural labourers are married but their families in majority of the cases live at their native places in separation. As a result, most of the migrants in their native places have limited number of children in their families, whereas the local labourers have large sized families.

Migrant streams are not only from the scheduled castes and the backward castes, but poverty and unemployment also compel the households of the general castes to migrate to Punjab to earn their livelihood. At the native places, one-third of the migrant labourers do not have a house of their own and those who have, they are having only one room *katcha* house. But the locals are having either semi-*pucca* or *pucca* house. As regards the availability of other facilities, the position is more or less the same in both the cases.

As regards the debt position, majority of the labourers are in the grip of moneylenders and farmers. Moreover, they have taken loans for meeting the basic necessities of life. The major chunk of the local agricultural labourers is also in the debt trap and that also for unproductive and unavoidable purposes. By and large, it can be said that rural labourers still rely on the mercy of their employers for their sustenance.

REFERENCES

De Haan; and Rogaly, B. (1996); "Eastward ho! Leap Frogging and Seasonal Migration in Eastern India", in G.Rodgeres et al. (eds.), *The Institutional Approach to Labour and Development*, London, Frank Cass, pp. 140-60

Rogaria, M.A. (1997), "Sudanese Migration to the New World: Socio-economic Characteristics", *International Migration*, Vol. 35(4), pp. 513-36.

Yadava, K.N.S. (1988), *Determinants, Patterns and Consequences of Rural Migration in India*, Independent Publishing Company, New Delhi, pp. 80-85

Yadava, K.N.S.; Yadava, S.S.; and Sinha, R.K. (1996-97), "Rural-Out-Migration and Its Economic Implications on Migrant Households in India—A Review", *The Indian Economic Journal* Vol. 44, No. 2, pp. 21-28.

Determinants, Trends and Factors Associated with Migration

Movement is an integral part of human existence. The factors associated with the movement of human beings are complex and intertwined. Motivation for migration can be explained by mechanical metaphors—centrifugal and centripetal forces. The centrifugal impulse does not have a strong effect if the centripetal impulse is weak. The centrifugal impulse attributes to 'push factors' operating at the place of origin whereas centripetal impulse relates to 'pull factors' that identify the positive characteristics at the place of destination (Datta, 2004).

Migration of any type, whether documented or undocumented, forced or voluntary can be explained in terms of these push and pull factors. It appears that the availability of work, wage rate and wage structure, social security and relatively cordial atmosphere in Punjab worked as a centripetal force for the migrants from the poor states of the country. The factors encouraging migration can be broadly classified into economic and non-economic factors.

The basic economic push factors that motivated the migrants to leave their native place are: poverty, lack of employment opportunities and struggle for livelihood, corruption, political instability and lack of industrialisation.

ECONOMIC FACTORS

In the process of human migration, economic factors play a crucial role. These factors can be divided into three categories:

(a) Demand pull factors;

(b) Supply push factors;

(c) Social Network.

NON-ECONOMIC FACTORS

Apart from above stated economic factors, there are certain social pull and push factors that also facilitate labour migration. Cordial behaviour and favourable social conditions are some of the social pull factors whereas low level of education, social insecurity, caste system and religious harassment are the social push factors. Apart from the development of the means of transport and communication, desire for new experience and adventure are the other factors which help labour migration.

SOCIAL NETWORK

The social and family network at the place of destination also strengthens the process of migration. The three types of factors encouraging labour migration do not usually have equal weights in migration decisions and the importance of each factor can change over time. Generally, the demand pull and supply push factors are strong at the beginning of a migration flow and the network becomes more important as migration streams mature. Network factors become more important in sustaining migration (Phillip, 2005).

With the advent of green revolution, Punjab economy has witnessed drastic changes in terms of inputs, outputs and demographic features. Before the introduction of 'seed-fertilizer-irrigation' technology, the Punjab agriculture was subsistence economy where the farmers cultivated with the help of family labour or with the help of local agricultural hired labour. But the green revolution, particularly the picking up of paddy cultivation, though was highly mechanised but some specific agronomic operations made it labour-intensive too. The labour-intensive operations such as transplantation, harvesting, reaping and chemical spraying, etc. highlighted the need of more farm labourers which may be ready to work at lower wage rate. This situation became the ground for the migrants to come to Punjab and work on farms. In general, it can be said that the phenomenon of the migrant labourers to Punjab picked up significantly around the mid 1970s when paddy cultivation picked up in the state and an image of prosperous Punjab spread in other states.

FACTORS OF MIGRATION

There are a number of factors which motivated the labourers to migrate to Punjab. These have been presented in Table 5.1 which shows that most important factor appeared to be the poverty among the labourers in their native state. This factor contributed towards migration in 70.68 per cent of the total respondents, while such percentages for Faridkot, Ludhiana and Hoshiarpur districts were 86.84, 74.27 and 53.75 respectively. However, the trend was somewhat different in Hoshiarpur district where the highest proportion of respondents, *i.e.* 58.75 per cent reported higher wages in Punjab as the major reason behind their migration. The higher wages factor as the second major reason behind migration was reported in 54.37 per cent respondents in Ludhiana and 52.63 per cent in Faridkot while the same was 55.25 per cent for the state as a whole. The third factor for migration was to repay debt. As many as 41.67 per cent of the migratory labourers migrated to Punjab to earn money to repay their debts which they had taken from the village moneylenders and/or the feudal landlords.

The next factor which contributed towards migration appeared to be unemployment in the native states of the

Table 5.1: Factors Associated with the Migration of Migrant Agricultural Labourers to Punjab

Factors	Ludhiana		Hoshiarpur		Faridkot		Punjab		Rank
	No.	%age	No.	%age	No.	%age	No.	%age	
1. Higher wages	112	54.37	47	58.75	20	52.63	179	55.25	II
2. Poverty	153	74.27	43	53.75	33	86.84	229	70.68	I
3. Unemployment	20	9.71	8	10.00	6	15.79	34	10.49	IV
4. To Repay Debt	81	39.32	37	46.25	17	44.75	135	41.67	III
5. Crime	9	4.37	0	0.00	0	0.00	9	2.78	VI
6. Corruption	18	8.74	0	0.00	2	5.26	20	6.17	V
7. Caste domination	3	1.46	0	0.00	0	0.00	3	0.93	VII
8. Exploitation	1	0.49	0	0.00	0	0.00	1	0.31	VIII

Source: Field Survey 2006

respondents. It was reported by 10.49 per cent of the total respondents, whereas it was 9.71 per cent in Ludhiana, 10.00 per cent in Hoshiarpur and 15.79 per cent in Faridkot districts.

There were some other factors also which motivated the labourers to migrate to Punjab, but their extent was not of much consideration. These factors appeared to be crime in the native state (2.78 per cent), corruption (6.17 per cent), caste domination (0.93 per cent), and exploitation (0.31 per cent).

Thus, the factors like poverty in the native state, higher wages in Punjab, and earning money to repay the debts led the labourers to migrate to Punjab. The poverty might be there due to unemployment, under employment, low wages and low earnings from their meagre owned assets of land due to low agricultural productivity.

SOURCE OF MOTIVATION FOR MIGRATION

A perusal of Table 5.2 (*See on page 125*) provides that the highest proportion of the migratory agricultural labourers (41.36 per cent) in Punjab came here at the instance of their friends, followed by 25.93 per cent who migrated at the instance of their relatives. There were only 13.27 per cent of them who migrated to Punjab on the advice of their parents, while 15.74 per cent of them came to Punjab on their own. Only 3.09 per cent of the migrants migrated to Punjab through agents, whereas 0.93 per cent came here through other sources, such as contractors, truck drivers, etc. who reported them about accessibility of agricultural employment opportunities and higher wage rate in Punjab.

The above analysis of the data brings out the fact that friends and relatives emerged as the major sources of motivation for the migration of labourers to Punjab who attracted them by reporting more employment and higher wages in the farm sector of Punjab. However, parents also played a considerable role, particularly in Faridkot district to motivate their wards to migrate to work as agricultural labour.

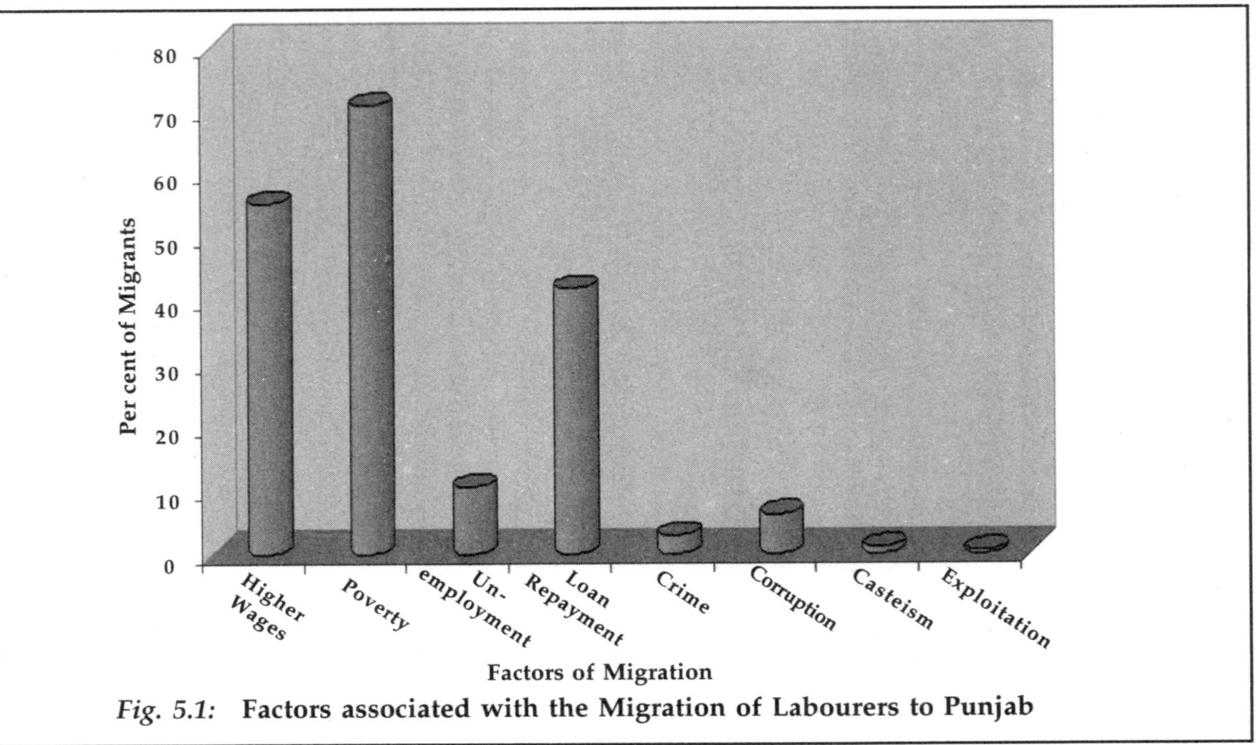

Fig. 5.1: Factors associated with the Migration of Labourers to Punjab

Table 5.2: Source of Motivation for the Migration of Migrant Agricultural Labourers of Punjab

Source of Motivation	Ludhiana		Hoshiarpur		Faridkot		Punjab		Rank
	No.	%age	No.	%age	No.	%age	No.	%age	
1. Agents	3	1.46	7	8.75	0	0.00	10	3.09	V
2. Friends	77	37.38	35	43.75	22	57.89	134	41.36	I
3. Parents	30	14.56	4	5.00	9	23.68	43	13.27	IV
4. Relatives	56	27.18	21	26.25	7	18.42	84	25.93	II
5. At Own	40	19.42	11	13.75	0	0.00	51	15.74	III
6. Any Other	1	0.49	2	2.50	0	0.00	3	0.93	VI

Source: Field Survey 2006

SOURCES OF SELECTION OF PRESENT PLACE IN PUNJAB

As per the data given in Table 5.3 (*See on next page*), the friends became a major source of selection to settle at a certain place in Punjab as reported by 35.80 per cent of the migrants. This proportion was 33.01 per cent in Ludhiana district, 33.75 per cent in Hoshiarpur district, and further as high as 55.26 per cent in Faridkot district. The second source of selecting the present place in Punjab appeared to be the farmers who brought the labourers to their farms from the respective railway stations. But in Faridkot district, other sources such as contractors and truck drivers were instrumental in the selection of place in Punjab for 28.95 per cent migrant agricultural labourers. As much as 4.32 per cent selected the present place through agents who took them from their native village to Punjab, while only a single person with a negligible percentage of 0.31 selected the present place in Punjab as a matter of chance getting in Ludhiana district. The selection of present place in Punjab on the advice of farmers, who took them to work from the railway station, was the highest (24.27 per cent) in Ludhiana district as Ludhiana city may be the destination of their railway journey.

Overall, it can be said that in selecting a place of work in Punjab friends and farmers played a major role.

MEANS OF TRANSPORTATION FOR COMING TO PUNJAB

The data given in Table 5.4 (*See on page 128*) exhibits that none of the migrants preferred to travel by bus to Punjab. The table brings out that almost 96 per cent of the migratory labourers while coming to Punjab used rail as a mode of transportation. This may be due to the low fare and heavy capacity to travel together in large numbers keeping in view the security in the rail as compared to other means of transportation. Only 3.40 per cent of them came to Punjab on trucks whose drivers attracted them to work in Punjab for

Table 5.3: Sources of Selecting the Present Place to Work in Punjab

Source of Selection	Ludhiana		Hoshiarpur		Faridkot		Punjab		Rank
	No.	%age	No.	%age	No.	%age	No.	%age	
1. Agents	2	0.97	12	15.00	0	0.00	14	4.32	V
2. Friends	68	33.01	27	33.75	21	55.26	116	35.80	I
3. Natives	53	25.73	8	10.00	3	7.89	64	19.75	III
4. Per chance	1	0.49	0	0.00	0	0.00	1	0.31	VI
5. Farmers (railway station)	50	24.27	17	21.25	3	7.89	70	21.60	II
6. Any other	31	15.05	15	18.75	11	28.95	57	17.59	IV

Source: Field Survey 2006

Table 5.4: Means of Transportation for Coming to Punjab and Back

Means of Transportation	Ludhiana		Hoshiarpur		Faridkot		Punjab		Rank
	No.	%age	No.	%age	No.	%age	No.	%age	
1. Rail	195	94.66	77	96.25	38	100.00	310	95.68	I
2. Bus	0	0.00	0	0.00	0	0.00	0	0.00	–
3. Truck	8	3.88	3	3.75	0	0.00	11	3.40	II
4. Any other	3	1.46	0	0.00	0	0.00	3	0.93	III

Source: Field Survey 2006

better wages. Due to long distance, bus journey was not preferred by these labourers. They, by and large, travel in rails without berth reservation. Due to heavy expenses involved in visiting their native places, the migrant labourers generally pay only a single visit in a year. It is during the lean period covering the months of January to March and mid-July to mid-September that majority of the migrant agricultural labourers go back to their native places. However, the seasonal migrant labourers go back after the peak period is over.

This is because after this period, wage rates decline comparatively and work is also not available regularly. Those who are employed permanently and have brought their families with them do not pay regular visits to their native places.

HARDSHIPS DURING JOURNEY

The migrant agricultural labourers face a number of hardships during their journey to Punjab and back home. As per data given in Table 5.5 (*See on next page*), 31.17 per cent of them blame the railway officials who create hardships for them. Keeping in view the extraordinary rush in the trains, the railway officials force them to travel on the roofs of the railway coaches and always put their lives in danger. Sometimes, mishaps also occur especially when after a long journey the labourers feel tired and fall asleep on the roof. This attitude of the railway officials towards migrants needs to be curbed on humanitarian grounds.

As high as 76.23 per cent of the migratory agricultural labourers reported that railway police officials are never considerate about their problems and rather create many more hardships for them during the journey. In the name of security, police personnel search their belongings such as bags, trunks, pockets etc. and snatch their valuable articles as well as cash from them which they earned by working hard in Punjab. They are used to take such articles and cash with them mainly

Table 5.5: Incidence of Hardship Faced by Migrant Agricultural Labourers during Journey

Hardship Creating Agency	Ludhiana		Hoshiarpur		Faridkot		Punjab	
	No.	%age	No.	%age	No.	%age	No.	%age
Railway Officials	66	32.04	18	22.50	17	44.74	101	31.17
Railway Police	151	73.30	63	78.75	33	86.84	247	76.23
Fellow Friends	11	5.34	2	2.50	0	0.00	13	4.01
Other Passengers	37	17.96	15	18.75	6	15.79	58	17.90
Any Other	6	2.91	1	1.25	0	0.00	7	2.16

Source: Field Survey 2006

for their families living in their native villages. Some of them also reported that any resistance means physical torture and even a threat to implicate them in a false criminal case.

Fellow friends also became problem creator for 4.01 per cent migrant agricultural labourers. Their fellow friends tried to snatch the valuables and cash with them after assaulting them physically, while similar problems by other passengers are reported by 17.90 per cent of the migratory agricultural labourers. However, 2.16 per cent of them reported that criminal gangs, pickpockets and beggars also create many problems for them. Sometimes, such unscrupulous persons in order to loot their belongings fraudulently take them into confidence and offer some eatables mixed with intoxicants. That is why they travel in groups of 5-6 persons known to one another to avoid such incidence of hardships during their train journey.

To sum up, the foregoing discussion brings out that the labour intensive agronomic practices, particularly of paddy picked up the rate of migration to Punjab, *i.e.* during and after the period of Green Revolution. Thus, the availability of work in the farm sector of Punjab, wage structure, social security and cordial atmosphere worked as centripetal force for migrants from other states. The economic distress operating at the place of origin motivated the migratory labourers for farm labour in Punjab. Poverty, low wage rate, unemployment at their native places are the push factors (centrifugal forces) which compel them to migrate. Apart from this, the migratory labourers generally being honest, docile, obedient, reliable and less costly are in more demand in the farm sector of Punjab.

The social and family network in Punjab also strengthens the process of migration. Parents, relatives and friends are the major sources of motivation to migrate as well as to select the present place in Punjab. These network factors are more important in sustaining migration. Migrants prefer to travel

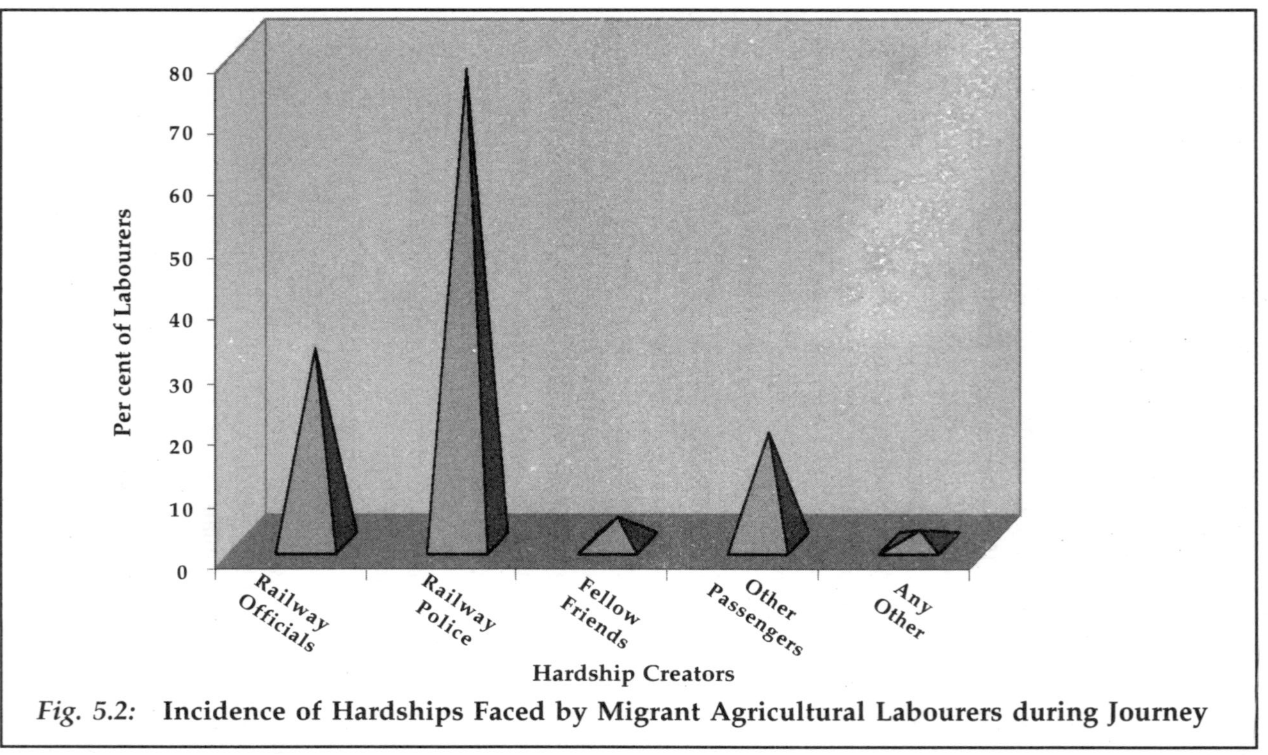

Fig. 5.2: Incidence of Hardships Faced by Migrant Agricultural Labourers during Journey

by trains. Railway police, railway officials and other passengers are the major hardship creating agencies during their journey.

REFERENCES

Datta, P (2004), "Push and Pull Factors of Undocumented Migration from Bangladesh to West Bengal: A Perception Study", *The Qualitative Report*, 9(2) pp. 335-58.

Phillip, Martin (2005), "Managing Labour Migration; Professionals, Guest Labourers and Recruiters", Downloaded From the website:http//www.un.org/es/population/meetings/illmigdev.2005/P01—PhilMartin.

Wage Structure of the Migrant and Local Labourers in the Agricultural Sector of Punjab

There are different patterns of labour employment in agriculture such as part time, daily wage basis and yearly/ seasonal contractual basis. The contract may be for the whole year or for a crop season of *rabi* and/or *kharif*. Part-time employment may be operation-specific such as paddy transplanting, paddy harvesting, wheat harvesting, threshing etc. Daily wage basis provides employment to the labourers as and when required by the farmers, *i.e.* for irrigation, fertilization, spraying, hoeing etc.

NATURE OF JOB

Distribution of migrant agricultural labourers in Table 6.1 (a) shows that the highest proportion, *i.e.* 45.37 per cent of the migratory agricultural labourers work on farms on daily wages basis followed by 33.33 per cent who work on the operation-specific contract basis while only 21.30 per cent of them work on yearly or *rabi/kharif* seasonal contract basis. It is worth-mentioning here that during the peak period of work-load, *i.e.* transplanting of paddy, harvesting and threshing of paddy and wheat, the daily wages basis labourers also prefer to work on contract basis.

Table 6.1 (a): Distribution of Migrant Agricultural Labourers according to the Nature of Present Job

Nature of Present Job	Ludhiana		Hoshiarpur		Faridkot		Punjab	
	No.	%age	No.	%age	No.	%age	No.	%age
Part-time contract	73	35.44	23	28.75	12	31.58	108	33.33
Daily wages basis	90	43.69	38	47.50	19	50.00	147	45.37
Yearly seasonal contract	43	20.87	19	23.75	7	18.42	69	21.30

Source: Field Survey 2006

According to the data contained in Table 6.1 (b), the highest proportion, *i.e.* 41.27 per cent of the local agricultural labourers work on yearly/seasonal contract basis followed by 34.94 per cent who work on daily wages basis while 23.79 per cent of the local agricultural labourers work on operation-specific contract basis.

Table 6.1 (b): Distribution of Local Agricultural Labourers according to the Nature of Present Job

Nature of Present Job	Ludhiana		Hoshiarpur		Faridkot		Punjab	
	No.	%age	No.	%age	No.	%age	No.	%age
Part-time contract	28	22.22	19	24.05	17	26.56	64	23.79
Daily wages basis	46	36.51	28	35.44	20	31.25	94	34.94
Yearly seasonal contract	52	41.27	32	40.51	27	42.19	111	41.27

Source: Field Survey 2006

Table 6.1 (c): A Comparison between Migrant and Local Agricultural Labourers

Nature of Present Job	z-value	p-value
Part-time contract	2.55	<0.05
Daily wages basis	2.58	<0.01
Yearly/seasonal contract	5.27	<0.01

The incidence of yearly/seasonal contract work pattern is significantly higher among the local labourers as compared to the migrant labourers. This may be due to age-old relations of the farmers with the local labourers and availability of all the family members to work on the farm as well as in the household work.

On the contrary, the incidence of work on daily wages basis and part-time contract is significantly higher among the migratory agricultural labourers as compared to the local agricultural labourers. This may be due to low wage rate accepted by the migrants and easy availability of groups of migrants for specific operations of paddy and wheat.

LENGTH OF WORKING DAY

Table 6.2 (a) (*See on page 138*) shows that majority of the migrant agricultural labourers, *i.e.* 62.97 per cent have to work for 10 hours a day, followed by 33.33 per cent who work for 12 hours a day. There are only 3.70 per cent of them who work for a specified length of 8 hours a day.

Similarly, Table 6.2(b) (*See on page 139*) reveals that 51.67 per cent of the local agricultural labourers have to work for 10 hours a day. Only 7.07 per cent of them work for 12 hours a day while 41.26 per cent of them work for 8 hours a day. District-wise analysis also depicts a similar pattern in the case of both the migratory as well as local agricultural labourers.

Table 6.2(a) further brings out that the average length of working day for the migratory agricultural labourers comes to 10.03 hours in Ludhiana district, 10.45 hours in Hoshiarpur district and 10.08 hours in Faridkot district while it was 10.59 hours in Punjab as a whole.

The corresponding length of working day for the local agricultural labourers works out to be 9.32, 9.16 and 9.50 hours in Ludhiana, Hoshiarpur and Faridkot districts respectively and 9.32 hours in the state as a whole (Table 6.2 b). There is no significant district to district variation regarding length of working day for the migratory as well as the local agricultural labourers. But a significant variation is found between average lengths of working day for the migrant and local agricultural labourers in all the districts as well as in the state (*See Table 6.2 (c) on page 141*). A migrant labourer has to work more for 1.31, 1.29 and 1.18 hours in Ludhiana, Hoshiarpur and Faridkot districts respectively as compared to the local labourers.

Table 6.2 (a): Length of Working Day for Migrant Agricultural Labourers in Punjab

Length of Working Day	Ludhiana		Hoshiarpur		Faridkot		Punjab	
	No.	%age	No.	%age	No.	%age	No.	%age
8 hrs.	3	1.46	9	11.25	0	0.00	12	3.70
10 hrs.	135	65.53	44	55.00	25	65.79	204	62.97
12 hrs.	68	33.01	27	33.75	13	34.21	108	33.33
Mean working day (hrs.)	10.63		10.45		10.68		10.59	
F-ratio = 1.37		p-value >0.10ns						

Source: Field Survey 2006

Table 6.2 (b): Length of Working Day for Local Agricultural Labourers in Punjab

Length of Working Day	Ludhiana		Hoshiarpur		Faridkot		Punjab	
	No.	%age	No.	%age	No.	%age	No.	%age
8 hrs	51	40.48	34	43.04	26	40.63	111	41.26
10 hrs	67	53.17	44	55.69	28	43.75	139	51.67
12 hrs	8	6.35	1	1.27	10	15.62	19	7.07
Mean working day (hrs.)	9.32		9.16		9.50		9.32	
F-ratio = 0.94	p-value >0.10ns							

Source: Field Survey 2006

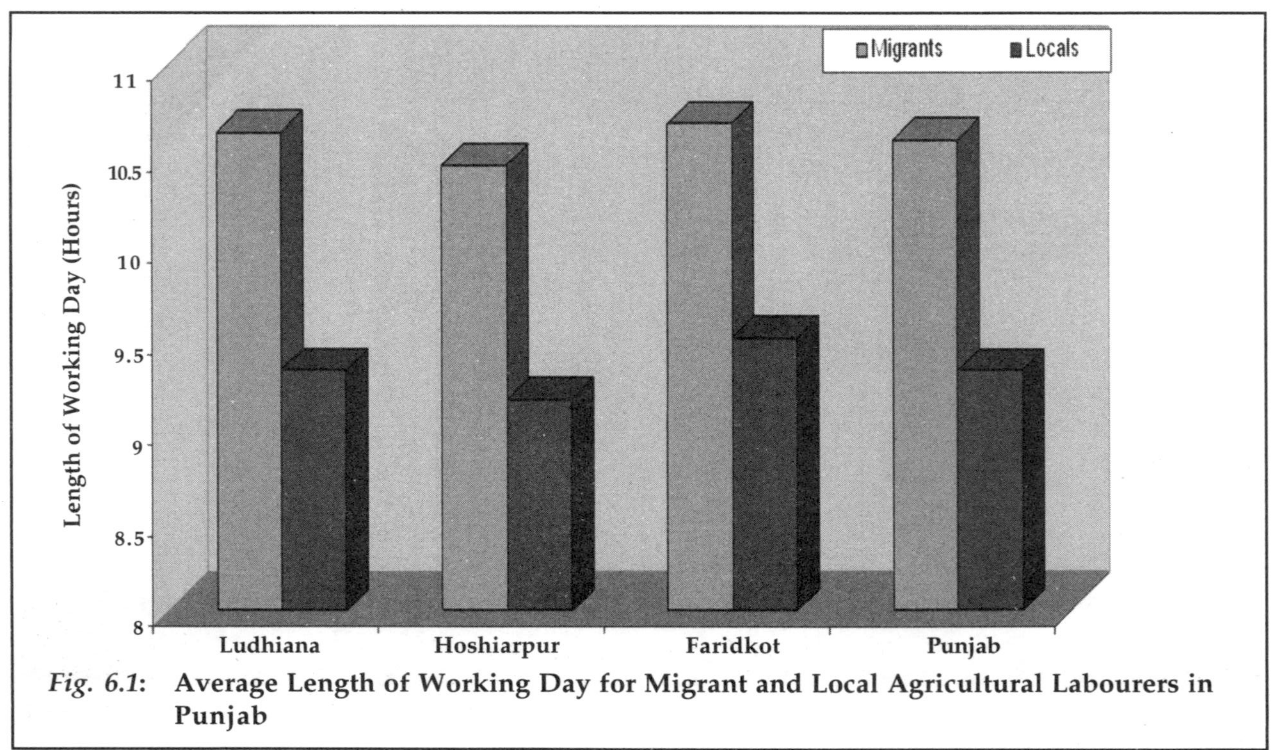

Fig. 6.1: Average Length of Working Day for Migrant and Local Agricultural Labourers in Punjab

Table 6.2 (c): Migrant Agricultural Labourers *vs.* Local Agricultural Labourers

Mean Working Day	Ludhiana	Hoshiarpur	Faridkot	Punjab
t-value	2.14	2.07	2.27	1.94
p-value	<.05	<.05	<.05	<.05

In the state as a whole, a migrant worker has to work for 1.27 hours more than a local worker. However, the field survey revealed a disturbing fact that the contractual migratory labourers are on call throughout the day and night.

This depicts the inverse relationship between length of working day and wage rate. The migrant agricultural labourers get lower wage rate for more work while the local agricultural labourers get higher wage rate for less work. This is because of easy availability of labourers out of the increasing unemployed reserve army of labourers.

WAGE RATES: PEAK PERIOD

The wage rates vary with the quantum of work load. Tables 6.3 and 6.4 present the wage rates for the migratory and local agricultural labourers during the peak and lean periods. During the peak period a migratory labourer gets Rs. 79.43 on an average per day while the same for a local labourer is Rs. 100.40 per day. A migrant labourer gets Rs. 20.97 per day less than a local agricultural labourer. The wage rate was the highest in Ludhiana district, *i.e.* Rs. 80.68 per day for a migratory labourer and Rs. 103.52 per day for a local labourer. By and large, the district-wise analysis also corresponds to the state analysis. The gap between the wage rates of the migrant and local agricultural labourers is found to be significant.

Table 6.3: Average Wage Rate for Migrant and Local Agricultural Labourers during Peak Period (Year)

District	Average Wage Rate (Rs./day)			t-value	p-value
	Migrants	Locals	Less		
Ludhiana	80.68	103.52	22.84	3.31	<.01
Hoshiarpur	76.84	98.67	21.83	2.99	<.01
Faridkot	78.13	96.39	18.26	2.53	<.05
Punjab	79.43	100.40	20.97	2.68	<.01

Source: Field Survey 2006

WAGE RATES: LEAN PERIOD

Table 6.4 shows that during the lean period of work load, the wage rate comes down. For the migratory labourers, it slashed down from Rs. 79.43 during the peak period to Rs. 55.49 during the lean period showing a decline of Rs. 23.94 per day.

Table 6.4: Average Wage Rate for Migrant and Local Agricultural Labourers during Lean Period (Year)

District	Average Wage Rate (Rs./day)			t-value	p-value
	Migrants	Locals	Less		
Ludhiana	57.02	78.96	21.94	3.17	<.01
Hoshiarpur	53.39	73.11	19.72	2.86	<.01
Faridkot	51.62	71.86	20.24	3.01	<.01
Punjab	55.49	75.55	20.06	3.09	<.01

Source: Field Survey 2006

In case of local agricultural labourers, the wage rate slashed down from Rs. 100.40 during the peak period to Rs. 75.55 during the lean period showing a cut of Rs. 24.85 per day in the state as a whole. The district-wise scenario

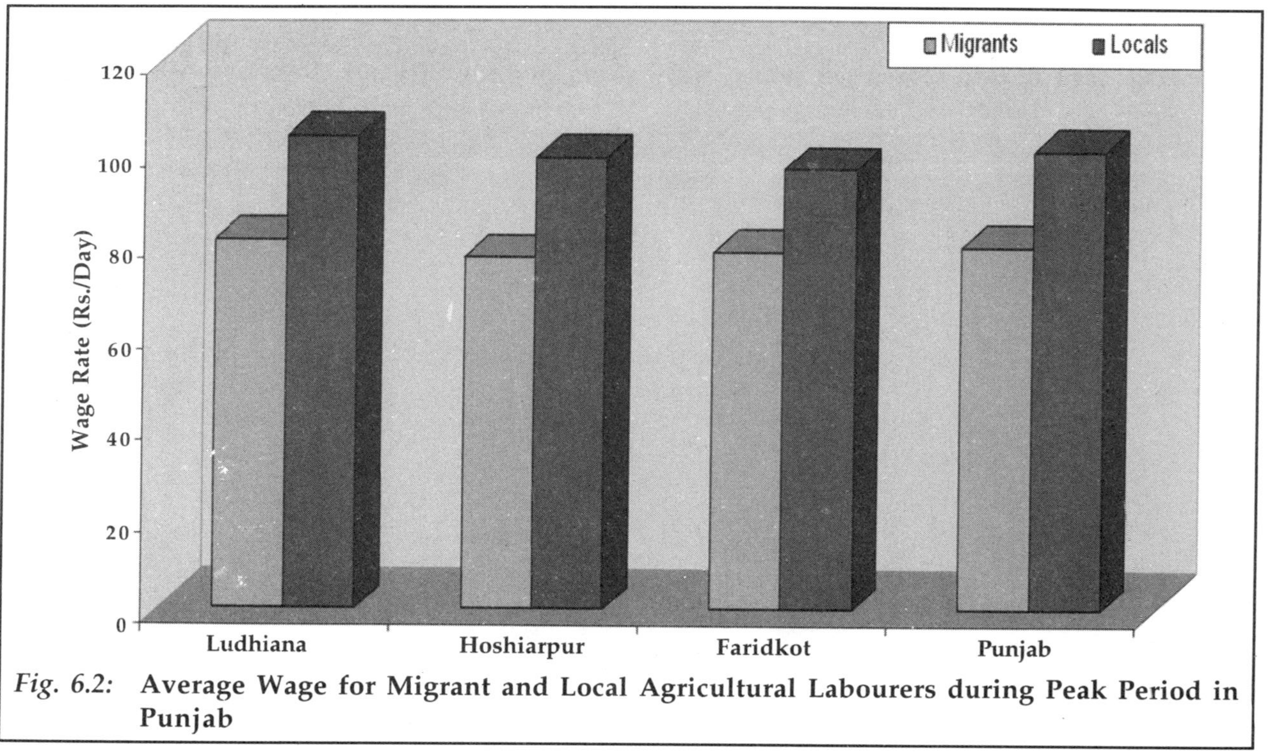

Fig. 6.2: Average Wage for Migrant and Local Agricultural Labourers during Peak Period in Punjab

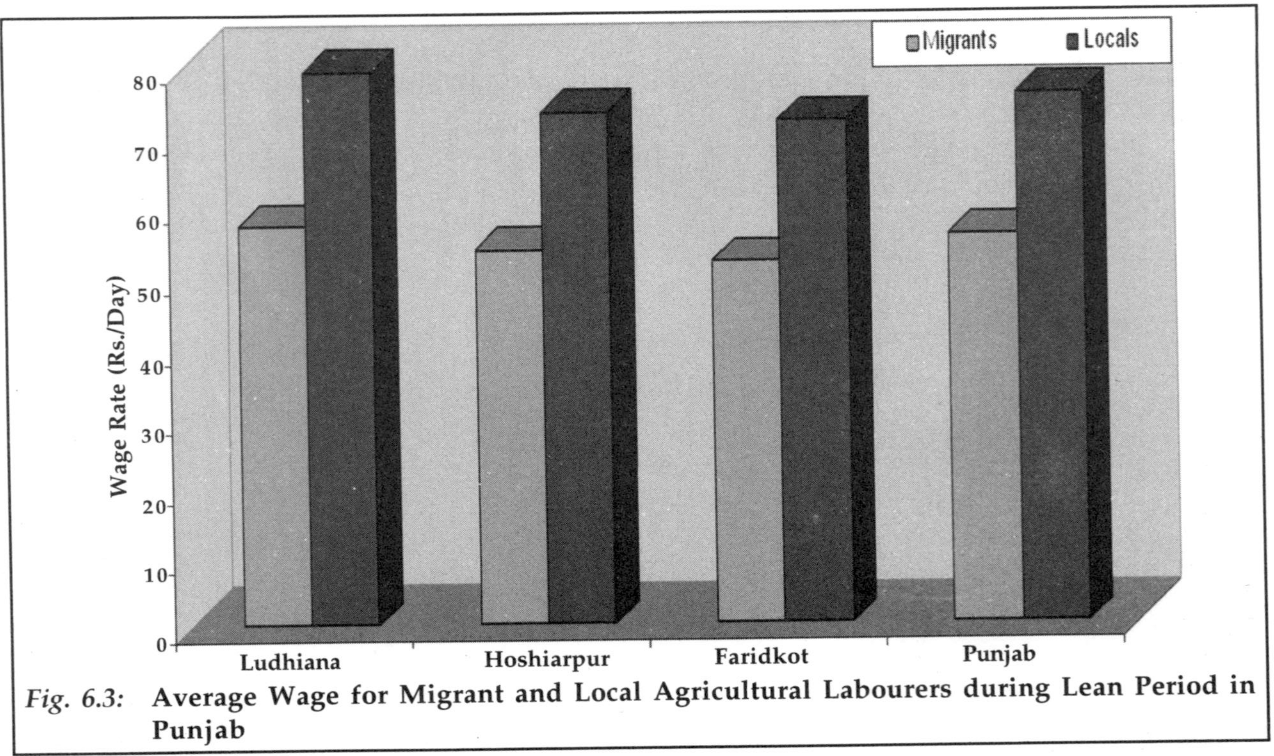

Fig. 6.3: Average Wage for Migrant and Local Agricultural Labourers during Lean Period in Punjab

follows the same pattern. The differences of wage rates for the migratory and local agricultural labourers are highly significant in all the districts as well as for the state as a whole. This shows that the migrant agricultural labourers get ready to work at lower wage rates in Punjab as these are still higher than those of their native places. But this competition results in further bringing down the wage rates in the wake of ever-increasing unemployment.

ANNUAL EARNINGS

The average annual earnings of the migrant and local agricultural labourers are shown in Table 6.5. In Punjab, the average annual earnings of the migrant agricultural labourers come to Rs. 17118.75, while those of the local agricultural labourers are Rs. 20156.71 showing a significant difference of Rs. 3037.96 per year. The earnings are the highest in Ludhiana district, *i.e.* Rs. 18087.50 for the migrant agricultural labourers and Rs. 21960.00 for the local agricultural labourers. The same are the lowest in Hoshiarpur district, i.e. Rs. 15147.60 for the migrant agricultural labourers and Rs. 18093.81 for the local agricultural labourers.

On one hand, the differences in the earnings of the migrant and local agricultural labourers are significant in all the districts under study, while on the other among the migrant agricultural labourers, district-wise differences are also significant. Similarly, among the local agricultural labourers, district-wise differences are also quite significant. This shows that the migrants are paid less than the local agricultural labourers. The annual earnings and the wage rates in different districts under study reveal a direct relationship with the soil productivity as these decreased from Ludhiana, the highest productive soil district to Faridkot, the medium productivity soil district and further to Hoshiarpur, the least productive soil district. Thus the wages are directly related to the productivity level of the districts.

Table 6.5: Annual Earnings of Migrant and Local Agricultural Labour

District	Average Earnings (Rs./Annum)			t-value	p-value
	Migrants	Local	Less		
Ludhiana	18087.50	21960.00	3872.50	3.52	<.01
Hoshiarpur	15147.60	18093.81	2946.21	2.89	<.01
Faridkot	16016.87	19152.88	3136.01	3.11	<.01
Punjab	17118.75	20156.71	3037.96	2.98	<.01
F-Ratio p-value	5.67 <.01	4.96 <.01			

Source: Field Survey 2006.

EXTRA WORK *Vs.* EXTRA WAGES

A glance at Tables 6.6 (a) and 6.6 (b) (*See on page 148*) provides that as many as 90.74 per cent of the migratory agricultural labourers have to work extra while this proportion is significantly low in the case of local agricultural labourers, i.e. 65.06 per cent as indicated by the significant z-value of 7.66 (*Table 6.6 (c) on page 149*).

The proportions for the migrant agricultural labourers who have to work extra do not differ significantly in the different districts while these differ significantly in the case of local agricultural labourers. This proportion is the highest in Faridkot district (82.81 per cent) and the lowest in Hoshiarpur district (44.30 per cent). In Ludhiana district, the incidence of extra work is 69.05 per cent. It may be due to highly labour intensive operations related to cotton such as spraying, hoeing, picking and uprooting of sticks in Faridkot district and low labour intensive operations related to maize in Hoshiarpur district.

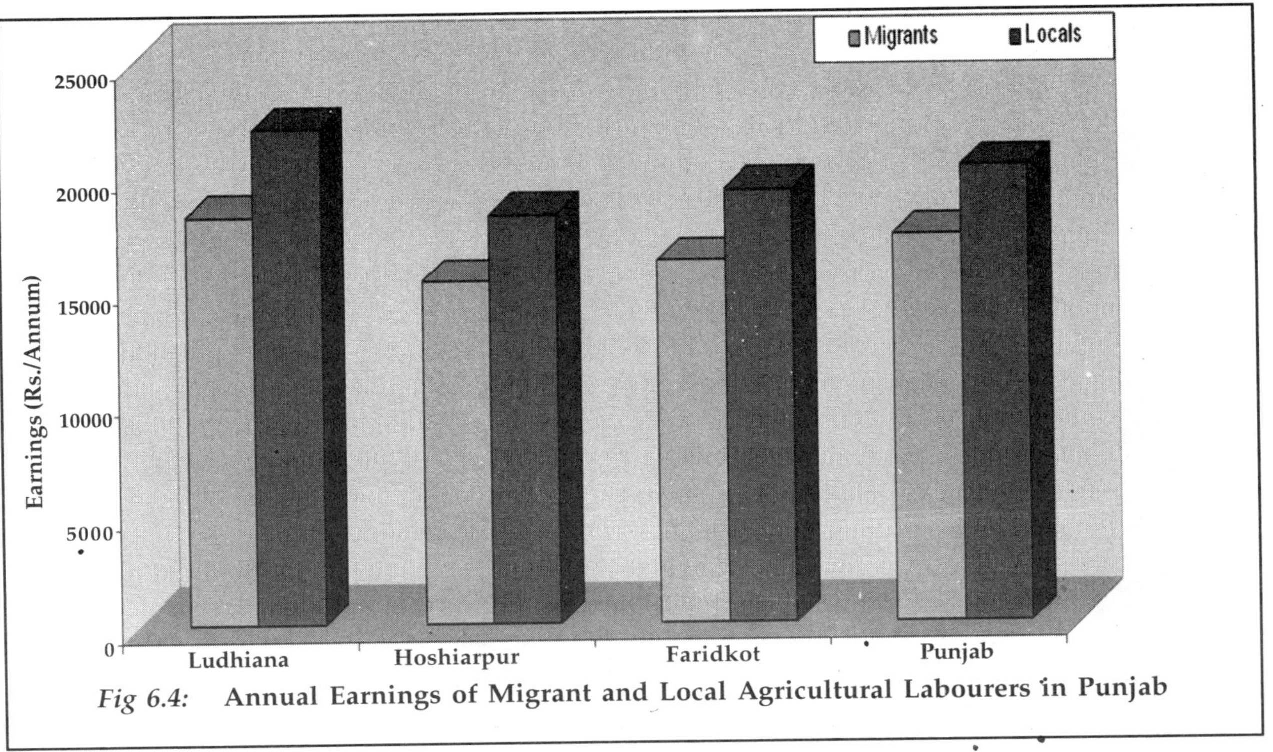

Fig 6.4: Annual Earnings of Migrant and Local Agricultural Labourers in Punjab

Table 6.6 (a): Distribution of Migrants according to Extra Work and Wages for Extra Work

District	Have to work extra		Get extra wages for extra work	
	Yes	No	Yes	No
Ludhiana	189 (91.75)	17 (8.25)	1 (0.53)	188 (99.47)
Hoshiarpur	69 (86.25)	11 (13.75)	2 (2.90)	67 (97.10)
Faridkot	36 (94.74)	2 (5.26)	0 (0.00)	36 (100.00)
Punjab	294 (90.74)	30 (9.26)	3 (1.02)	291 (98.98)
χ^2 value p-value	2.89 >0.10ns			

Source : Field Survey 2006

Note : The figures given in parentheses represent percentages.

Table 6.6 (b): Distribution of Locals according to Extra Work and Wages for Extra Work

District	Have to work extra		Get extra wages for extra work	
	Yes	No	Yes	No
Ludhiana	87 (69.05)	39 (30.95)	1 (1.15)	86 (98.85)
Hoshiarpur	35 (44.30)	44 (55.70)	0 (0.00)	35 (100.00)
Faridkot	53 (82.81)	11 (17.19)	0 (0.00)	53 (100.00)
Punjab	175 (65.06)	94 (34.94)	1 (0.68)	174 (99.32)
χ^2 value p-value	24.73 <0.01			

Source : Field Survey 2006

Note : The figures given in parentheses represent percentages.

Table 6.6 (c): Migrant Agricultural Labourers *Vs.* Local Agricultural Labourers

	Have to work extra	Get extra wages for extra work
z-value	7.66	0.51
p-value	<.01	>0.10 ns

The dark side of the picture emerged when 99.32 per cent and 98.98 per cent of the local and migrant agricultural labourers respectively reported that the farmers do not pay them for extra work. This must have resulted in further bringing down the wage rates on man-day equivalent basis. It means the labourers have to work beyond the specified length of 8 hrs. a day without any extra payment. The data contained in Table 6.2 has already proved that the length of working day for the migrant agricultural labourers is 2.59 hours longer than the standardized 8 hours working day, while the same is 1.32 hours longer in the case of the local agricultural labourers.

DISCRIMINATION REGARDING WORK AND WAGES

The data shown in Table 6.7 (a) (*See on page 151*) indicates that majority of the migrant agricultural labourers (64.51 per cent) face discrimination in working hours as they are forced to work for a longer duration than their local counterparts in Punjab. The proportion of the migrant agricultural labourers who reported discrimination in working hours comes out to 68.75 per cent in Hoshiarpur district, 65.79 per cent in Faridkot district and 62.62 per cent in Ludhiana district. The non-significant value of chi-square indicates that statistically the extent of discrimination in working hours in all the districts under study is almost the same.

Apart from the discrimination against migrant agricultural labourers regarding working hours, they are not even given wages equal to the local agricultural labourers.

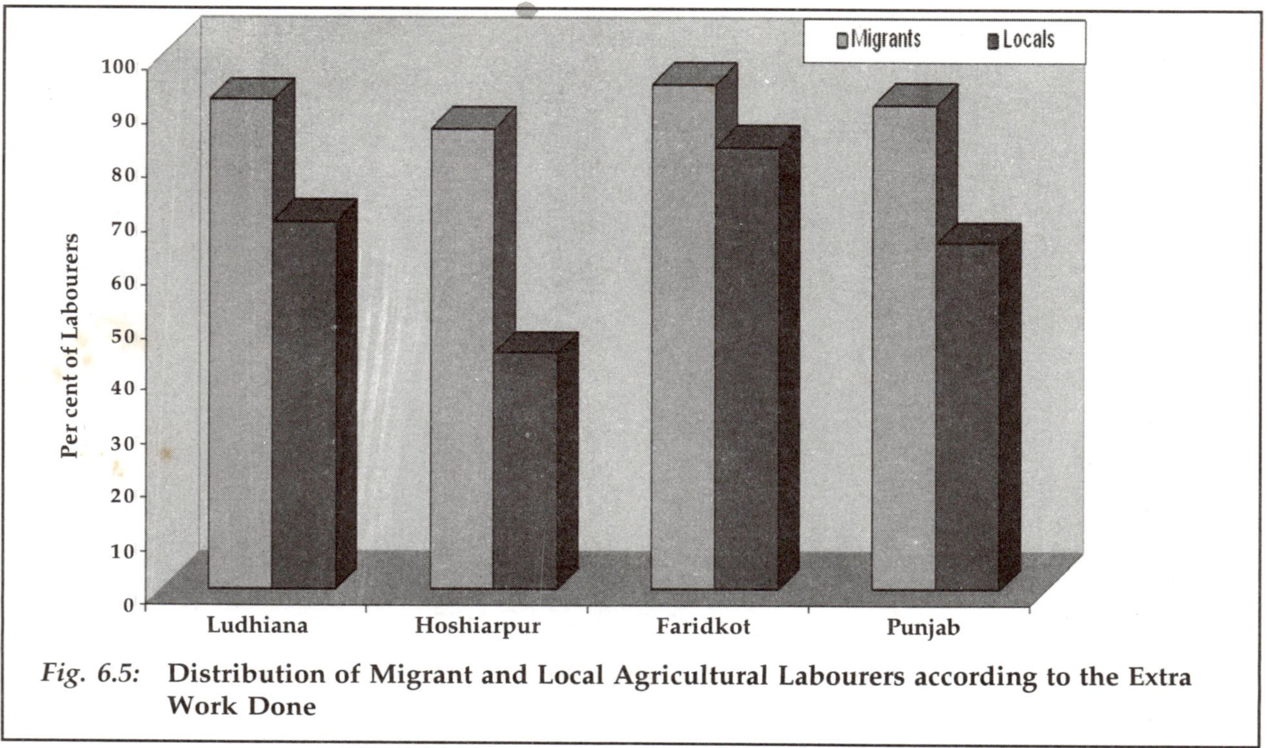

Fig. 6.5: Distribution of Migrant and Local Agricultural Labourers according to the Extra Work Done

Table 6.7 (a): Discrimination against Migratory Agricultural Labourers regarding Working Hours and Wages

Labour Strata District wise	Face discrimination in working hours		Wages equal to the local labourers	
	No	Yes	Yes	No
Ludhiana	77 (37.38)	129 (62.62)	63 (30.58)	143 (69.42)
Hoshiarpur	25 (31.25)	55 (68.75)	21 (26.25)	59 (73.75)
Faridkot	13 (34.21)	25 (65.79)	14 (36.84)	24 (63.16)
Punjab	115 (35.49)	209 (64.51)	98 (30.25)	226 (69.75)
χ^2 value p-value	1.01 >.10ns		1.38 >.10ns	

Source: Field Survey 2006

Note : The figures given in parentheses represent percentages.

Only 30.25 per cent of the migrant agricultural labourers are given wages equal to the local agricultural labourers, whereas the remaining 69.75 per cent are discriminated in this regard. The district-wise pattern of discrimination against the migrant agricultural labourers regarding wages is found to be similar as the discrimination in wages is reported by 73.75 per cent, 69.42 per cent and 63.16 per cent in Hoshiarpur, Ludhiana and Faridkot districts respectively. The non-significant value of chi-square has also established this fact.

The reasons for discrimination against the migrant agricultural labourers regarding wages are shown in Table 6.7 (b) (*See on page 152*). The major reasons are uncertainty of employment (87.17 per cent), and pressure of daily consumption needs (80.53 per cent) The migrant labourers fear to face unemployment if they refuse to work at low wage rates at the present place.

Table 6.7 (b): Reasons for Discrimination against Migrant Agricultural Labourers Regarding Wages (Multiple Responses)

District	Discrimination Reported by	Reasons of Discrimination				
		Locals more productive	Less supply of locals	Influence of trade unions	Daily needs pressure	Uncertainty of employment
Ludhiana	143	0 (0.00)	43 (30.07)	10 (6.99)	117 (81.82)	124 (86.71)
Hoshiarpur	59	2 (3.39)	29 (49.15)	2 (3.39)	47 (79.66)	51 (86.44)
Faridkot	24	0 (0.00)	10 (41.67)	4 (16.67)	18 (75.00)	22 (91.67)
Punjab	226	2 (0.88)	82 (36.28)	16 (7.08)	182 (80.53)	197 (87.17)

Source : Field Survey 2006

Note : The figures given in parentheses represent percentages.

It seems quite difficult and disturbing to settle at another place in Punjab as the factor of uncertainty of employment always looms large on the mind of the labourers. So, they are compelled to accept work at lower wage rates as compared to their local counterparts.

A migrant labourer knows that a refusal to work at even lower wages would mean losing the work as the reserve army of unemployed is always there to replace him. He also knows that it is difficult to fulfil his daily needs without the wages. This has emerged as one of the major reasons of discrimination against the migrant agricultural labourers as reported by 80.53 per cent of the affected labourers.

The third reason for discrimination is insufficient supply of the local agricultural labourers, which when interacted with its demand; carries the wages to higher levels. This is reported by 36.28 per cent of the migratory labourers. The field survey brought out the fact that in the absence of migrant labourers having any trade unions the influence of trade unions of the local agricultural labourers helps them in getting higher wages than the migrant labourers.

The different reasons for discrimination against migrant agricultural labourers regarding wages have shown a similar pattern in all the three districts under study.

BEHAVIOUR OF FARMERS REGARDING PAYMENT OF WAGES

The data contained in Table 6.8 highlights the behaviour of the farmers towards the migrant agricultural labourers at the time of making payment of wages to them. As many as 65.43 per cent migrant agricultural labourers showed their satisfaction over the time of payment of wages to them. But it is a matter of great concern that more than one-third of them are not paid their wages well in time or at the time of their need. District-wise analysis also indicates no significant variation in this regard.

Table 6.8: Behaviour of Farmers towards Migrants Regarding Payment of Wages

Particulars	Districts				χ^2 value	p-value
	Ludhiana	Hoshiarpur	Faridkot	Punjab		
Payment well in time	134 (65.05)	55 (68.75)	23 (60.57)	212 (65.43)	0.81	>.10ns
Wages refused by farmer	25 (12.14)	17 (21.25)	10 (26.32)	52 (16.25)	6.92	<.01
Abused/manhandled by farmers	37 (17.96)	12 (15.00)	8 (21.05)	57 (17.59)	0.70	>.10ns
Favouritism in recruitment	5 (2.43)	4 (5.00)	2 (5.26)	11 (3.40)	1.62	>.10ns

Source : Field Survey 2006

Note : The figures given in parentheses represent percentages.

As many as 16.25 per cent of the migrant agricultural labourers reported that the farmers refused to pay them the wages after completion of the job. However, the district-wise analysis reveals significant variation. The situation in this regard is worst in Faridkot district where more than one-fourth, *i.e.* 26.32 per cent of the migrant labourers were refused the payment of wages by the farmers. This incidence comes to 21.25 per cent in Hoshiarpur district and 12.14 per cent in Ludhiana district. In Faridkot district, the highest incidence of refusing wages to the labourers may be due to cotton crop failure year after year, whereas the low level of crop productivity in Hoshiarpur district may be responsible for refusing the wages to the migrant agricultural labourers.

It is disturbing that the migrant agricultural labourers are even abused, ill-treated and manhandled when they demand their wages from the farmers. The occurrence of such incidents to the extent of 17.59 per cent in Punjab as a whole and 21.05, 17.96 and 15.00 per cent in Faridkot, Ludhiana and Hoshiarpur districts respectively is quite considerable. The incidence of favouritism in recruitment is reported by only 3.40 per cent of the migratory labourers. In some cases, the farmers preferred to employ the local agricultural labourers. This may be due to the inefficiency of some migratory labourers or related to certain specific agronomic operations such as marketing of inputs as well as the produce, driving tractors etc.

Overall, it can be said there is a lot of discrimination against the migratory labourers regarding wage rate and payment of wages. They are sometimes refused the payment of wages in time, even abused and manhandled by the farmers whenever they ask for their wages.

IMPACT OF THE MIGRANT AGRICULTURAL LABOURERS ON EMPLOYMENT OF THE LOCAL AGRICULTURAL LABOURERS

According to the data given in Table 6.9, only 2.23 per cent of the local agricultural labourers view that there is no effect of the migrant agricultural labourers on their employment, while the vast majority, *i.e.* 97.77 per cent of the

Table 6.9: Impact of Migrant Agricultural Labourers on Employment of Local Agricultural Labourers

District	Effect of Migrants on Employment of Locals			Average Level of Effect	% Effect
	No Effect	Low Wages	Less Employment		
Ludhiana	4 (3.17)	86 (68.25)	68 (53.97)	0.97	97.47
Hoshiarpur	0 (0.00)	67 (84.81)	49 (62.03)	1.00	100.00
Faridkot	2 (3.13)	56 (87.50)	36 (56.25)	0.98	97.87
Punjab	6 (2.23)	209 (77.70)	153 (56.88)	0.98	98.37
			F-ratio p-value	1.16 >0.10ns	

Source : Field Survey 2006

Note : The figures given in parentheses represent percentages.

local agricultural labourers view that the influx of migrant agricultural labourers has an adverse effect on their employment opportunities. They find the migrant agricultural labourers to be their competitors in narrowing down the farm employment opportunities (56.88 per cent) and also depressing the wage rates (77.70 per cent). Though there is no open manifestation of this in the form of any dispute or confrontation between the two types of labourers, but the local agricultural labourers are having a bitter feeling that the migrant agricultural labourers have affected their employment opportunities and wages rates adversely.

To sum up, since most of the migratory labourers have a rural base, they generally prefer to work in the farms. Majority of the migratory labourers work on daily wage basis, whereas majority of the local agricultural labourers prefer to work on yearly or seasonal contract basis.

Although the wage rate during the peak period is higher than that of the lean period, yet during these periods, the average daily wage rate of the migrant agricultural labourers is lower than that of the local agricultural labourers. Apart from this, there is a significant variation between the average length of working day for the migrant and the local agricultural labourers. Though, the migrants have to work for longer hours in a day, yet they are hardly paid for their extra work. As a result of this, the average annual earnings of the locals exceed those of the migrants. The migratory labourers in the absence of any trade unions of their own face discrimination. Although majority of the farmers were cordial and sympathetic towards the migrant agricultural labourers, yet, in certain cases, they were refused wages; and even abused and manhandled.

The local agricultural labourers do not like the migratory agricultural labourers as they consider them their main competitors on the farms. The influx of migratory agricultural labour in Punjab has reduced their capacity to assert. Moreover, the local farm labourers feel that because of the easy availability of the migrant agricultural labourers their own real wages have decreased and the chances of their employment have shrinked.

Socio-cultural Changes in the Migrant Agricultural Labourers

Migration, being an independent human activity, is considered to be a good indicator of socio-cultural change in a country like India comprising different castes, cultures, languages and religions. The migrant and local agricultural labourers differ in many aspects such as language, complexion, food habits, behavioural traits etc. But migration offers a number of opportunities to change and adopt new ways and means of life, which ultimately bring qualitative changes in terms of socio-cultural and economic conditions. The migration of labourers from various states of India to Punjab in the agricultural sector caused socio-cultural and economic changes in them.

IDENTITY OF THE MIGRANT AGRICULTURAL LABOURERS

It has been found that majority of the migrant agricultural labourers (66.36 per cent) are called not by their actual names but by the name convenient to the locals such as *bhaiya, Ramu, Shamu,* etc. in Punjab. The districts under study have also shown a similar trend in this regard. There are only 35.92, 30.00 and 28.95 per cent of the migrant agricultural labourers in Ludhiana, Hoshiarpur and Faridkot districts

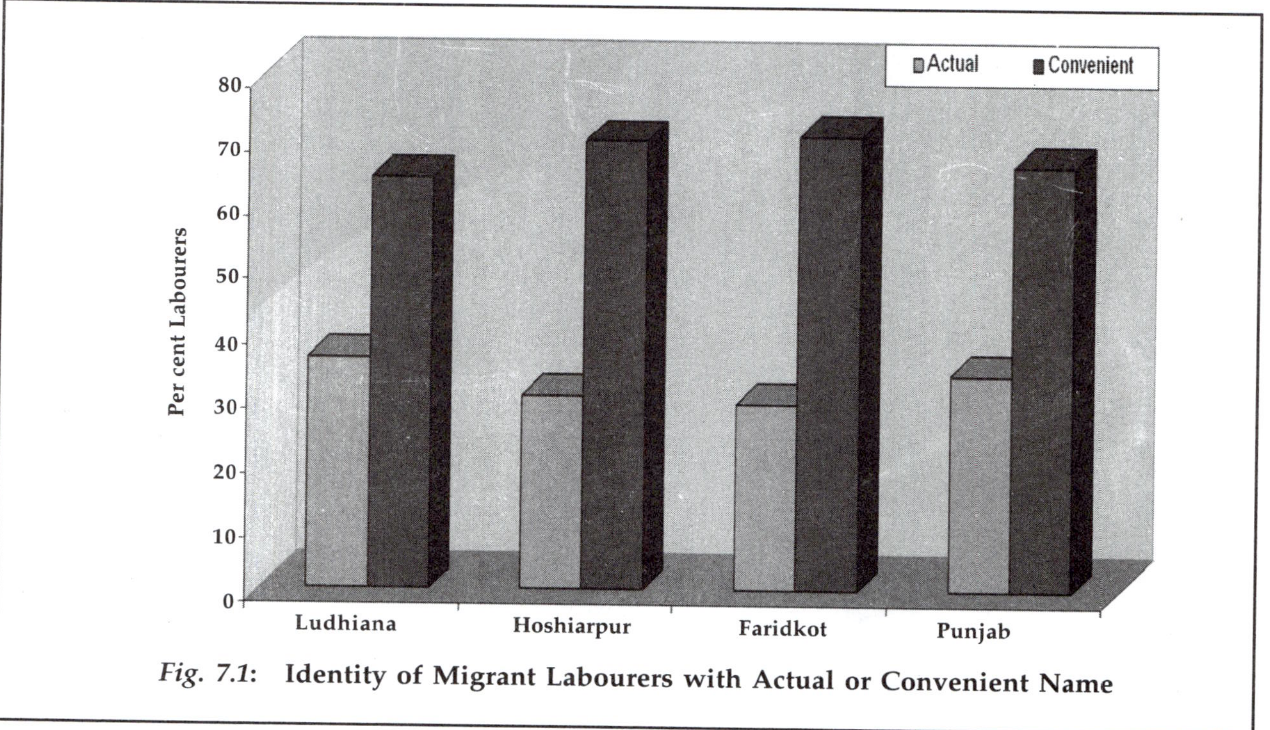

Fig. 7.1: Identity of Migrant Labourers with Actual or Convenient Name

respectively who are called by their actual names by the locals. The proportions of those called by their actual names are significantly lower than those called by the convenience of the locals. Though this is a change in the migrants' cultural aspect yet the change is not favourable because one should be called with respect by one's actual name. The migrants also do not protest being called by other names.

Table 7.1: Identity of Migrant Agricultural Labourers with the Actual or Convenient Name

District	Identity (Name)		Z-value	p-value
	Actual	Convenient		
Ludhiana	74 (35.92)	132 (64.08)	5.72	<0.01
Hoshiarpur	24 (30.00)	56 (70.00)	5.06	<0.01
Faridkot	11 (28.95)	27 (71.05)	3.67	<0.01
Punjab	109 (33.64)	215 (66.36)	8.33	<0.01

Source : Field Survey 2006

Note : The figures given in parentheses represent percentages.

FOOD PATTERN

In the study area, three types of food preparation patterns are found. As shown in Table 7.2(a), majority of the migratory labourers *i.e.* 59.26 per cent get their food from their farmer's house in the state followed by 22.84 per cent who prepare their food collectively while 17.90 per cent of them prepare it individually. But the pattern differs significantly across the districts under study. Majority of the migrant agricultural labourers from Faridkot and Ludhiana districts with the percentages of 76.31 and 64.07 respectively get their food from the respective farmer's house, whereas this percentage in the case of Hoshiarpur district is only 38.75. Further, it has been found that the migrant agricultural labourers from the Hoshiarpur district with the highest percentage of 42.50 prepare their food collectively.

Table 7.2(a): Food Preparation Pattern among Migratory Labourers in Punjab

District	Food Preparation Pattern		
	Individually	Collectively	From Farmer's House
Ludhiana	40 (19.42)	34 (16.51)	132 (64.07)
Hoshiarpur	15 (18.75)	34 (42.50)	31 (38.75)
Faridkot	3 (7.90)	6 (15.79)	29 (76.31)
Punjab	58 (17.90)	74 (22.84)	192 (59.26)
χ^2 value = 28.76	p value < .01		

Source : Field Survey 2006

Note : The figures given in parentheses represent percentages.

The farmers in Hoshiarpur district are having low level of income due to relatively low land productivity. This may be the reason that the farmers in Hoshiarpur district cannot offer food to the migrant labourers. In Ludhiana district, individual food preparation pattern is the second major pattern (19.42 per cent) while it is collective food preparation pattern in Faridkot district (15.79 per cent). The high significant value of chi-square establishes a close relationship between food preparation pattern and the regions.

A glance at Table 7.2 (b) provides that as high as 77.16 per cent of the migrant agricultural labourers reported a change in their consumption pattern. The extent of change varies from district to district; Faridkot district showing a change with the highest percentage of 94.74 followed by Hoshiarpur and Ludhiana districts with the percentages of 81.25 and 72.33 respectively. This difference from district to district may be attributed to the varied wage rates, earnings, culture etc.

In the state as a whole, 76.00 per cent of the migrant agricultural labourers who reported a change in their consumption pattern took the change as 'good' while 23.60 per cent could not give any response to the quality of change. Only 0.40 per cent of them reported that change in the consumption pattern was bad. The overall score of quality of change comes to 75.60 per cent which points towards a good change in the consumption pattern.

The proportions of those migratory labourers who termed the change as good differ significantly from district to district, *i.e.* 80.54 per cent in Ludhiana, 77.78 per cent in Faridkot and 64.61 per cent in Hoshiarpur districts. The score of quality of change comes to be 80.54, 77.78 and 63.08 per cent in Ludhiana, Faridkot and Hoshiarpur districts respectively. The variation in the score of quality of change in consumption pattern of the migrant agricultural labourers is found to be significant as indicated by the F-ratio. The low score of quality of change in the consumption pattern in Hoshiarpur district may be due to the reason that only a small proportion of them get their food from the respective farmer's house which is always of better quality and taste as compared to the food prepared by them.

LIKING FOR PUNJABI LANGUAGE

Table 7.3(a) carries the data about the migrant agricultural labourers showing their liking for Punjabi language, songs and dances. As many as 18.83 per cent of the

Table 7.2 (b): Trends of Change in the Consumption Pattern among Migratory Labourers

District	Change	Quality of Change			Mean Score of Quality	% Extent
Ludhiana	149 (72.33)	120 (80.54)	0 (0.00)	29 (19.46)	0.81	80.54
Hoshiarpur	65 (81.25)	42 (64.61)	1 (1.54)	22 (33.85)	0.63	63.08
Faridkot	36 (94.74)	28 (77.78)	0 (0.00)	8 (22.22)	0.78	77.78
Punjab	250 (77.16)	190 (76.00)	1 (0.40)	59 (23.60)	0.76	75.60
χ^2 value p-value	10.15 <0.01			F-ratio p-value	4.31 <0.05	

Source : Field Survey 2006

Note : The figures given in parentheses represent percentages.

migrant agricultural labourers have learnt to speak Punjabi frequently. This percentage varies from district to district in Punjab; Faridkot district showing the maximum percentage of 36.84 followed by Ludhiana and Hoshiarpur districts with the percentages of 17.96 and 12.50 respectively. The significant value of chi-square also establishes this fact.

The percentage of migrants using both Punjabi and Hindi languages for conversation with the locals varies from district to district. However, in Punjab about 40 per cent of them use Hindi only, while 51 per cent of them converse with the locals in Punjabi only. A small proportion of about 9 per cent of the remaining migrants use both the languages as per convenience. The survey revealed that majority of the migrant agricultural labourers belong to the Hindi speaking or some local dialect areas but in Punjab, they have learnt to speak Punjabi for conversation with Punjabi people.

District-wise analysis of using language for conversation with the locals shows that there are significant differences in the pattern. In Ludhiana district, 48.06 per cent of migrant agricultural labourers talk in Hindi with the locals, while in Faridkot and Hoshiarpur districts, as high as 65.78 per cent and 60 per cent respectively use Punjabi language for conversation with the locals. The association of the languages used by the migrant agricultural labourers for conversation with the locals is significant with districts as conveyed by the significant value of chi-square.

This pattern is found to be in correspondence with that presented in Table 7.3 (b). In Ludhiana district, majority of the local agricultural labourers *i.e.* 61.11 per cent use Hindi for conversation with the migrant agricultural labourers while in Hoshiarpur and Faridkot districts, majority of the local agricultural labourers use Punjabi language for conversation with the migrant agricultural labourers. The association between languages used by the local agricultural labourers for conversation with migrant agricultural labourers in the districts of Punjab is found to be significant as conveyed by

Table 7.3 (a): Liking for Punjabi Language and Punjabi Songs

District	Speaking Punjabi Frequently	Conversation with Locals			Liking for Punjabi Songs/Dance	Prefer to Sing Punjabi Songs
		Hindi	Punjabi	Both		
Ludhiana	37 (17.96)	99 (48.06)	93 (45.14)	14 (6.80)	147 (71.36)	27 (13.11)
Hoshiarpur	10 (12.50)	20 (25.00)	48 (60.00)	12 (15.00)	63 (78.75)	26 (32.50)
Faridkot	14 (36.84)	10 (26.32)	25 (65.78)	3 (7.90)	31 (81.58)	11 (28.95)
Punjab	61 (18.83)	129 (39.82)	166 (51.23)	29 (8.95)	241 (74.38)	64 (19.75)
χ^2 value p-value	10.27 <.01		18.31 <.01		2.82 >.10 ns	15.97 <.01

Source : Field Survey 2006

Note : The figures given in parentheses represent percentages.

the significant value of chi-square. Thus, there is similarity in the pattern of using languages by the local and migrant agricultural labourers for conversation with one another.

Table 7.3 (b): Language Used by Local Agricultural Labourers for Conversation with Migrant Agricultural Labourers and Reasons for Using Language Other than the Mother Tongue

District	Language Used		Reasons For Using Hindi	
	Punjabi	Hindi	Migrants Not Knowing Punjabi	Locals Try to Speak Hindi
Ludhiana	49 (38.89)	77 (61.11)	39 (50.65)	45 (58.44)
Hoshiarpur	43 (54.43)	36 (45.57)	15 (41.67)	32 (88.89)
Faridkot	45 (70.31)	19 (29.69)	6 (31.58)	17 (89.47)
Punjab	137 (50.93)	132 (49.07)	60 (45.45)	94 (71.21)
χ^2 value p-value	17.31 <.01			

Source : Field Survey 2006

Note : The figures given in parentheses represent percentages.

Majority of the local agricultural labourers use Hindi for conversation with the migrant agricultural labourers due to their willingness to try to speak Hindi (71.21 per cent) while 45.45 per cent of them use Hindi as the migrant agricultural labourers could not understand Punjabi.

BATHING AND WASHING PATTERN

Tables 7.4(a) and 7.4(b) present the data showing the distribution of the migratory labourers as per their frequency of bathing and interval of washing clothes.

Table 7.4(a) brings out that all the migrant agricultural labourers in all the districts under study take bath daily during the summer season. But during the winter season, only 15.43 per cent of them take bath daily. The highest proportions, *i.e.* 33.95 per cent of the migrant agricultural labourers take their bath after 4-6 days in winter followed by 26.23 per cent who take their bath after 2-4 days. As many as 14.20 per cent of them were reported to take bath after 6-8 days, *i.e.* only once a week, while 10.19 per cent were in the habit of taking bath not even once a week but as and when required in a fortnight. The average score of bathing frequency comes to 3.23 which works out to 64.60 per cent by giving weights to different frequencies, *i.e.* 5 for daily, 4 for 2-4 days, 3 for 4-6 days, 2 for 6-8 days and 1 for as and when required. Thus, the overall score falls in 4-6 days frequency of taking bath in the state, as a whole. The district-wise analysis could not depict any significant variations in the bathing pattern. The mean score of frequency of taking bath by the migratory labourers came to be 3.38 (67.60 per cent), 3.21 (64.20 per cent) and 3.17 (63.40 per cent) in Hoshiarpur, Faridkot and Ludhiana districts respectively. The non-significant value of F-ratio signifies that there was no regional variation in the bathing pattern of the migrant agricultural labourers.

It is evident from the data shown in Table 7.4 (b) that only 14.81 per cent of the migratory labourers used to wash clothes daily while majority of them, *i.e.* 53.70 per cent used to wash clothes after a gap of 2-4 days. This was followed by 24.07 per cent who were in the habit of washing clothes after a gap of 4-6 days. There were 4.32 per cent migrants who used to wash clothes once a week, i.e. after a gap of 6-8 days, while 3.09 per cent of them washed their clothes as and when required. The mean score of frequency of washing clothes by the migrant agricultural labourers in the state came to be 3.73 (74.60 per cent) which falls in the category of 2 to 4 days interval of washing clothes.

Table 7.4 (a): Distribution of Migratory Labourers according to the Frequency of Bathing

District	Summer	During Winter					Mean Score	%Score
	Daily	Daily (5)	2-4 Days (4)	4-6 Days (3)	6-8 Days (2)	As & When Required (1)		
Ludhiana	206 (100.00)	28 (13.59)	52 (25.24)	73 (35.44)	33 (16.02)	20 (9.71)	3.17	63.40
Hoshiarpur	80 (100.00)	15 (18.75)	23 (28.75)	24 (30.00)	13 (16.25)	5 (6.25)	3.38	67.60
Faridkot	38 (100.00)	7 (18.42)	10 (26.32)	13 (34.21)	0 (0.00)	8 (21.05)	3.21	64.20
Punjab	324 (100.00)	50 (15.43)	85 (26.23)	110 (33.95)	46 (14.20)	33 (10.19)	3.23	64.60
						F-ratio p-value	1.09 >.10ns	

Source: Field Survey 2006

Note : The figures given in parentheses represent percentages.

Table 7.4 (b): Distribution of Migratory Labourers according to the Interval of Washing Clothes

District	Interval of Washing Clothes (Days)					Mean Interval	% Interval
	Daily (5)	2-4 Days (4)	4-6 Days (3)	6-8 Days (2)	As & When Required (1)		
Ludhiana	22 (10.68)	115 (55.83)	54 (26.21)	9 (4.37)	6 (2.91)	3.67	73.40
Hoshiarpur	13 (16.25)	41 (51.25)	20 (25.00)	3 (3.75)	3 (3.75)	3.73	74.60
Faridkot	13 (34.21)	18 (47.37)	4 (10.53)	2 (5.26)	1 (2.63)	4.05	81.00
Punjab	48 (14.81)	174 (53.70)	78 (24.07)	14 (4.32)	10 (3.09)	3.73	74.60
					F-ratio p-value	5.11 <0.05	

Source : Field Survey 2006

Note : The figures given in parentheses represent percentages.

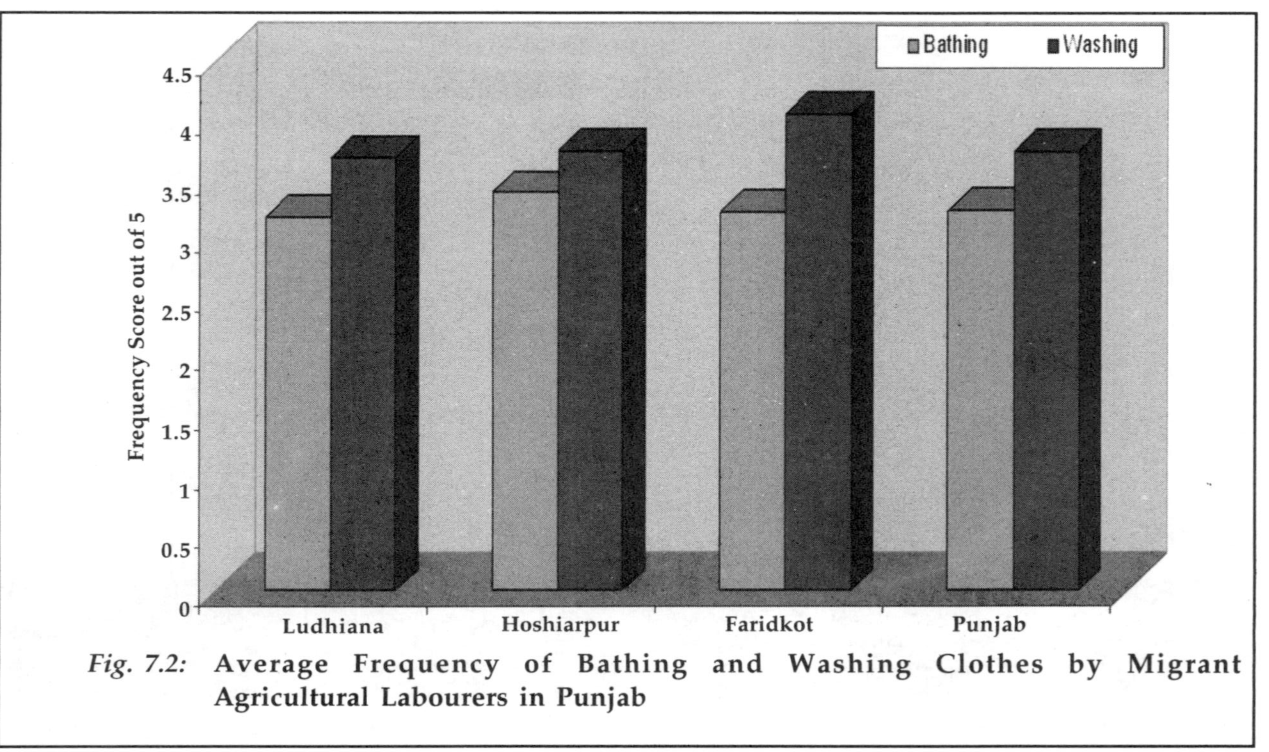

Fig. 7.2: Average Frequency of Bathing and Washing Clothes by Migrant Agricultural Labourers in Punjab

The district-wise analysis indicated a significant variation in the frequency of washing clothes. The higher proportion of the migrant agricultural labourers, *i.e.* 34.21 per cent used to wash clothes daily in Faridkot district, and the lowest to the tune of 10.68 per cent in Ludhiana district. This led to the highest mean score of interval of washing clothes, i.e. 4.05 (81.00 per cent) in Faridkot district which was found to be significantly higher than the other districts. It was 3.73 (74.60 per cent) in Hoshiarpur district and 3.67 (73.40 per cent) in Ludhiana district. The possible reasons for regional variation in washing clothes may be due to the variation in work load, possession of clothes and shortage of time.

SLEEPING SPOT

The analysis presented in Table 7.5 shows that a significant majority of the migrant agricultural labourers, *i.e.* 57.10 per cent used to sleep on a cot as compared to the remaining 42.90 per cent who had no cot and used to sleep on the floor. There were significant regional variations in the sleeping pattern. In Ludhiana and Faridkot districts, majority of the migrants, *i.e.* 62.62 per cent and 60.53 per cent respectively used to sleep on a cot, while a majority of them in Hoshiarpur district, *i.e.* 58.75 per cent used to sleep on the floor for want of any cot. This may again be attributed to the lower wages in Hoshiarpur district as compared to Ludhiana and Faridkot districts.

Table 7.5 further reveals that majority of the migrant agricultural labourers, *i.e.* 57.72 per cent were having a quilt for sleeping during the winter nights, while the remaining 42.28 per cent were having only a blanket. The proportion of the migrant agricultural labourers having quilts was significantly higher than those having blankets in the state. Ludhiana district also showed the same pattern, whereas the differences were non-significant in Hoshiarpur and Faridkot districts.

Table 7.5: Sleeping Spot and Possession of Clothes for Sleeping During Winter

District	Sleep at Night			Possess During Winter		
	On Floor	Cot	Z-value	Quilt	Blanket	Z-value
Ludhiana	77 (37.38)	129 (62.62)	5.12***	122 (59.22)	84 (40.78)	3.74***
Hoshiarpur	47 (58.75)	33 (41.25)	2.21**	43 (53.75)	37 (46.25)	0.95ns
Faridkot	15 (39.47)	23 (60.53)	1.84*	22 (57.90)	16 (42.10)	1.38ns
Punjab	139 (42.90)	185 (57.10)	3.61***	187 (57.72)	137 (42.28)	3.93***
χ^2 value p-value	10.95 <0.01			0.70 >0.10ns		

*** p<.01; ** p<0.5; * p<.10.

Source : Field Survey 2006.

Note : The figures given in parentheses represent percentages.

HEALTH SERVICES

The different aspects of health related services among the migratory labourers are presented in Table 7.6. As high as 80.25 per cent of the migrant agricultural labourers used to have medical treatment from the government dispensary or Primary Health Centre located in their village, followed by 17.28 per cent and 2.47 per cent who got medical treatment from the registered medical practitioners and *hakims* respectively. There was no significant regional variation in the pattern of getting medical treatment, as indicated by the non-significant value of chi-square. It is encouraging to note that migrant agricultural labourers, who were getting medical treatment from quacks in their native villages, are now

Table 7.6: Pattern of Health Services among Migratory Agricultural Labourers in Punjab

District	Mode of Treatment			Discrimination at Dispensary/PHC	Type of Discrimination (Multiple Response)	
	Dispensary or PHC	RMP	Hakim		No Medicine	Misbehave
Ludhiana	172 (83.50)	28 (13.59)	6 (2.91)	98 (56.98)	21 (21.43)	85 (86.73)
Hoshiarpur	59 (73.75)	20 (25.00)	1 (1.25)	39 (66.10)	10 (25.64)	32 (82.05)
Faridkot	29 (76.32)	8 (21.05)	1 (2.63)	22 (57.19)	13 (59.09)	17 (77.27)
Punjab	260 (80.25)	56 (17.28)	8 (2.47)	159 (61.15)	44 (27.67)	134 (84.28)
χ^2 value p value	6.11 >0.10 ns			4.50 > 0.10 ns		

Source: Field Survey 2006

Note : The figures given in parentheses represent percentages.

availing better medical services in Punjab. But it is unfortunate that the migrant agricultural labourers are being discriminated at the dispensaries or primary health centers. As high as 61.15 per cent of the migrant agricultural labourers, who used to have medical treatment from the government dispensaries, reported that they are often misbehaved (84.28 per cent) by the dispensary staff and no medicine (27.67 per cent) is given to them. A similar trend was noticed in all the districts under study. But the discrimination pattern significantly differed in all the three districts as the highest percentage of respondents, *i.e.* 59.09 from Faridkot district followed by 25.64 from Hoshiarpur district and 21.43 from Ludhiana district reported that they got no medicine from the respective dispensaries or primary health centers. On the contrary, the incidence of misbehaviour by the staff was higher in Ludhiana district (86.73 per cent) followed by Hoshiarpur (82.05 per cent) and Faridkot (77.27 per cent) districts.

The unhygienic bathing and washing patterns and lack of proper sleeping facilities, (Tables 7.4 and 7.5) indicated the morbid conditions prevalent among the migrant agricultural labourers. Their bad living conditions are related to the incidence of infectious diseases such as malaria, hepatitis, typhoid and respiratory infections.

No doubt, majority of the migrant agricultural labourers (80.25 per cent) avail medical facilities provided by the Govt. dispensaries and Primary Health Centres, but they are ill-treated and no proper medicine is provided to them there. Majority of the migrants surveyed fall prey to many diseases because they have to live in overcrowded rooms; they do not get nutritional food, they have to drink water not suitable for human consumption; and their environmental conditions are never healthy.

SAVINGS PATTERN

Table 7.7 exhibits the data regarding different savings patterns among the migratory labourers and local labourers.

Table 7.7: Distribution of Respondents according to Methods of Savings

Savings Deposit Methods	Ludhiana		Hoshiarpur		Faridkot		Punjab	
	No.	%age	No.	%age	No.	%age	No.	%age
A. Migratory Labourers								
1. No Savings	0	0.00	0	0.00	0	0.00	0	0.00
2. Bank/Post Office	31	15.05	4	5.00	2	5.26	37	11.42
3. Own Level	53	25.73	9	11.25	5	13.16	67	20.68
4. With Farmer	122	59.22	67	83.75	31	81.58	220	67.90
χ^2 value (Between regions) = 19.84***								
B. Local Labourers								
1. No Savings	49	38.90	58	73.42	38	59.37	145	53.91
2. Bank/Post Office	42	33.33	14	17.72	18	28.12	74	27.51
3. Own Level	31	24.60	5	6.33	6	9.38	42	15.61
4. With Farmer	4	3.17	2	2.53	2	3.13	8	2.97
χ^2 value (Between regions) = 47.82***								

(Contd...)

Savings Deposit Methods	Ludhiana		Hoshiarpur		Faridkot		Punjab	
	No.	%age	No.	%age	No.	%age	No.	%age
Z-value (Migrants *Vs.* Locals)								
1. No Savings	9.69***		9.62***		6.00**		15.20***	
2. Bank/Post Office	3.90***		2.53**		2.81***		5.00**	
3. Own Level	0.23ns		1.10ns		0.60ns		1.59ns	
4. With Farmer	10.21***		10.33***		8.19***		16.12***	

Source: Field Survey 2006

*** Significant at 1% level; ** Significant at 5% level; ns: Non-significant.

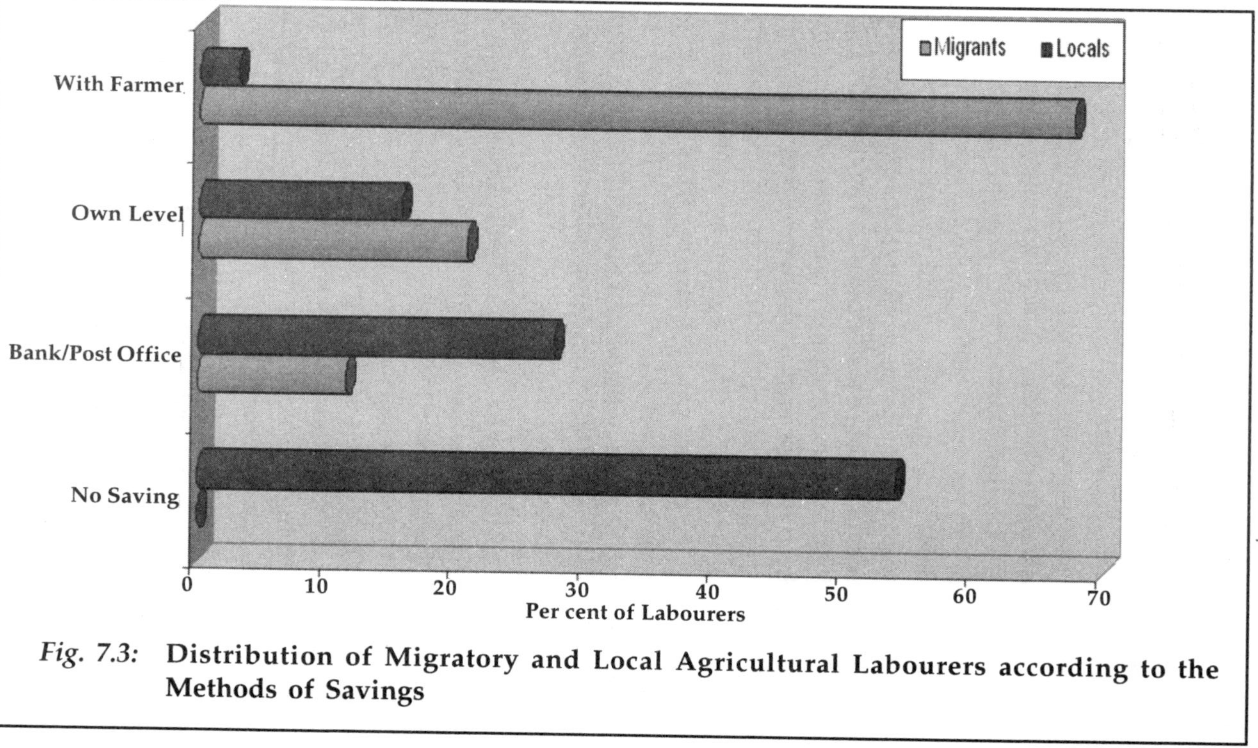

Fig. 7.3: **Distribution of Migratory and Local Agricultural Labourers according to the Methods of Savings**

A glance at the table provides that all the migratory labourers used to save something for the future although to the varying extents. On the other hand, significantly as high as 53.90 per cent of the local agricultural labourers were not saving at all. This may be due to their extravagant nature and family compulsions as compared to those of migrant agricultural labourers. The standard of living of local agricultural labourers is significantly higher than that of migrant agricultural labourers which leaves them nothing to save. The table further reveals that only 11.42 per cent of the migratory labourers and 27.51 per cent of the local agricultural labourers had their savings accounts in banks or post offices. A significantly high proportion of the migrant agricultural labourers, *i.e.* 67.90 per cent used to keep their savings with their respective farmers, while this proportion was only 2.97 per cent in the case of the local agricultural labourers. The migrants consider it safe and secure to keep the money with the farmers. They used to get their money back as and when required. However, the remaining 20.68 per cent of the migrant agricultural labourers and 15.61 per cent of the local agricultural labourers managed the savings at their own level.

District-wise, there has been a significant variation in the savings deposit methods. In the districts of Ludhiana, Faridkot and Hoshiarpur, 15.05 per cent, 5.26 per cent and 5.00 per cent migratory agricultural labourers respectively preferred to deposit their savings in the banks/post offices. Ludhiana being a relatively more developed district, banking services gained higher recognition here as compared to the other districts. On the other hand, in Hoshiarpur district significantly the highest majority of the migrant agricultural labourers, *i.e.* 83.75 per cent used to keep their savings with the farmers, followed by 81.58 per cent and 59.22 per cent in the districts of Faridkot and Ludhiana respectively.

Among the local agricultural labourers, savings methods differed significantly across the districts. The proportion of the local agricultural labourers who had no savings came to be 73.42 per cent in Hoshiarpur district, followed by 59.37 per cent in Faridkot district and only 38.90 per cent in Ludhiana district. These figures correspond to the pattern of wage rates and earnings in the different districts under study. In order to deposit their savings, the banking facility was again availed by 33.33 per cent of the local agricultural labourers in Ludhiana district while it was 28.12 per cent in Faridkot district and only 17.72 per cent in Hoshiarpur district. Most of the agricultural labourers being illiterate avoided to avail the banking facility as they found it difficult to fill up the deposit and withdrawal slips. Even they had no spare time to stand in the queues of the banks. The association between methods of savings deposit and districts was found to be significant as indicated by the significant value of chi-square.

On the basis of above analysis it can be said that the migrant agricultural labourers preferred to deposit their savings, with the farmers whereas the local agricultural labourers preferred the banks/post offices.. As a result of relatively higher standard of living, majority of the local agricultural labourers failed to save at all.

ASPECTS RELATED TO SAVINGS

Table 7.8 indicates that about 91 per cent of the migratory labourers used to send their savings to support their families living at their native villages. However, the remaining about 9 per cent did not follow this practice as their families were either staying with them in Punjab or they were unmarried. But there had been a significant district-wise variation in this regard. In Faridkot district, 100 per cent of the migratory labourers used to send money to their families, while it was 93.75 per cent in Hoshiarpur district and 87.86 per cent in Ludhiana district.

Table 7.8: Various Aspects related to Savings among Migratory Labourers

Aspects Related to Savings	Ludhiana		Hoshiarpur		Faridkot		Punjab	
	No.	%age	No.	%age	No.	%age	No.	%age
A. Remittance to Family:								
No	25	12.14	5	6.25	0	0.00	30	9.26
Yes	181	87.86	75	93.75	38	100.00	294	90.74
χ^2 value = 6.76**								
B. Mode of Remittance								
Bank	39	21.55	20	26.67	5	13.16	64	21.77
Money Order	136	75.14	49	65.33	33	86.84	218	74.15
Any other	6	3.31	6	8.00	0	0.00	12	4.08
χ^2 value = 8.39***								

(Contd...)

Aspects Related to Savings	Ludhiana		Hoshiarpur		Faridkot		Punjab	
	No.	%age	No.	%age	No.	%age	No.	%age
C. Lost/Delay of Money Order	51	37.50	14	28.57	13	39.39	78	35.78
D. Lost Money during Travelling	30	14.56	8	10.00	6	15.79	44	13.58
E. Relatives/Natives Stolen Money	21	10.19	3	3.75	8	21.05	32	9.88

Source : Field Survey 2006

*** : Significant at 1% level.

** : Significant at 5% level.

The table further shows that the highest proportion of the migrant agricultural labourers, *i.e.* 74.15 per cent sent the remittances to their families through money order followed by 21.77 per cent who utilised banking services and only 4.08 per cent used other methods. The maximum use of money order service may be for the reason of security and low postal charges.

Though the pattern for the mode of remittances was found to be similar in all the three districts under study, yet the proportion of the migrant agricultural labourers adopting one or the other mode showed a significant difference as the use of money order was made by as high as 86.84 per cent of the migrants in Faridkot district, 75.14 per cent in Ludhiana district and 65.33 per cent in Hoshiarpur district.

As many as 35.78 per cent of the migratory labourers reported loss/delay of money sent through money order. About 14 per cent of the migrants reported loss of money during travelling, whereas in the case of about 10 per cent the money was stolen by their relatives/natives. The complaints of money stolen by relatives/natives were more in Faridkot district (21.05 per cent) followed by Ludhiana district (10.19 per cent) and Hoshiarpur district (3.75 per cent). This shows that the money sent by the migrants to their families at their native places through different modes is never free from the risk of being lost or stolen.

PURPOSES OF REMITTANCES

The data given in Table 7.9 reveals that in most of the cases,i.e.94.56 per cent the money sent by the migrants to their families living at the native places use such remittances for their daily consumption needs. The second purpose of remittances came to be the repayment of debt taken from landlords and/or money-lenders (38.10 per cent), followed by the purchase of domestic articles (30.95 per cent) such as cots, almirah, TVs, transistors, watches, table, chairs, sewing machine, bicycle, garments, toiletries etc. The remittances were also used for house repair/construction by 19.05 per

Table 7.9: Distribution of Migrant Labourers according to the Purpose for which the Remittances are used (Multiple Responses)

Purpose for which Remittances are Used	Ludhiana 181		Hoshiarpur 75		Faridkot 38		Punjab 294	
	No.	%age	No.	%age	No.	%age	No.	%age
1. Buying Land	4	2.21	3	4.00	1	2.63	8	2.72
2. House Repair/Construction	18	9.94	21	28.00	17	44.74	56	19.05
3. Buying Domestic Articles	65	35.91	17	22.67	9	23.68	91	30.95
4. Buying Livestock	20	11.05	6	8.00	7	18.42	33	11.22
5. Business Investments	0	0.00	0	0.00	0	0.00	0	0.00
6. Marriages of Children	6	3.31	3	4.00	3	7.89	12	4.08
7. Education of Children	2	1.10	2	2.67	4	10.53	8	2.72
8. Repayment of Loan	62	34.25	34	45.33	16	42.11	112	38.10
9. Daily Consumption Needs	174	96.13	68	90.67	36	94.74	278	94.56

Source: Field Survey 2006

cent while only 4.08 per cent incurred expenditure out of remittances for the marriage of their children.

The survey further revealed that not even in a single case such remittances could be used as business investment. The use of remittances for the purchase of land and livestock was to the tune of 2.72 and 11.22 per cent respectively. Education could secure the least priority as only 2.72 per cent of them spent a meagre amount of remittances on education of their children. Thus the remittances were mainly used for unproductive purposes such as daily consumption needs, house construction, marriage of the children, and repayment of loans.

PREFERENCE FOR TECHNIQUES OF FARMING

Table 7.10 brings out that as high as 77.47 per cent of the migrant agricultural labourers preferred to work with modern farming techniques as against a significantly lower proportion, i.e. 60.22 per cent of the local agricultural labourers. The modern techniques include the handling and operating the farm machinery and implements such as tractor, seed-drill, thresher etc. As many as 17.59 per cent of the migrant agricultural labourers and 32.34 per cent of the local agricultural labourers preferred to work with both, modern as well as traditional techniques depending upon the nature of agronomic operations, such as land preparation with tractor and transplanting of paddy manually. The migrant agricultural labourers reported that they were unable to use the advanced skills and knowledge at their native villages due to financial constraints, unmatching irrigation facilities, poor marketing infrastructure and overall backwardness of the agriculture sector.

The above discussion leads us to conclude that the socio-cultural matrix among the migratory labourers underwent significant changes over a period of time. They have adopted the convenient names, local food habits by replacing rice with wheat and maize, Punjabi language, getting medical facilities from government dispensaries, etc.

Table 7.10: Distribution of Labourers according to their Preference to Work with Different Techniques

Techniques	Ludhiana		Hoshiarpur		Faridkot		Punjab	
	No.	%age	No.	%age	No.	%age	No.	%age
(A) The Migratory Labourers								
Modern	155	75.24	66	82.50	30	78.95	251	77.47
Traditional	12	5.83	3	3.75	1	2.63	16	4.94
Both	39	18.93	11	13.75	7	18.42	57	17.59
χ^2 value (between regions) = 2.27ns								
(B) The Local Labourers								
Modern	86	68.25	42	53.16	34	53.13	162	60.22
Traditional	8	6.35	3	3.80	9	14.06	20	7.43
Both	32	25.40	34	43.04	21	32.81	87	32.34
χ^2 value (between regions) = 12.60***								
z-value (Migrants vs. Locals)								
Modern	1.39ns		3.96***		2.61***		4.55***	
Traditional	0.20ns		0.02ns		1.88*		1.27ns	
Both	1.39ns		4.10***		1.58ns		4.17***	

Source : Field Survey 2006.

*** : Significant at 1% level; * Significant at 10% level; ns: Non-significant

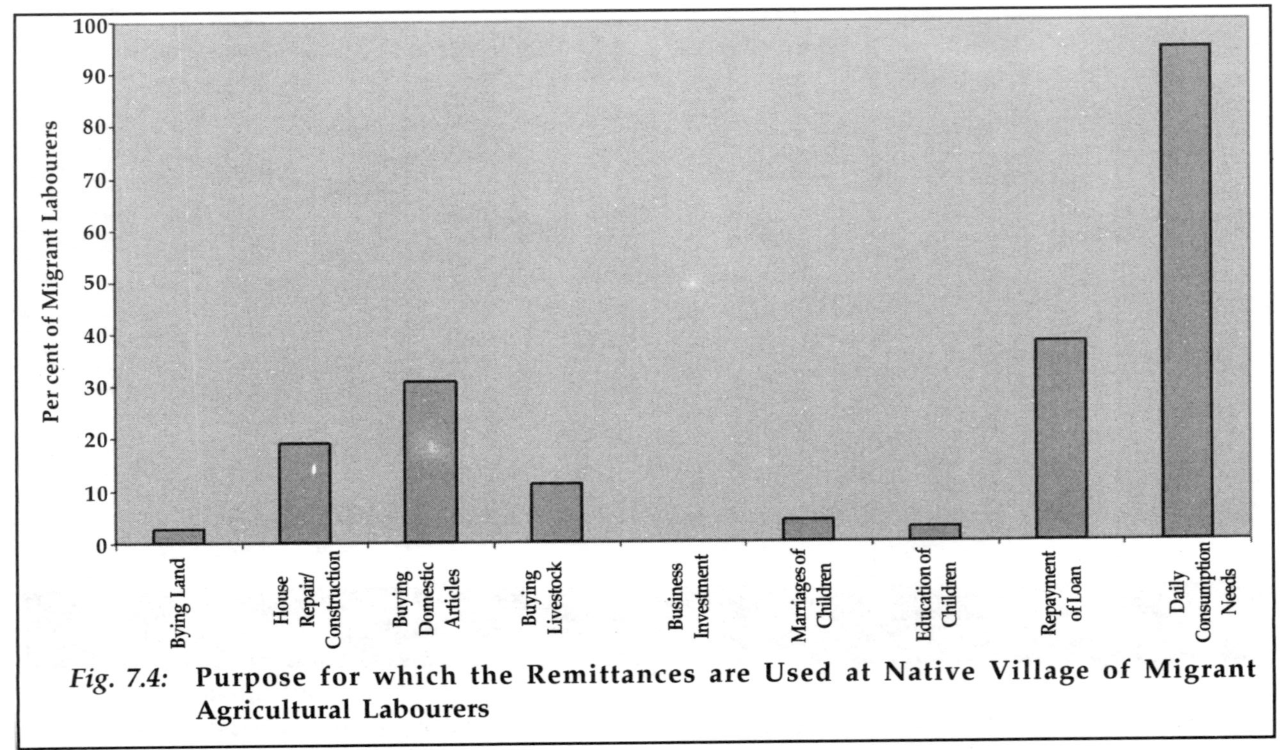

Fig. 7.4: **Purpose for which the Remittances are Used at Native Village of Migrant Agricultural Labourers**

To sum up, economic distress is the major factor which motivated the migrant agricultural labourers from the poor states to work as farm labour in Punjab. Generally the migratory farm labourers have a rural background, so while working in the agricultural fields of Punjab, they do not feel any major change in the nature of their work.

Migration prepares a migrant to face any kind of adversity and gives the hope of a better living.

Better transportation and communication means serve to underscore the linkage between migration and development as well as improvement of the economic and social conditions of the migrant agricultural labourers and their families both at the place of origin and destination.

The analysis shows that migration has brought a change in the socio-cultural aspect of the migratory agricultural labourers. Majority of the migrants have lost their actual identity and are called by the convenient names by the locals. As regards the consumption pattern, a large section of the migrant agricultural labourers accepted that they not only find the changes in their consumption pattern as good but they are also in a position to take full meal up to their desire in Punjab. The interaction with the locals has enabled them to learn the Punjabi language. It is astonishing to note that majority of the migrant agricultural labourers prefer to listen Punjabi songs and drum beats. A few of them also know the art of singing Punjabi songs, but with their native accent.

Although the poor migrants have contributed significantly in the farm sector of Punjab, and also gained from relatively higher wages, yet they remain economically excluded from the wider benefits of economic well-being such as access to health facilities, education, housing and sanitation. Some of the migrants who have their families with them in Punjab face the problem of schooling for their children. Their children have to spend the whole day along with their parents in the dusty fields.

Poor living conditions such as unhygienic bathing and washing patterns, lack of proper sleeping facilities, lack of pure drinking water facility, and poor and deplorable drainage system expose the migrants to various kinds of diseases. All these factors give rise to morbidity not only among the migrant agricultural labourers but also the local people as both categories of agricultural labourers work together throughout the day, and also share the intoxicants with one another.

The socio-cultural changes in the migrant agricultural labourers also reveal an important fact that all the migrants save for the future although to varying extents. Most of them prefer to keep their savings with the farmers. A large proportion of the migrant agricultural labourers also remit the money to their families staying in their native villages. It shows that migration is not a *zero-sum* game. It benefits the receiving area, the area of origin, the migrant agricultural labourers and their families. As regards the mode of remitting money, about three-fourths of the migrants prefer to send money through money order. This remitted money is mainly used for the daily consumption needs, repayment of debt, purchase of domestic articles, marriage of children etc. However, a very small amount of the money is spent on the education of the children.

Last but not the least, another significant change is the adoption of advanced technical know-how and knowledge by the migrant agricultural labourers. They try to apply these modern agricultural techniques in their native villages so as to transform the traditional agriculture of those areas.

Assimilation of the Migrants, Farmers and Local Agricultural Labourers

Assimilation is a continuous process in a society, and it is directly related to the level of development. In the era of subsistence economy under feudalism, assimilation of different classes, strata of society could hardly be materialised because subsistence economy does not offer objective conditions to interact. Production and consumption were the two aspects of economy under feudalism. When another, the most important factor of development, *i.e.* marketing adds up to production and consumption, the interaction of masses increases significantly and qualitatively. The pace of development of various sectors leads towards interaction, not confined to state boundaries but across the states of the country. The commercialisation of agriculture in India has made the process of interaction among various sections of people in agriculture such as farmers, migrant agricultural labourers and local agricultural labourers highly rapid. The commercialisation of agriculture resulted in increasing the employment opportunities at a much faster rate than that during the era of subsistence. The logic of development establishes two facts, *i.e.* capital flows from low rate of profit areas to high rate of profit areas; and labour goes from low wage rate areas to high wage rate areas. These trends have been confirmed by the history as Punjabis go to Europe, West etc. to seek higher wages and the residents of Bihar, Uttar Pradesh and other states and even the neighbouring poor countries prefer to come to Punjab for higher wages. This process of national as well as international interaction leads towards higher and higher levels of assimilation among various strata of masses in the society.

Since the advent of green revolution and advancement in technology in Punjab agriculture, the labourers from backward states of India have migrated to Punjab in search of higher earnings, where they have interactions with the locals. This interaction leads to different kinds of assimilation among them and the extent of participation also varies which have been taken up for study in the present chapter.

PARTICIPATION IN SOCIAL GATHERINGS

The data given in Table 8.1 shows that majority of the migrant agricultural labourers, *i.e.* 55.25 per cent never participate in social gatherings arranged by the local agricultural labourers. These social gatherings include bhog ceremonies, marriage functions etc. There were 2.47 per cent of them who used to participate regularly in the social gatherings, while about 34 per cent participated in the social gatherings occasionally. The overall score of participation in social gatherings came to be 0.58 out of maximum score of 3 which was only 19.33 per cent. This shows that the extent of participation of the migratory labourers in the social gatherings organised by the locals was extremely low.

There were significant regional variations in the extent of participation of the migratory agricultural labourers in social gatherings. Though, the extent of participation was very low in all the districts under study, yet it was relatively higher in Faridkot district (24.67 per cent) as compared to Hoshiarpur (18.67 per cent) and Ludhiana districts (17.00 per cent).

Table 8.1: Extent of Participation in Social Gatherings by Migrant Agricultural Labourers

District	Extent of Participation				Average Extent	% Extent
	Never (0)	Occasionally (1)	Sometimes (2)	Regularly (3)		
Ludhiana	118 (57.28)	66 (32.04)	17 (8.25)	5 (2.43)	0.51	17.00
Hoshiarpur	45 (56.25)	28 (35.00)	4 (5.00)	3 (3.75)	0.56	18.67
Faridkot	16 (42.11)	16 (42.11)	6 (15.78)	0 (0.00)	0.74	24.67
Punjab	179 (55.25)	110 (33.95)	27 (8.33)	8 (2.47)	0.58	19.33
				F-ratio p-value	4.51 <0.05	

Source : Field Survey 2006

Note : The figures given in parentheses represent percentages.

PARTICIPATION IN FESTIVALS/FAIRS

Festivals include mainly *diwali, dussehra, lohri, baisakhi, gurpurbs*, etc. and fairs include sports, religious and cultural fairs, etc. Table 8.2(a) highlights the extent of participation of the migrant agricultural labourers in these local festivals and fairs. Majority of the migrant agricultural labourers, *i.e.* 52.77 per cent never participated in local festivals/fairs while only 5.56 per cent of them participated regularly. As many as 29.63 per cent participated in local festivals/fairs occasionally. The overall score of extent of participation came to be 23.33 per cent.

Table 8.2 (a): Extent of Participation in Local Festivals/Fairs by Migrant Agricultural Labourers

District	Extent of Participation				Average Extent	% Extent
	Never (0)	Occasionally (1)	Sometimes (2)	Regularly (3)		
Ludhiana	110 (53.40)	58 (28.15)	23 (11.17)	15 (7.28)	0.72	24.00
Hoshiarpur	48 (60.00)	23 (28.75)	6 (7.50)	3 (3.75)	0.55	18.33
Faridkot	13 (34.21)	15 (39.47)	10 (26.32)	0 (0.00)	0.92	30.67
Punjab	171 (52.77)	96 (29.63)	39 (12.04)	18 (5.56)	0.70	23.33
				F-ratio p-value	7.91 <0.01	

Source : Field Survey 2006

Note : The figures given in parentheses represent percentages.

District-wise analysis highlights significant variations in the extent of participation of the migrant agricultural labourers in local festivals and fairs. It was relatively the highest, *i.e.* 30.67 per cent in Faridkot district, followed by 24.00 per cent in Ludhiana district and 18.33 per cent in Hoshiarpur district. This shows that the locals in Faridkot district are more open-hearted towards the migrant agricultural labourers as compared to the other districts under study.

On the whole, it can be said that the extent of participation of the migrant agricultural labourers in local social gatherings, festivals and fairs is extremely low which indicates that assimilation between migrant agricultural labourers and locals stands at a low ebb.

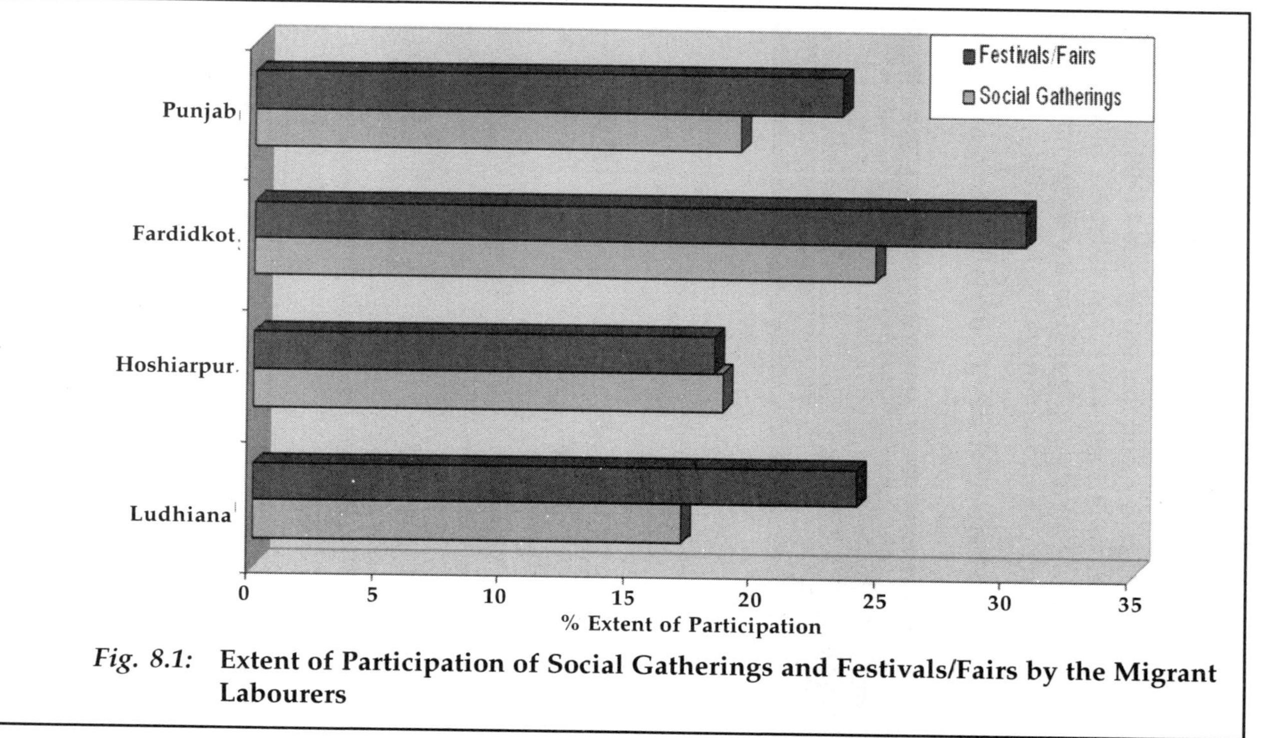

Fig. 8.1: **Extent of Participation of Social Gatherings and Festivals/Fairs by the Migrant Labourers**

The data given in Table 8.2 (b) shows that only 3 out of 269, *i.e.* 1.12 per cent of the local agricultural labourers participated in the social functions arranged by the migrant agricultural labourers, and that too only in Ludhiana district. In Hoshiarpur and Faridkot districts, none of the local agricultural labourers participated in the social functions of the migrant agricultural labourers.

Table 8.2 (b): Participation of Locals in Migrants' Social Functions

District	Participation		Feeling During Participation		Liking Migrants' Culture	
	Yes	No	Comfortable	Ignored	Yes	No
Ludhiana	3 (2.38)	123 (97.62)	3 (100.00)	0 (0.00)	2 (1.59)	124 (98.41)
Hoshiarpur	0 (0.00)	79 (100.00)	—	—	0 (0.00)	79 (100.0)
Faridkot	0 (0.00)	64 (100.00)	—	—	0 (0.00)	64 (100.0)
Punjab	3 (1.12)	266 (98.88)	3 (100.00)	0 (0.00)	2 (0.74)	267 (99.26)

Source : Field Survey 2006

Note : The figures given in parentheses represent percentages.

Of the three local agricultural labourers who felt comfortable during the functions, only 2 of the 269, *i.e.* 0.74 per cent liked migrants' culture. This may be the main reason of negligible participation of the local agricultural labourers in migrants' social gatherings along with the non-invitation to the locals by the migrant agricultural labourers. This shows that the social assimilation between the migrants and local labourers is prevailing at a very low level.

PERCEPTION OF THE FARMERS ABOUT THE MIGRANT AGRICULTURAL LABOURERS

The interaction of farmers with the migrant agricultural labourers on different aspects is shown in Table 8.3. It is evident from the table that a vast majority of the farmers *i.e.* 81.25 per cent had employed the migrant agricultural labourers on their farms in Punjab. This proportion ranged between 73.33 per cent in Hoshiarpur district to 92.86 per cent in Faridkot district. Relatively low incidence of employing migrant agricultural labourers in Hoshiarpur district may be the less labour requiring agronomic operations in maize crop, for which family labour is sufficient.

In response to the question whether the farmers faced any problem while communicating with the migrant agricultural labourers, only 1.92 per cent of them reported that they really faced such a problem. This problem might have arisen in those cases where the migrant agricultural labourers were either new to the place of their migration or in certain cases they could not understand the language spoken by the farmers and vice-versa.

The table further revealed that only 19.23 per cent of the farmers invited the migrant agricultural labourers on social gatherings organised by them. It was the lowest to the tune of 15.91 per cent in Hoshiarpur district and the highest of the order of 23.08 per cent in Faridkot district. This low incidence of inviting the migrant agricultural labourers in social gatherings was despite the fact that almost 100 per cent of farmers provided accommodation to them, either a servant room in the dwelling house or a tube-well room at the farm.

As many as 23.08 per cent of the farmers used to offer liquor to the migrant agricultural labourers working on their farms. This offer was the highest in Faridkot district (30.77 per cent), followed by Ludhiana district (23.26 per cent) while it was found to be the lowest in Hoshiarpur district (18.18 per cent). Relatively high incidence of offering liquor to the

Table 8.3: Extent of Interaction of Farmers with Migrants in Different Aspects

District	No. of Farmers Employing Migrants	Problems in Conversation	Invitation in Social Gatherings	Providing Accommodation	Offering Liquor	Force to Cast Illegal Votes	Keeping Savings with Farmers
Ludhiana	86 (82.69)	2 (2.33)	17 (19.77)	85 (98.84)	20 (23.26)	4 (4.65)	74 (86.05)
Hoshiarpur	44 (73.33)	0 (0.00)	7 (15.91)	44 (100.00)	8 (18.18)	1 (2.27)	40 (90.91)
Faridkot	26 (92.86)	1 (3.85)	6 (23.08)	26 (100.00)	8 (30.77)	2 (7.69)	25 (96.15)
Punjab	156 (81.25)	3 (1.92)	30 (19.23)	155 (99.36)	36 (23.08)	7 (4.49)	139 (89.10)

Source : Field Survey 2006

Note : The figures given in parentheses represent percentages.

migrant agricultural labourers in Faridkot district may be due to the open-mindedness of the farmers and preparation of *desi* country made liquor in the district.

It was reported only by 4.49 per cent of the farmers who forced the migrant agricultural labourers to cast illegal or bogus votes in various elections. Further, 89.10 per cent of the farmers reported that the migrant agricultural labourers used to keep their savings with them which they (migrants) take as and when required.

The foregoing analysis clearly brings out the fact that there is very low incidence of cultural assimilation in terms of conversation, attending/inviting at social gatherings, festivals, fairs, sharing liquor etc. but there is quite high incidence of social assimilation in terms of providing employment, providing accommodation, keeping savings with the farmers etc. Thus, the economic needs have helped to bring social assimilation but not the cultural assimilation.

DRUG ADDICTION AND SHARING

A glance at Table 8.4 (a) provides that as high as 76.54 per cent of the migrant agricultural labourers were drug addicts in the state as a whole, out of which about 70 per cent were already in the habit of addiction at their native villages while the remaining 30 per cent got addicted to drugs at the present place. As high as 77.02 per cent of the addicted migrant agricultural labourers used to share drugs with the local agricultural labourers. However, this assimilation had got negative implications.

Though drug addiction was relatively higher in Hoshiarpur district (86.25 per cent) as compared to other districts, yet the sharing pattern of drugs with the locals was found to be statistically similar in all the districts under study. This kind of assimilation needs to be discouraged in order to have a healthy society.

The data shown in Table 8.4 (b) indicates that only about 19 per cent of the local agricultural labourers were not in the habit of using intoxicants in the state while 33.09 per cent of them were addicted to tobacco and as high as 72.49 per cent were found to be addicted to *zarda*, another form of tobacco. Out of 81 per cent of the local labourers, who were addicted either to tobacco or *zarda* or both, 82.65 per cent reported that they used to take these intoxicants in the company of the migrant agricultural labourers while the remaining only 17.35 per cent of them used these intoxicants on their own

Table 8.4 (a): Drug Addiction among Migrant Agricultural Labourers and its Sharing with Local Agricultural Labourers

District	Drug Addiction	Addiction Started From		Sharing Drugs with Local Labour
		Native Village	Present Place	
Ludhiana	147 (71.36)	104 (70.75)	43 (29.25)	118 (80.27)
Hoshiarpur	69 (86.25)	45 (65.22)	24 (34.78)	47 (68.12)
Faridkot	32 (84.21)	24 (75.00)	8 (25.00)	26 (81.25)
Punjab	248 (76.54)	173 (69.76)	75 (30.24)	191 (77.02)
χ^2 value p-value	8.53 <0.05	1.16 >0.10ns		4.29 >0.10ns

Source : Field Survey 2006

Note : The figures given in parentheses represent percentages.

Table 8.4 (b):Pattern of Taking Intoxicants among Local Labourers (Multiple Responses)

District	Intoxicants Used			Intoxicants in the Company of		z-value	p-value
	No	Tobacco	Zarda	Migrants	Own		
Ludhiana	27 (21.43)	41 (32.54)	86 (68.25)	77 (77.78)	22 (22.22)	7.82	<0.01
Hoshiarpur	15 (18.99)	29 (36.71)	58 (73.42)	52 (81.25)	12 (18.75)	7.07	<0.01
Faridkot	8 (12.50)	19 (29.69)	51 (79.69)	52 (92.86)	4 (7.41)	9.07	<0.01
Punjab	50 (18.59)	89 (33.09)	195 (72.49)	181 (82.65)	38 (17.35)	13.67	<0.01

Source: Field Survey 2006

Note : The figures given in parentheses represent percentages.

The district-wise analysis shows that a significant majority of the local agricultural labourers in all the districts as well as in the state used to consume tobacco and *zarda* in the company of the migrant agricultural labourers while working together.

It can be said that assimilation between the migrant agricultural labourers and the locals emerged in the form of sharing drugs and intoxicants which is not a healthy trend for the rural society. However, the reasons behind such a high incidence of taking drugs and intoxicants ought to be explored for further investigations.

RELATIONS BETWEEN THE MIGRANT AND LOCAL AGRICULTURAL LABOURERS

The relations between the migrant and local agricultural labourers were also studied as response to their attributes to the quality of relations in terms of 'good', 'bad', 'can't say'. Then the average quality of relations was worked out by giving weightage to the attributes such as '1' for 'good', '-1' for 'bad' and '0' for 'can't say'. The results are presented in Tables 8.5 (a), 8.5 (b) and 8.5 (c).

Table 8.5 (a) shows that majority of the migrant agricultural labourers, *i.e.* 76.23 per cent had 'good' relations with the locals, while only 5.56 per cent of them were having 'bad' relations with the locals. However, 18.21 per cent of the migrant agricultural labourers failed to say anything in this regard. They were of the view that their relations with the locals were neither good nor bad; rather these were quite normal.

There was not much district to district variation as the average level of relations of the migrant agricultural labourers with the locals came to be 0.84 in Faridkot, 0.72 in Ludhiana, and 0.61 in Hoshiarpur districts.

The relations with migrant agricultural labourers as viewed by the locals were at the lower level than that viewed by the migrant agricultural labourers with the locals. In this case 54.65 per cent of the local agricultural labourers had 'good' relations with the migrants, while 11.90 per cent of them were having 'bad' relations, and the remaining 33.45 per cent failed to say anything in this regard.

The mean score of relations of the locals with the migrant agricultural labourers came to be 0.43 which was significantly lower than 0.71 in the case of migrant agricultural labourers with the locals. The district-wise analysis also showed a similar trend but the mean score of relations of the locals with the migrant agricultural labourers in each district was significantly lower than the score of relations of the migrant agricultural labourers with the locals.

Table 8.5 (a): Relations between Migrants and Local Agricultural Labourers

District	Migrants with Locals			Average Level
	Good (1)	Bad (-1)	Can't Say (0)	
Ludhiana	158 (76.70)	10 (4.85)	38 (18.45)	0.72
Hoshiarpur	56 (70.00)	7 (8.75)	17 (21.25)	0.61
Faridkot	33 (86.84)	1 (2.63)	4 (10.53)	0.84
Punjab	247 (76.23)	18 (5.56)	59 (18.21)	0.71
Locals with Migrants				
Ludhiana	75 (59.52)	15 (11.91)	36 (28.57)	0.48
Hoshiarpur	39 (49.37)	11 (13.92)	29 (36.71)	0.35
Faridkot	33 (51.56)	6 (9.38)	25 (39.06)	0.42
Punjab	147 (54.65)	32 (11.90)	90 (33.45)	0.43
Migrants *Vs.* Locals				
	Ludhiana	**Hoshiarpur**	**Faridkot**	**Punjab**
t-value	3.96	3.74	4.21	4.01
p-value	<0.01	<0.01	<0.01	<0.01

Source : Field Survey 2006

Note : The figures given in parentheses represent percentages.

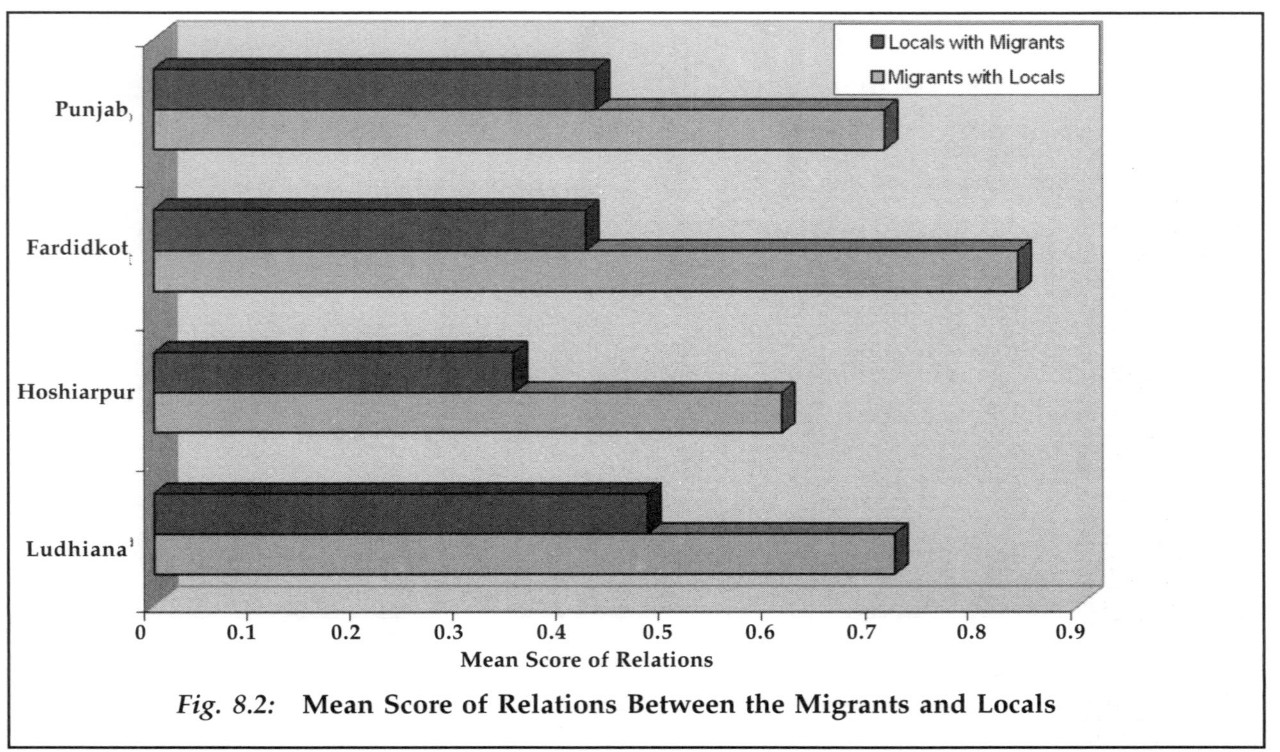

Fig. 8.2: **Mean Score of Relations Between the Migrants and Locals**

The survey brings out that keeping good relations with the locals may be an objective need of the migrants due to the reason of social security. But the locals bother less than the migrant agricultural labourers to have good relations with them because they have many other relations in Punjab and a prepossessed complex of being the natives of the land.

The data given in Table 8.5 (b) shows that as many as 53.90 per cent of the local agricultural labourers felt good to work with the migrant agricultural labourers, while 11.90 per cent of them had a bad feeling and the remaining 34.20 per cent failed to say anything in this regard.

Table 8.5 (b): Chance and Feeling of Local Agricultural Labourers to work with Migratory Agricultural Labourers

District	Feeling to work with Migrants			Average Extent of Feeling
	Good (1)	Bad (-1)	Can't Say (0)	
Ludhiana	72 (57.14)	10 (7.94)	44 (34.92)	0.49
Hoshiarpur	39 (49.37)	15 (18.98)	25 (31.65)	0.30
Faridkot	34 (53.13)	7 (10.94)	23 (35.93)	0.42
Punjab	145 (53.90)	32 (11.90)	92 (34.20)	0.42
			F-ratio p-value	6.78 <0.01

Source : Field Survey 2006

Note : The figures given in parentheses represent percentages.

Table 8.5 (c): Reasons for Feeling Good or Bad to Work with Migrants (Multiple Responses)

District	Reasons for Feeling Good				Reasons for Feeling Bad			
	Docile	Obedient	Less Quarrelsome	Helpful	Competition	Drugs	Personality	Revengeful
Ludhiana	34 (47.22)	41 (56.94)	36 (50.00)	43 (59.72)	6 (60.00)	3 (30.00)	4 (40.00)	6 (60.00)
Hoshiarpur	18 (46.15)	21 (53.85)	11 (28.20)	15 (38.46)	9 (60.00)	7 (46.67)	7 (46.67)	8 (53.33)
Faridkot	19 (55.88)	23 (67.65)	16 (47.06)	20 (58.82)	4 (57.14)	2 (28.57)	3 (42.86)	4 (57.14)
Punjab	71 (48.97)	85 (58.62)	63 (43.45)	78 (53.79)	19 (59.38)	12 (37.50)	14 (43.75)	18 (56.25)

Source : Field Survey 2006

Note : The figures given in parentheses represent percentages.

The mean extent of this feeling came to be 0.42 in Punjab, *i.e.* less than half of the local labourers feel good to work with the migrant agricultural labourers. The feeling to work was significantly low, *i.e.* only 0.30 in Hoshiarpur district because relatively a higher number of local agricultural labourers felt bad while working with the migrant agricultural labourers than those in other districts. This may be due to the prevailing less employment opportunities in farm sector in Hoshiarpur district which leads to jealousy against the migrant agricultural labourers.

The reasons for feeling good or bad to work with the migrant agricultural labourers are shown in Table 8.5 (c). Table 8.5(b) brings out that as many as 145 (53.90 per cent) local agricultural labourers in Punjab felt good to work with the migrant agricultural labourers. Out of these 145 labourers the highest proportion, *i.e.* 58.62 per cent felt good to work with the migrant agricultural labourers for their obedient nature, followed by 53.79 per cent who considered them as helping, 48.97 per cent reported them as docile and 43.45 per cent of the local agricultural labourers were having a good feeling to work with the migrant agricultural labourers due to their less quarrelsome nature. The incidence of terming the migrant agricultural labourers as less quarrelsome and helping was considerably low in Hoshiarpur district.

There were only 32 local agricultural labourers who felt bad while working with the migrant agricultural labourers due to various reasons. The highest proportion, *i.e.* 59.38 per cent of these 32 labourers, felt bad to work with the migrant agricultural labourers as they considered them as their competitors in the field of employment. The acceptance of low wages by the migrant agricultural labourers badly affected the employment opportunities of the local agricultural labourers. The reason of bad feeling was followed by other reasons, *viz.* the revengeful nature (56.25 per cent), personality (43.75 per cent), and drug addiction among the migrant agricultural labourers (37.50 per cent). The district-wise analysis also showed a similar pattern for the reasons mentioned above.

PREFERENCE OF FARMERS FOR MIGRANT AGRICULTURAL LABOURERS

Table 8.6 reveals that the most common reason for preferring the migrant agricultural labourers appeared to be low wages as reported by 83.85 per cent of the farmers followed by the migrants' readiness for extra work (69.27 per cent), their easy availability (57.29 per cent), less problematic (44.79 per cent) and submissive nature (41.67 per cent). Only 7.29 per cent and 4.69 per cent of the farmers reported that they preferred the migrant agricultural labourers to the local agricultural labourers as the migrants were more reliable and dependable respectively than the local agricultural labourers. This shows that farmers preferred the migrant agricultural labourers mainly due to the economic reasons, *i.e.* low wages and extra work. The interaction of these factors always leads to the higher net returns for the farmers in Punjab. The district-wise analysis, by and large, depicted a similar pattern as observed in the state as a whole. However, the proportion of those farmers who preferred the migrant agricultural labourers due to low wages was significantly lower in Hoshiarpur district (73.33 per cent) as compared to Faridkot district (96.43 per cent) and Ludhiana district (86.54 per cent). Another reason *viz.* readiness for extra work by the migrant agricultural labourers also showed a similar pattern. In Hoshiarpur district, the relative level of farm employment is low due to less labour involving operations in maize crop as compared to labour intensive specific operations in paddy and cotton crops.

CATEGORY OF LABOUR EMPLOYED AND PREFERENCE OF FARMERS FOR THE STATE OF MIGRANT LABOUR

Table 8.7 presents both the categories of labour employed by the farmers and their preference for the state to which the migrants belong. Majority of the farmers, *i.e.* 81.25 per cent

Table 8.6: Reasons for Preferring Migratory Agricultural Labour by Farmers in Punjab

District	Easy Availability	Less Problematic	More Reliable	Dependable	Submissive	Low Wages	Extra Work
Ludhiana	60 (57.69)	46 (44.23)	7 (6.73)	4 (3.85)	43 (41.35)	90 (86.54)	73 (70.19)
Hoshiarpur	33 (55.00)	29 (48.33)	5 (8.33)	3 (5.00)	25 (41.67)	44 (73.33)	37 (61.67)
Faridkot	17 (60.71)	11 (39.29)	2 (7.14)	2 (7.14)	12 (42.86)	27 (96.43)	23 (82.14)
Punjab	110 (57.29)	86 (44.79)	14 (7.29)	9 (4.69)	80 (41.67)	161 (83.85)	133 (69.27)

Source : Field Survey 2006

Note : The figures given in parentheses represent percentages.

employed the migratory agricultural labour on their farms. However, the relative proportion of the farmers who preferred the migrant agricultural labourers was the highest in Faridkot district (92.86 per cent) followed by Ludhiana (82.69 per cent) and Hoshiarpur districts (73.33 per cent).

As high as 82.69 per cent of the farmers in Punjab preferred to employ labour from Bihar on their farms, followed by 12.82 per cent from U.P. and 4.49 per cent from Nepal. In Faridkot district all the farmers preferred to employ the migrant agricultural labourers from Bihar, whereas 81.40 per cent of the farmers in Ludhiana district preferred migrant agricultural labourers from Bihar followed by 16.27 per cent from Uttar Pradesh and only 2.33 per cent from Nepal. In case of Hoshiarpur district, 75 per cent of the farmers preferred labour from Bihar, 13.64 per cent from Uttar Pradesh, and the remaining 11.36 per cent from Nepal.

FARMERS' OPINION ABOUT THE CRIMINAL ACTIVITIES OF THE MIGRANT AGRICULTURAL LABOURERS

The data contained in Table 8.8 carries the opinion of the farmers about the criminal activities of the migrant agricultural labourers. As many as 75 per cent of the farmers reported that the migrant agricultural labourers are not prone to criminal activities; 23.96 per cent of the farmers were of the view that the migrant agricultural labourers are falsely implicated in criminal cases, whereas 65.63 per cent of the farmers didn't give any clear response to this question. About 57 per cent of the farmers came to the rescue of the migrant agricultural labourers when they were falsely implicated in criminal cases.

District-wise analysis about the criminal activities of the migrant agricultural labourers shows almost a similar pattern as observed in the case of Punjab as a whole. But as high as 35.71 per cent of the farmers of Faridkot district reported that the migrant agricultural labourers are falsely implicated, whereas 57.15 per cent failed to give their opinion in this

Table 8.7: Category of Labour Employed and Preference of Farmers for the State of Migrant Agricultural Labour

District	Category of Employment		Preference for State of Migrant Agricultural Labour			
	Local	Migrant	Bihar	U.P.	M.P.	Nepal
Ludhiana	20 (19.23)	86 (82.69)	70 (81.40)	14 (16.27)	0 (0.00)	2 (2.33)
Hoshiarpur	20 (33.33)	44 (73.33)	33 (75.00)	6 (13.64)	0 (0.00)	5 (11.36)
Faridkot	8 (28.57)	26 (92.86)	26 (100.00)	0 (0.00)	0 (0.00)	0 (0.00)
Punjab	48 (25.00)	156 (81.25)	129 (82.69)	20 (12.82)	0 (0.00)	7 (4.49)

Source : Field Survey 2006

Note : The figures given in parentheses represent percentages.

Table 8.8: Distribution of Farmers according to their Opinion about Criminal Activities of Migrant Agricultural Labourers

District	Migrants Prone to Criminal Activities		Migrants Suffer Due to False Allegations			When Falsely Implicated, Do You Help Them	
	Yes	No	Yes	No	Can't Say	Yes	No
Ludhiana	28 (26.92)	76 (73.08)	21 (20.19)	10 (9.62)	73 (70.19)	13 (61.90)	8 (38.10)
Hoshiarpur	13 (21.67)	47 (78.33)	15 (25.00)	8 (13.33)	37 (61.67)	9 (60.00)	6 (40.00)
Faridkot	7 (25.00)	21 (75.00)	10 (35.71)	2 (7.14)	16 (57.15)	4 (40.00)	6 (60.00)
Punjab	48 (25.00)	144 (75.00)	46 (23.96)	20 (10.42)	126 (65.62)	26 (56.52)	20 (43.48)

Source : Field Survey 2006

Note : The figures given in parentheses represent percentages.

regard. However, in Ludhiana district, as low as 20.19 per cent of the respondent farmers opined that migrant agricultural labourers are falsely implicated, whereas 70.19 per cent failed to give their opinion in this regard.. But in Ludhiana district, 61.90 per cent of the farmers came forward to help the migrant agricultural labourers who were falsely implicated, whereas this proportion of the farmers in Hoshiarpur and Faridkot districts is 60 per cent and 40 per cent respectively.

In this era of globalisation and commercialisation, the pace of development of various sectors of the economy is not only confined to the state boundaries but across different states of the country. The commercialisation of agriculture has accelerated the process of interaction among the various sections of the people such as the farmers, migrant agricultural labourers and local agricultural labourers. Their interaction has formed an assimilation among them in a variety of manners.

The migratory agricultural labourers working in the Punjab agriculture are not only from the different states, religions, castes and communities, but also from the neighbouring country like Nepal. They are unable to constitute a homogenous entity of their own because the migrant agricultural labourers with varied social base are forced to interact with the local agricultural labourers and employers (farmers) in the rural society of Punjab. After migrating to Punjab, the migrant agricultural labourers find themselves in a wonderful position as they earn more in comparison to their counterparts in their native villages, so they have compromised over their relations with the employers (farmers) and the local agricultural labourers. Only a small segment of the migrant agricultural labourers take part in social gatherings, festivals and local fairs of that area. The difference in the culture and religion of both the migratory agricultural labour and the Punjabis has restricted their social and cultural assimilation to a large extent.

Work culture assimilation of the migrant agricultural labourers with the local agricultural labourers is highly significant as majority of the farmers prefer to engage the migrant labourers on their fields. Although there is no proper yardstick to measure the degree of efficiency of the migrant and local agricultural labourers, yet the migrants are considered to be more efficient in terms of their regularity and longer work duration Above all, they are honest, obedient, docile, reliable and helpful in domestic work. But the incidence of inviting the migrant agricultural labourers to social gatherings organised by the farmers is very low. Despite this, the migrant agricultural labourers have full confidence in their employers as they prefer to keep their savings with them. The economic need of the farmers has played a significant role in establishing social assimilation but not cultural assimilation. The adverse effect of work culture assimilation is that the Punjabi farmer once known for his hard working nature is now losing his dignity because of the availability of cheap migratory labour.

Both the migrant and local agricultural labourers belong to the poor strata of the society. They have to work together at the farms of their employers for the sake of earning wages. Since the migrant agricultural labourers are alien to the land, so they prefer to keep their relations with the local agricultural labourers cordial, whereas the local agricultural labourers do not bother to have such relations. The local agricultural labourers have a grudge against the migrant agricultural labourers as they consider the migrants responsible for the deterioration in their terms and conditions of work and wages. In spite of all this, there has never been a conflict between these two categories of labourers.

Another adverse effect of assimilation is that frequent mobility of the migrant agricultural labourers to and from their native states can cause many infectious diseases. The study also reveals that the addiction of drugs and intoxicants among both the locals and migrants has not been good for the rural society.

Summary, Conclusions and Policy Implications

This study has been organised into nine chapters. The first chapter provides an introduction to the concepts of labour migration and other associated issues. It is well argued that the problem of labour migration cannot be studied in isolation and therefore, the problem requires an integrated approach. Hence, the discourses on the laws of migration, nature of migration, pattern of migration and factors causing and affecting migration find place in this chapter. Also, the main objectives of the study, the explanation of the basic concepts about labour migration and chapter scheme in brief have been outlined in this chapter.

The second chapter is devoted to the analysis of review of the related literature. As labour migration is not confined to any specific region, so quite naturally, the chapter is divided into three sections: review of literature relating to international studies, national studies and state level studies. In all the three sections, the theoretical as well as empirical views of economists and other social scientists have been presented and examined in the light of the analysis of these studies. The essence of the present study and domain of its significance has also been presented in this chapter.

The issues relating to study area, data size and methodology have been discussed in the third chapter. An attempt has been made to explain the selection of the study area and the statistical techniques employed to analyse the collected data for fulfilling the requirements of the study.

In the following chapter, the assessment of the socio-economic background of the migratory agricultural labourers is presented. In this connection the basic discussion is on native state, caste, age, marital status, number of children, nature of employment, education level and possession of other basic facilities along with the debt position of the migrants. Thereafter a comparative study of the socio-economic background of the migrant and the local agricultural labourers has been outlined in this chapter.

The fifth chapter deals with the determinants, trends and factors associated with migration. Apart from push and pull factors, the social network also finds place for discussion in this chapter.

The wage structure of the migrant and the local agricultural labourers in the agricultural sector have been discussed in the sixth chapter. Along with it, the behaviour of the farmers regarding payment of wages, impact of the supply of the migratory agricultural labourers on the wage rate and level of employment of the local agricultural labourers is supplemented in this chapter.

Socio-cultural changes in the migrant agricultural labourers have been discussed in chapter seventh of the study. An endeavour has been made to unravel their social identity, food pattern, living conditions, health facilities and factors causing morbidity among the migrant agricultural labourers. Apart from the savings pattern, various aspects relating to savings and the purpose of remittances have been dealt herewith.

The study also presents the assimilation of the migrant agricultural labourers, farmers and the local agricultural labourers in the eighth chapter. It deals with the perception of the farmers about the migrant agricultural labourers, relations between the migrant and the local agricultural labourers and the causes of preference of farmers for migrant agricultural labourers.

The last chapter presents the main issues examined in the study and highlights the general conclusions emerging from the analysis of the collected data.

Migration of human beings is a complex phenomenon. Ever since the dawn of human civilization, the growing uneven and imbalanced pattern of economic, social, political and cultural development of various parts and regions of the earth has initiated the process of migration of people from one place to another. In the present era of globalisation and liberalisation, the study of migration has become one of the most dynamic aspects of human beings. Nowadays, the process of human migration is analysed in a broader perspective. The migration phenomenon cannot be understood without analysing the dynamics and interplay of economic, demographic, social, and socio-psychological and many other factors. The migrated population put forth many socio-economic implications for the society. Agriculturally, Punjab is the most advanced state, particularly after the implementation of green revolution technology. It generated higher employment opportunities with higher wage rates for the labourers than any other state in India. That is why there has been rapid migration from different states to Punjab. This migration has many socio-economic implications for the rural society in Punjab which need to be studied periodically so as to develop rational policy formulations for the development of the state.

SALIENT FINDINGS OF THE STUDY

SOCIO-ECONOMIC BACKGROUND OF THE MIGRANT AGRICULTURAL LABOURERS

The socio-economic background of migrant agricultural labourers made an important impact on the labour supply curve, labour productivity status and assimilation with locals. The state-wise classification of migrant agricultural labourers shows that majority of the migrants, *i.e.* 60.80 per cent belonged to Bihar followed by 18.52 per cent from Uttar Pradesh, 11.11 per cent from Jharkhand, 5.86 per cent from Nepal and 1.85 per cent each from Bengal and other states of India. The obvious reason for migration may be poverty and lack of employment opportunities in their native states.

Majority of the migratory agricultural labourers, *i.e.* 74.07 per cent belong to the age group of 15-35 years, which is the most labour productive age group. Out of this, 47.53 per cent of them fall in the age group of 15-20 years which is the age of schooling. It is a matter of concern that about 23 per cent of the migrant agricultural labourers were less than 15 years of age. There were only about 2.50 per cent of the migrant agricultural labourers who were above the age of 35 years. It reveals that the younger migratory labourers attract the labour market more than the older ones due to the level of labour productivity while the older people would be a better option to stay at the native place back home to look after the family affairs. The average age of the migrant agricultural labourers in Punjab was found to be 18.63 years. Among the local agricultural labourers, none was found to be below the age of 15 years, while 20.45 per cent of them were above the age of 50 years. The mean age of the migratory labourers was found to be significantly lower than that of the local agricultural labourers. It leads us to say that the migratory labourers have to do work for their livelihood and to support their families in a much younger age. They have to work hard in the fields at an age when they are expected to have books in their hands for study.

It is a matter of pity that about three-fourths (72.54 per cent) of the migratory agricultural labourers were illiterate and only 1.54 per cent of them were matriculates. No one was reported to be above matric. The mean score worked out by assigning the weight zero to illiterate, one to primary, two to middle and three to matric, comes out to be only 1.58 for the state as a whole. Among the local agricultural labourers, 55.01 per cent were illiterate while 1.49 per cent of them were matriculates. A comparison between these two categories shows that the local agricultural labourers were somehow more educated than the migratory agricultural labourers as the mean score of education among the local agricultural labourers came to be 2.64 for the state as a whole. But it is pertinent to say that labourers, either migratory or local, have to abandon their studies in search of employment amidst poverty.

As much as 68.21 per cent of the migratory agricultural labourers were married. Out of this only 17.65 per cent used to reside with their spouses. The remaining bulk proportion, *i.e.* 82.35 per cent of them could not enjoy the company of their life-partners due to high cost of living in Punjab and to take care of children and parents there at native village. The average number of children among the married migratory agricultural labourers was found to be 1.61.However; the average number of children among the married local agricultural labourers was 3.03. The average number of children was significantly higher among the local labourers as compared to that among the migratory agricultural labourers. The lesser number of children among the migratory agricultural labourers seems obviously due to their separation from their wives under the pressure of poverty.

Majority of the migratory agricultural labourers *i.e.* 58.64 per cent belonged to the scheduled castes followed by 31.17 per cent from the backward classes. It is revealing that as many as 10.19 per cent of the migratory agricultural labourers belonged to the general upper castes in the society. This shows that poverty and unemployment forced the agricultural labourers from all the castes to migrate to Punjab for their livelihood. However, the data highlighted that none among the local agricultural labourers was reported to be from the general (upper) castes, while a vast majority of the local agricultural labourers, *i.e.* 94.05 per cent belonged to the scheduled castes. In Punjab, generally, the backward castes have adopted parental self-employment pattern such as construction, repairing of farm implements and tools, tailoring and weaving, pottery etc. However, some people from the backward castes who could not survive themselves in these self-employment occupations were forced to join the rank of the farm labour force.

It is not feasible for every migrant agricultural labourer to live in an independent house or construct his own house for want of surplus income. Therefore, the migratory agricultural labourers, by and large, live jointly in the groups in accommodation provided either by the farmers at their tube-well rooms at farmhouses or in village community places such as *dharamshala*, temple, etc. Thus, the housing conditions of the migratory labourers in Punjab cannot be compared with those of the local agricultural labourers in Punjab because the local agricultural labourers, generally, own their houses in whatsoever condition these may be.

The provisions relating to housing, entertainment, information technology, conveyance, etc. among the migratory and the local agricultural labourers showed that labourers, in general, have insufficient facilities but the migratory labourers are deprived of these facilities to a significantly larger extent as compared to the local agricultural labourers. It is disturbing to note that for 7.41 per cent of the migratory labourers and 2.60 per cent of the local agricultural labourers wells are the only source of drinking water. Such water is mostly contaminated and always poses a danger to the health of the labourers. The analysis also shows that majority of the labourers belonging to both the categories are still deprived of the most common entertainment devices due to their low level of income.

The data revealed that about 55 per cent of the migratory agricultural labourers were under debt. Most of them, i.e. 96.63 per cent had taken loans from the money-lenders and landlords of their native state. The non-repayment of debt may be one of the major reasons to migrate to Punjab to earn and repay the debt. The highest proportion, *i.e.* 32.58 per cent of the indebted labourers had taken loan for daily consumption needs, while only 10.67 per cent and 5.06 per cent of them had been taken loan for production and educational purposes respectively. As far as the local agricultural labourers are concerned, 64.31 per cent of them were found to be under debt. Out of the indebted local agricultural labourers, as high as 71.68 per cent take loan from landlords, followed by 24.86 per cent from money-lenders. This shows that the landlords emerged as the major source of obtaining loan by the migratory as well as the local agricultural labourers. By advancing loan at exorbitant rate of interest to the farm labourers, the landlords used this tool for dictating illogical and suppressive terms and conditions on labourers, even up to the extent of using them as bonded labour in some cases. In case of the local agricultural labourers, only 28.90 per cent of the indebted labourers took loan for starting a work project, while the remaining vast majority took loan for social and religious ceremonies like marriages, deaths and other social obligations. Thus, it can be said that as the loans taken by the labourers are mainly used for unproductive purposes, so it becomes quite difficult for them to repay the same. Consequently, the labourers are caught in a vicious cycle of debt, poverty and oppression throughout their life.

DETERMINANTS, TRENDS AND FACTORS ASSOCIATED WITH MIGRATION

With the advent of green revolution, though the agriculture became highly mechanized yet some specific agronomic operations made it labour-intensive too. The labour-intensive operations such as transplantation, harvesting and chemical spraying, etc. highlighted the need of more farm labourers which may be ready to work at lower wage rate. This situation prepares the ground for the migrants to come to Punjab and work on farms.

Poverty emerged as the most important factor of migration among the migrant agricultural labourers. The second major reason for migration was the higher wages in Punjab, followed by the reasons like repayment of debt and unemployment. There were some other reasons also which motivated the labourers to migrate to Punjab, but their extent was not of much consideration. These reasons include crime in the native state, corruption, caste domination and exploitation.

The highest proportion of the migratory agricultural labourers (41.36 per cent) came to Punjab at the instance of their friends, followed by 25.93 per cent at the instance of their relatives, 15.74 per cent on their own, and 13.27 per cent on the advice of their parents. Only 3.09 per cent of the migrant agricultural labourers came to Punjab through agents, whereas 0.93 per cent of them came here through some other sources, such as contractors, truck drivers and others who reported them about accessibility of agricultural employment opportunities and higher wage rates in Punjab.

None of the migrant agricultural labourers preferred to travel by bus for while coming to Punjab. The data brings out that about 96 per cent of the migratory agricultural labourers used to come to Punjab through rail. This may be due to the reasons like low fare and heavy capacity to travel together in large numbers and keeping in view the level of security in the rail as compared to other means of transportation. As reported by the migratory labourers, sometimes certain railway officials create hardships for them. Keeping in view the extraordinary rush in the trains, the railway officials force them to travel on the roof of the railway coaches and always put their lives in danger. Sometimes, mishaps also occur especially when after a long journey the labourers feel tired and fall asleep on the roof. This attitude of the railway officials towards migrants needs to be curbed on humanitarian grounds. In certain cases, under the grab of security checking, the police personnel searched their belongings such as bags, trunks, pockets etc. and snatched their valuable articles as well as hard earned money from them which were meant for their family members living in their native villages. Some of them also reported that their resistance resulted in physical torture and even a threat to implicate them in false cases of different kinds. Their fellow friends tried to snatch their valuables and cash after assaulting them physically, while similar problems created by other passengers were also reported.

WAGE STRUCTURE OF MIGRANT AND LOCAL AGRICULTURAL LABOURERS IN THE AGRICULTURAL SECTOR OF PUNJAB

There are different patterns of labour employment in agriculture such as part time, daily wage basis and yearly/ seasonal contractual basis. The highest proportion *i.e.* 45.37 per cent of the migratory agricultural labourers worked on farms on daily wage basis followed by 33.33 per cent who worked on the operation-specific contract basis while only 21.30 per cent of them worked on yearly or *rabi/kharif* seasonal contract basis. It is worth-mentioning here that during the peak period of work-load, *i.e.* transplanting of paddy, harvesting and threshing of paddy and wheat, the daily wage basis labourers also preferred to work on contract basis. While the highest proportion of the local agricultural labourers, *i.e.* 41.27 per cent worked on yearly/seasonal contract basis followed by 34.94 per cent and 23.79 per cent who worked on daily wages and operation-specific contract basis respectively. The incidence of yearly/seasonal contract work pattern was significantly higher among the local agricultural labourers as compared to the migrant agricultural labourers. This may be due to age-old relations of the farmers with the local agricultural labourers and availability of all the family members to work on the farm as well as in the household work.

Majority of the migrant agricultural labourers *i.e.* 62.97 per cent had to work for 10 hours a day, followed by 33.33 per cent who worked for 12 hours a day. There were only 3.70 per cent of them who worked for a specified length of 8 hours a day. Similarly, 51.67 per cent of the local agricultural labourers had to work for 10 hours a day. Only 7.07 per cent of them worked for 12 hours a day while 41.26 per cent of them worked for 8 hours a day. The average length of working day for the migratory agricultural labourers came to be 10.59 hours. The corresponding length of working day for the local agricultural labourers worked out to be 9.32 hours in the state. A migrant agricultural labourer had to work for 1.27 hours more than a local agricultural labourer. This depicted the inverse relationship between length of working day and wage rate. The migrant agricultural labourers got lower rate for higher work while the local agricultural labourers got higher wage rate for less work. This is because of easy availability of labourers out of the increasing unemployed reserve army of labourers.

The wage rates vary with the quantum of work load. During the peak period a migratory agricultural labourer got Rs. 79.43 on an average per day while the same for a local agricultural labourer was Rs. 100.40 per day. A migrant agricultural labourer got Rs. 20.97 per day less than a local labourer. During the lean period of work load, the wage rate came down. For the migratory agricultural labourers, it slashed down from Rs. 79.43 during the peak period to Rs. 55.49 during the lean period showing a decline of Rs. 23.94 per day. In case of the local agricultural labourers, the wage rate slashed down from Rs. 100.40 during the peak period to

Rs. 75.55 during the lean period showing a cut of Rs. 24.85 per day in the state as a whole. This shows that the migrant agricultural labourers got ready to work at lower wage rates in Punjab as these are still higher than those of their native places. But competition resulted in further lowering down the wage rates in the wake of ever-increasing unemployment. The average annual earnings of the migrant agricultural labourers came to be Rs. 17118.75, while those of the local agricultural labourers were Rs. 20156.71 showing a significant difference of Rs. 3037.96 per year.

As many as 90.74 per cent of the migratory agricultural labourers had to work extra while this proportion was significantly low in the case of the local agricultural labourers, *i.e.* 65.06 per cent. The dark side of the picture emerged when 99.32 per cent and 98.98 per cent of the local and migrant agricultural labourers respectively reported that they were never paid by the farmers for the extra work. This must have resulted in further bringing down the wage rates on man-day equivalent basis. It means the labourers had to work beyond the specified length of 8 hours a day without any extra payment. Majority of the migrant agricultural labourers, *i.e.* 64.51 per cent faced discrimination in working hours as they were forced to do work for a longer duration than their local counterparts in Punjab. Apart from the discrimination against the migrant agricultural labourers regarding working hours, they were not even given wages equal to the local agricultural labourers. Only 30.25 per cent of migrant agricultural labourers were given wages equal to the local agricultural labourers, whereas the remaining 69.75 per cent had been discriminated in this regard. The major reasons for discrimination against the migrant agricultural labourers regarding wages appeared to be uncertainty of employment (87.17 per cent), and pressure of daily consumption needs (80.53 per cent). The migrant agricultural labourers feared to face unemployment if they refuse to do work at low wage rates at the present place. It seems quite difficult and disturbing to settle at another place in Punjab as the factor of uncertainty of employment always looms large on the minds of the migrant agricultural labourers. So, they are compelled to accept work at lower wage rates as compared to their local counterparts. It was observed that as many as 65.43 per cent of the migrant agricultural labourers showed their satisfaction over the time of payment of wages to them. But it is a matter of great concern that more than one-third of them were not paid their wage well in time or at the time of their need. As many as 16.25 per cent of the migrant agricultural labourers reported that the farmers refused to pay them the wages after the completion of the job. It is disturbing to highlight that the migrant agricultural labourers were even abused and manhandled at the time when they demanded their wages from the farmers. The occurence of such incidents to the extent of 17.59 per cent in Punjab is quite considerable.

A vast majority of the local agricultural labourers, *i.e.* 97.77 per cent viewed that the influx of migrant agricultural labourers had an adverse effect on their employment opportunities. They considered the migrant agricultural labourers to be their competitors in narrowing down the farm employment opportunities (56.88 per cent) and also depressing the wage rates (77.70 per cent). Though there was no open manifestation of this in the form of any dispute or confrontation between the local and migrant agricultural labourers, yet the local labourers were having a bitter feeling against them as their presence adversely affected the employment opportunities and wage rates.

SOCIO-CULTURAL CHANGES IN THE MIGRANT AGRICULTURAL LABOURERS

Migration, being an independent human activity, is considered to be a good indicator of socio-cultural change in a country like India comprising different castes, cultures, languages and religions. The migrant and local agricultural labourers differ in many aspects such as language, mother tongue, complexion, food habits, etc. But migration offers a number of chances to change and adopt new ways and means in life, which ultimately bring qualitative changes in terms of socio-cultural and economic conditions. The migration of labourers from various states of India to Punjab in the agricultural sector caused socio-cultural and economic changes in them.

It was found that majority of the migrant agricultural labourers, *i.e.* 66.36 per cent were called not by their actual names but by the term convenient to the locals such as *bhaiya*, Ramu, Shamu, etc. Though, this is a change in the migrants' cultural aspect but the change is not favourable because one should be called with respect by one's actual name. As high as 77.16 per cent of the migrant agricultural labourers reported change in their consumption pattern. In the state as a whole, 76.00 per cent of those, who reported change in their consumption pattern, took the change as 'good', while 23.60 per cent could not give any response to the quality of change. Only 0.40 per cent of them reported that change in consumption pattern was bad. The overall score of quality of change came to be 75.60 per cent, which pointed towards a good change in the consumption pattern.

As many as 18.83 per cent of the migratory agricultural labourers learnt to speak Punjabi frequently. The migrant agricultural labourers used both Punjabi and Hindi for conversation with the locals. It should be noted that majority of the migrant agricultural labourers belonged to the Hindi speaking or some local dialect areas, but in Punjab, they learnt to speak Punjabi for conversation with the local people.

All the migrant agricultural labourers in all the districts under study used to take bath daily during summer season. But during winter season, only 15.43 per cent of them used to take bath daily. Only 14.81 per cent of the migratory agricultural labourers used to wash clothes daily, while majority of them, *i.e.* 53.70 per cent used to wash clothes after a gap of 2-4 days.

A significant majority of the migrant agricultural labourers, *i.e.* 57.10 per cent used to sleep on the cots as compared to the remaining 42.90 per cent who had no cot and used to sleep on the floor. Majority of the migrant agricultural labourers, *i.e.* 57.72 per cent, were having quilts for sleeping during the winter nights, while the remaining 42.28 per cent were having only the blankets.

As high as 80.25 per cent of the migrant agricultural labourers used to have medical treatment from the government dispensary or Primary Health Centre located in their village, followed by 17.28 per cent who got medical treatment from the quacks. Only 2.47 per cent of them used to go to *hakims* for medical treatment. But it is a matter of concern that the migrant agricultural labourers are not attended properly at the dispensaries or Primary Health Centres As high as 61.15 per cent of the migrant agricultural labourers, who used to have medical treatment from the government dispensaries, reported that they were misbehaved (84.28 per cent) by the dispensary staff and no medicine was given to them (27.67 per cent). The study brings out that the behaviour of the dispensary staff towards the migrant agricultural labourers is never good which ought to be discouraged. The unhygienic bathing and washing patterns, and lack of proper and adequate medical facilities expose the migrants to infectious diseases such as malaria, hepatitis, typhoid and respiratory problems. These are the basic factors which led to morbidity among the migrant agricultural labourers.

The migrant agricultural labourers preferred to deposit their savings with the farmers, while the local agricultural labourers preferred the banks and post offices for the purpose. Due to a relatively higher standard of living of Punjabis, majority of the local labourers failed to save at all. About 91 per cent of the migratory agricultural labourers sent their savings to their families living in their native village.

However, the remaining 9 per cent migrant agricultural labourers kept their savings with them as their families were either staying with them in Punjab or they were still unmarried. Almost 95 per cent of the families of migrant agricultural labourers living in their native village spent the remittances to fulfil their daily consumption needs. The second major purpose of remittances appeared to be the repayment of debt taken from landlords and/or money-lenders (38.10 per cent). Not even a single was able to use such remittances for business investments. Thus, the remittances were mainly used for unproductive purposes such as daily consumption needs, house construction, marriage of the children and repayment of loan.

Therefore, the socio-cultural matrix among the migratory agricultural labourers underwent a significant change over the period of time. They have adopted the convenient names, local food habits by replacing rice with wheat and maize, Punjabi language, getting medical services from the government dispensaries, etc.

ASSIMILATION AMONG THE MIGRANTS, FARMERS AND LOCAL AGRICULTURAL LABOURERS

Assimilation is a continuous process in a society, and it is directly related to the level of development. The commercialisation of agriculture in India has made the process of interaction highly rapid. Since the advent of green revolution and advancement in technology in Punjab agriculture, the labourers from backward states of India have migrated to Punjab in search of higher earnings, where they have interactions with the locals.

Majority of the migrant agricultural labourers, *i.e.* 55.25 per cent never participated in social gatherings arranged by the locals. These social gatherings include bhog ceremonies, marriage functions, etc. There were 2.47 per cent of them who used to participate regularly in the social gatherings while about 34 per cent participated in the social gatherings occasionally. The overall score of participation in social gatherings was found to be 0.58 out of maximum score of 3 which became only 19.33 per cent. This shows that the extent of participation of the migratory agricultural labourers in the social gatherings organised by the locals was extremely low. The extent of participation of the migratory agricultural labourers in local festivals such as *Diwali, Dussehra, Lohri, Baisakhi, Gurpurbs,* etc. and fairs like as sports, religious and cultural fairs, etc. came to be 23.33 per cent. On the other hand, only 3 out of 269, *i.e.* 1.12 per cent of the local agricultural labourers participated in the social functions arranged by the migrant agricultural labourers. This shows that the social assimilation between the migrant and local agricultural labourers prevails at a very low level. A vast majority of the farmers, *i.e.* 81.25 per cent had employed migrant agricultural labourers on their farms in Punjab. In response to the question whether any difficulty was faced by the farmers while conversing with the migrant agricultural labourers, only 1.92 per cent of them responded that they really faced such a difficulty. This problem may have arisen in those cases only where the migrants were new to the place that they could not understand the language spoken by the farmers and vice-versa. The analysis further revealed that only 19.23 per cent of the farmers used to invite the migrant agricultural labourers on social gatherings organised by them, in spite of the fact that almost 100 per cent of the farmers provided accommodation to them. As many as 23.08 per cent of the farmers used to offer liquor to the migrant agricultural labourers working on their farms. It was found that 4.49 per cent of the farmers forced the migrant agricultural labourers to cast illegal or bogus votes in various elections. Further, 89.10 per cent of the farmers reported that the migrant agricultural labourers used to keep their savings with them, which they (migrants) used to take as and when required.

As high as 76.54 per cent of the migrant agricultural labourers were found to be drug addicts, out of which about 70 per cent of them started taking to drugs at their native villages whereas the remaining 30 per cent started to take drugs at the place of their migration. As high as 77.02 per cent of the addicted migrant agricultural labourers used to share drugs with the local agricultural labourers. However, this assimilation has got negative implications. Out of 81 per cent of the local agricultural labourers, who were addicted either to tobacco or *zarda* or both, 82.65 per cent of them reported that they started to take these intoxicants in the company of migrant agricultural labourers, while the remaining 17.35 per cent started to take such intoxicants on their own.

It is established that assimilation between the migrant and local agricultural labourers emerged in the form of sharing drugs and intoxicants which is not a healthy trend for the rural society. However, the reasons behind such a high incidence of taking drugs and intoxicants ought to be explored for further investigations.

Majority of the migrant agricultural labourers, *i.e.* 76.23 per cent reported their relations with locals as 'good', while only 5.56 per cent of them found their relations with the locals as 'bad'. However, the remaining 18.21 per cent of the migrant agricultural labourers could say nothing on this aspect. They took their relations with the locals as neither good nor bad. The relations of the locals with the migrant agricultural labourers as viewed by the locals were at lower level than that viewed by the migrant agricultural labourers with the locals. In this case 54.65 per cent of the local agricultural labourers reported their relations with migrants as 'good' while 11.90 per cent of them termed it as 'bad' and the remaining 33.45 per cent were found neutral in this regard.

It is averred that keeping good relations with the locals may be an objective need of the migrant agricultural labourers for the reason of social security. But on the other hand, the locals bother less than the migrants to have good relations with them because the locals have many other relations in Punjab.

As many as 53.90 per cent of the local agricultural labourers felt good to work with the migrant agricultural labourers, while 11.90 per cent of them had a bad feeling, and the remaining 34.20 per cent were found neutral in this regard. It was due to the obedient nature of the migrants that the highest proportion of the local agricultural labourers felt good to work with them. However, a small proportion of local agricultural labourers who took it bad to work with the migrants considered them to be their competitors in the field of employment.

The most common reason for preferring the migrant agricultural labourers came to be low wages as reported by 83.85 per cent of the farmers followed by migrants' readiness to do extra work (69.27 per cent), their easy availability (57.29 per cent), less problematic (44.79 per cent) and submissive nature (41.67 per cent). Only 7.29 per cent and 4.69 per cent of the farmers reported that they preferred the migrants to the local agricultural labourers as they were more reliable and dependable respectively than the local agricultural labourers. This shows that the farmers preferred the migrant agricultural labourers mainly due to the economic reasons *i.e.* low wages and extra work. The interaction of these factors always leads to the higher net returns for the farmers in Punjab.

The study highlights the fact that the migratory agricultural labourers have to start working at a younger age with a low level of education, leaving their spouses at their native places. They are paid less wages than the local agricultural labourers which also affects their annual earnings adversely. The migrant agricultural labourers have to face discrimination regarding wage rate, payment of wages, length of working day, medical facilities, etc. Their relations with the local agricultural labourers are found to be unsatisfactory. The assimilation among migrants, locals and farmers is also found to be insignificant.

POLICY IMPLICATIONS

Since every socio-politico-economic study posits some policy implications, which can be utilized for the betterment of that section of the society that has provided data base to the study, an effort has been made to spell out policy implications of the present study.

It is observed that the migratory labour has to work at the age of schooling due to poverty. This situation leads towards the curse of illiteracy in the society. Therefore, for the migratory labour, the facilities like free education and better employment opportunities in their native states should be provided. As far as lack of education and employment opportunities are concerned, local labour is no exception.

Though majority of the migrant agricultural labourers belong to the scheduled castes and backward classes, yet about 10 per cent of them belong to general castes, which is not true for the local agricultural labourers. This implies that all sections of the society in the labour exporting states are facing severe economic crisis. Therefore, for the development of these states, government should generate employment opportunities there.

The study shows that more than 80 per cent of the migratory agricultural labourers could not enjoy their marital life due to separation from their wives, who have to live at their native places in order to take care of the parents, children and household assets what so ever they have. This leads to many familial, psychological and physical distortions among the migratory labourers. Such a state of affairs is unavoidable because labourers have chosen this option to serve in the other state to overcome the economic crisis.

About 32 per cent of the migratory agricultural labourers do not own their house even at their native place. Their families have to live in *jhuggis*, where no civic amenity prevails, which leads to severe health hazards. In case of local agricultural labourers, only 22 per cent are having *pucca* houses. Concerned governments should arrange houses for them.

About 63 per cent of the migrant agricultural labourers do not possess any livestock, which hinders their income enhancement. Governments should extend credit free of interest for them in order to make them able to purchase dairy animals, so that they can enhance their meagre income levels.

Majority of the local as well as the migrant agricultural labourers are forced to take loan from non-institutional sources. This implies that they have no access to the institutional loan and have to take loan at higher rate of interest and tough terms of repayment. This adds up to their economic misery. Therefore, governments should arrange institutional loan for them at subsidised or at nominal rate of interest.

The study highlights that most common factor responsible for migration is poverty followed by higher wages than those in their native states. This implies that poverty and low wage rate are inter-related and inter-dependent. Therefore, in order to eradicate poverty to some extent, government should implement the provision of minimum Wages Act, which should be revised periodically keeping in view the cost of standard of living.

The railway police is taken responsible for creating hardships for the migratory labour during their visits to their native villages and back. Thus, the law maintainers are the law breakers. This trend should be curbed strictly.

Majority of the local as well as the migrant agricultural labourers are either part-time labourers or working on daily wage basis. This implies that the sword of uncertainty always hangs over their heads. This vast chunk of the labour force should be provided job security so that they may work more efficiently and consistently.

The migrant agricultural labourers have to work for about 11 hours a day, while the time for local agricultural labourers is 9.32 hours. This implies that law of 8 hours working day is not implemented in the agrarian sector. This should be implemented strictly.

The wage rate of the migratory agricultural labour is significantly lesser than that of the local agricultural labour. This shows that there are two scales to measure for the same work in a society. They should be treated at par with the local agricultural labourers and their wages should be raised according to rising trends of inflation.

Almost all the local as well as the migrant agricultural labourers have to work extra, but they are not paid for it. This is a gross violation of labour laws in the agriculture sector, which should be severely dealt with.

Majority of the migrant agricultural labourers face discrimination during working hours. A civilised society cannot allow such practices. Thus every labourer should be treated honourably.

Majority of the migrant agricultural labourers never attend social gatherings and local festivals/fairs. This implies that their assimilation rate in Punjab is very low. This is reaffirmed by the fact that locals are also not participating in their social functions. If the government and the social organisations arrange national and cultural functions/festivals and a committed effort is made to create communal harmony, national unity and brotherhood, it will create an atmosphere of amity, co-operation and mutual love.

About 83 per cent of the local agricultural labourers are used to take intoxicants in the company of the migrants. This has grave social and health implications for rural Punjab. The tendency to take intoxicants needs to be curbed strictly in order to have a healthy and sound Punjab.

In the light of the above policy implications the state government should have a separate cell for the migratory labourers at the secretariat level to solve any dispute, grievances and problems concerning these labourers.

Glossary

Baisakhi	The harvest festival of Punjab.
Bhaiya	A common name for migrants.
Bidis	A cigarette made by rolling tobacco by hand in a dried leaf from the tendu tree.
Desi	Country made.
Dharamshala	A common living place in a village.
Diwali	A festival that is held in the autumn/fall, celebrated by lighting candles and clay lamps and with fireworks.
Dussehra	A festival to mark the victory of good over evil.
Gurpurb	Sikh festival celebrating a special event associated with the lives of gurus.
Hakim	Local doctor (Quack).
Jat	A race.
Katcha house	Mud house

Kharif	First crop (Rice) after monsoon *i.e.* June to November.
Lohri	Lohri is fundamentally an agricultural festival filled with merry making. It is celebrated in the state of Punjab on 13th of January every year.
Pucca house	A house made of cement and bricks.
Rabi	Second crop (wheat) following *kharif,* usually between December-March.
Siri	A servant on contract for a year or six months to look after the crops of the owner/ farmer.
Tolidar	A head person of the migrants.

Bibliography

Abbi, B.L.; and Singh Kesar (1997), *Post Green Revolution Rural Punjab: A Profile of Economic and Socio-cultural Change (1965-1995)*, Centre for Research in Rural and Industrial Development, Chandigarh, October, pp. 115-16.

Afsar, Rita (2004), "Dynamics of Poverty, Development and Population Mobility: The Bangladesh Case", *Asia Pacific Population Journal*, Vol. 19, No. 2, June, pp. 69-87.

Agarwal, S.N. (1968), "Socio-economic and Demographic Characteristics of Rural Migrants", *Journal of Institute of Economic Research,* Vol. 3 No. 2, July, pp. 39-45.

Amin, S. (1974), *Modern Migration in Western Africa,* Oxford University Press, London, p. 03.

Arora, D.R. and Kumar Balbir (1980), *Agricultural Development and Rural to Rural Labour Migration,* Department of Economics and Sociology, Punjab Agricultural University, Ludhiana, p. 5.

Azam, F. (1991), "Emigration Dynamics in Pakistan", *Regional Development Dialogue,* Vol. 12 No. 3, pp. 729-62.

Ballard, R. (1983), "The Contexts and Consequences of Migration: Jullunder and Mirpur Compared", *New Community* Vol. 11 No. 1 & 2, pp. 117-36.

Bartle, P.F.W. (1971), African *Rural-Urban Migration: A Decision Making Perspective*, Master Thesis, University of Columbia.

Beijer, G., (1967), "The Brain-drain from the Developing Countries", *International Migration*, Vol. 5, Nos. 3 & 4, pp. 228-36.

Bhatia, Ajit Singh (1992), *Rural Urban Migration*, Deep & Deep Publications, New Delhi pp. 79-131.

Bogue, D.J. (1959), "Internal Migration" in O.D. Duncan and P. Houser (eds.), *The Study of Population: An Inventory and Appraisal*, The University of Chicago Press, Chicago, pp. 486-560.

Bose, A. (1965), "Why do People Migrate to Cities", *Yojana*, Vol. 26, pp. 25-26.

Caldwell, John C. (1968), "Determinants of Rural-Urban Migration in Ghana", *Population Studies*, Canberra, Vol. 2, pp. 361-76.

Caldwell, J.C. and Okenjo, C. (1968), "The Population of Tropical Africa", *Longman*, London, pp. 116-30.

Castles, S.; and Kosak G. (1973), *Immigrant Workers and Class Structure in Western Europe*, Oxford University Press, London, pp. 106-16.

Chand, Himal (2005), "Migration in India—An Overview of Recent Evidences", September, *Man and Development*, Vol. XXVII, No. 3, pp. 51-71.

Chand, Krishan (2002), *Migrant Labour and Trade Union Movement in Punjab*, Centre for Research in Rural and Industrial Development, Chandigarh, July, pp. 162-73.

Chandna, R.C. (1986), *A Geography of Population*, Kalyani Publishers, New Delhi, pp. 103-29.

Chatterjee, B.; and. Kundu, A (2001), "Changing Agrarian Structure and the Choice between Local Labour and Migrant Labour", *The Indian Journal of Labour Economics*, Vol. 44, No. 4, pp. 873-80.

Choudhri, Anil Kumar (1998), "Seasonal Migration—A Technique for Self-Preservation by the Rural Poor—A Case Study of West Bengal", *Demography India*, Vol. 27. No. 2, pp. 327-36.

Compton, P. (1969), "Internal Migration and Population Change in Hungary between 1959 and 1965", *Transactions of the Institute of British Geographers*, Vol. 47, pp. 111-30.

Davis, K. (1974), "The Migration of Human Population", *Scientific American*, Vol. 231, No. 3, pp. 92-104.

Deshingkar, Priya (2006), *Internal Migration, Poverty and Development in Asia, Downloaded* from the website www.asia2015conferenceorg/pdhs/Deshingkar.pdf

Eisenstadt, S.N. (1954), *The Absorption of Immigrants: A Comparative Study Based Mainly on the Jewish Community in Palestine and the State of Israel*, London.

Fei, J.C.H.; and Ranis, G. (1953), "Innovation, Capital Accumulation and Economic Development", *American Economic Review*, Vol. 53, pp. 283-312.

Foot, D.K.; and Milne W.J. (1984), "Net Migration Estimation in an Extended Multiregional Gravity Model", *Journal of Regional Science*, pp. 119-34.

Gill, Indermit (1983), "Migrant Labour: A Mirror Survey of Jalandhar and East Champaran", *Economic and Political Weekly*, June, pp. 961-64.

Gill, Sucha Singh, (1980), Migrant *Labour in Rural Punjab: A Project Report* Punjabi University, Patiala, pp. 116-27.

Gill, Sucha Singh, (1982), "Migratory Labour in Punjab Agriculture: A Study of its Implications for Agricultural Labour", *Economic Analyst*, Vol., No. 2, December, p. 120.

Gosal, G.S. (1961), "International Migration in India—A Regional Analysis", The *Indian Geographical Journal* Vol. 36, No. 3, July-September, pp. 106-21.

Gosal, G.S. and Krishan, G. (1975), "Patterns of Internal Migration in India", *in L.A. Kosinski and R.M. Prothero (eds.), People on the Move*, Methuen and Co. Ltd., London, pp. 193-206.

Grewal, S.S.; and Sidhu, M.S. (1984) *A Study on Migrant Agricultural Labour in Punjab*, Department of Economics and Sociology, Punjab Agricultural University, Ludhiana, pp. 45-49.

Gould, W.T.S. and Prothero, R.M. (1975), "Space and Time in African Population Mobility" in *People on the Move*, Methuen and Co. Ltd., London, pp. 39-50.

Gupta, A.K. (1986), *Sociological Implications of Rural to Rural Migration: A Case Study of Rural In-migrants in Punjab*, Ph.D. Thesis, Punjab Agriculture University, Ludhiana, September, pp. 126-36.

Gupta, A.K.; Arora, D.R.; Aggarwal, B.K. (1988), "Sociological Analysis of Migration of Agricultural Labourers from Eastern to North Western Region of India", *Indian Journal of Industrial Relations*, Vol. 23, No. 4, April, pp. 429-45.

Gupta, B. Das and Laishly R. (1975), "Migration from Villages: An Indian Case Study", *Economic and Political Weekly*, Annual Number, pp. 23-34.

Gupta I. and Mitra, A.(2002), "Rural Migrants and Labour Segmentation : Micro Level Evidence from Delhi Slums", *Economic and Political Weekly*, January, pp. 163-68.

Gupta, M.P. and Sharma, S. (2003), "Economic Contributions of In-migrants in Korba City, India", *Annals of the National Association of Geographers*, India, Vol. XXIII, No. 1, June, pp. 46-57.

Haan, Arjen de, (2000) "Livelihoods and Poverty: The Role of Migration—A Critical Review of Migration Literature", *The Journal of Development Studies*, Vol. 36, No. 2.

Hamsaleelavathy, V. (1970), Migration *Differentials in the Metropolitan Cities in India*, Ph.D. Thesis, University of Bombay, pp. 21-30.

Jones, H.R. (1981), A *Geography of Population*, Harper and Row Publishers, London, pp. 201-55.

Joseph, G. (1975), "A Markov Analysis of Age/Sex differences in Inter-regional Migration in Great Britain", *Regional Studies*, Vol. 9, pp. 69-78.

Joshi, Y.G. and Verma, D.K. (2004), *In Search of Livelihood: Labour Migration from Chattisgarh*, Manak Publications Pvt. Ltd., New Delhi, pp. 137-46.

Kamble, N.D. (1983), *Labour Migration in Indian States*, Ashish Publishing House, New Delhi, pp. 1-2.

Kaur, Gurinder (2004), "Rural-Rural Male Migration in Punjab 1991", *Geographical Review of India* Vol. 66, No. 2, June, pp. 179-93.

Kaur, Gurinderjit (1999), Migratory *Labour in Punjab Agriculture*, Ph.D. Thesis, Department of Economics, Punjabi University, Patiala, July, p. 45.

Kaur, Gurinderjit (1999), *Migratory Labour in Punjab Agriculture*, Ph.D. Thesis, Department of Economics, Punjabi University, Patiala, July, pp. 190-205.

Khairkar, V.P. (2003), "Factors Affecting Volume of Migration to Pune City", *Geographical Review of India*, Vol. 65, No. 1, March, pp. 23-33.

Kothari, D.K.,(1980), *Patterns of Rural-Urban Migration—A Case Study of Four Villages in Rajasthan, (India)*, Australian National University, Canberra, Ph.D. Thesis, p. 41.

Kulischer, E.M.; and Price, D.O. (1963), "Migration", Encyclopaedia Britannica, p. 463.

Kumar, A and N. Sharma, (1979), "Bihar's Population on Move: Issues on Inter-district Migration", in Sinha, V.N.P. and Mandal R.B. (eds.), *Dimensions in Geography*, Associated Book Agency, Patna.

Ladinsky, J. (1967), "The Geographical Mobility of Professional and Technical Manpower", *Journal of Human Resources*, Vo1. 2, pp. 475-94.

Lee, Everett S. (1966), "A Theory of Migration", *Demography*, Vol. 3, No. 1, pp. 47-57 & 288-97.

Lee, Everett S.(1970),"A Theory of Migration", *in Population Geography—A Reader*, ed. by G.J. Demko and others, McGraw-Hill Book Co., New York, p. 290.

Lewis, W.A. (1954), *Economic Development with Unlimited Supplies of Labour*, The Manchester School of Economics and Social Studies, Vol. 22, pp. 139-91.

Mahesh, R (2004), "Labour Mobility and Paradox of Rural Unemployment—Farm Labour Shortage (A Micro Level Study)", *The Indian Journal of Labour Economics*, Vol. 47, No. 1, January-March, pp.115-33.

Mahmood, Zafar (1991), "Emigration and Wages in an Open Economy: Some Evidence from Pakistan, *The Pakistan Development Review*, Vol. 30, No. 3, pp. 243-62.

Mangalam, J.J (1968), *Human Migration", A Guide to Migration Literature in English*, 1955-1962, Lexington, University of Kentucky Press.

Mehta, G.S. (2003), *Non-Farm Economy and Rural Development*, Anmol Publications, New Delhi, pp. 284-85.

Mehta, S. (1971), "Patterns of Migration in the Bist-Doab, 1951-61", Panjab *University Research Bulletin (Arts)*, Panjab University, Chandigarh, pp. 17-33.

Mittar, Vishwa (1984), Growth of Informal Sector in Punjab's Urban Economy: A Case Study of Patiala District, Ph.D. Thesis, Punjabi University, Patiala, pp. 3-10.

Moore, R. (1977), *Migrants and Class Structure of Western Europe*, George Allen and Unwin Ltd., London, pp. 137-49.

Mukherjee, S. (2001), "Low Quality Migration in India: The Phenomenon of Distressed Migration and Acute Urban Decay", 24th IUSSP Conference, Salvador, Brazil, August, Downloaded from the website http//www.iussp.org/brazi/2001/s80/s8004mukherjee;pdf.

Nair,P.R.G.(1986), "India", in Godfrey Gunatilleke (ed.),Migration of Asian Labourers to the Arab World, Tokyo, The UN University, p. 74.

Namasivayam, N.; and Kumar, Vijay S. (2004), "Socio-economic Factors influencing Migration of Labour with special reference to Melur Taluk, Tamil Nadu: A Case Study", Downloaded from the website http://www.kli.re.kr./iira2004/pro/ papers/namasivianopdf.

Oberoi, A.S.; and Singh, H.K. Manmohan (1981), "Migration, Employment and Urban Labour Market—A Case Study of Ludhiana in the Indian Punjab", Population and Labour Policies Programme, Working Paper No. 113, Geneva, ILO, pp. 509-10.

Oberoi, A.S.; and Singh, H.K. Manmohan(1983) *Causes and Consequences of Internal Migration; A Study in the Indian Punjab*, Oxford University Press, New Delhi, pp. 399-416.

Odaman, O.M. (1988), "Migration and Rural Development: An Empirical Investigation of Migrants", Participation in Rural Community Development Projects in Nigeria; *Demography India*, Vol. 18, No. 1 & 2, pp. 191-99.

Paris, T. Singh; A. Luis, J.; and Hussain, M. (2005), "Labour Out-Migration, Likelihood of Rice Farming Household and Women Left Behind: A Case Study of Eastern Uttar Pradesh", *Economic and Political Weekly*, June 18, pp. 2522-2529.

Paul, R.R. (1989), *Rural-Urban Migration in Punjab,* Himalaya Publishing House, New Delhi, pp. 174-82.

Peterson, W. (1968), "Migration; Social Aspects", *International Encyclopaedia of Social Sciences,* p. 10.

Pooley, C. (1979), "Residential Mobility in Victorian City", Institute *of British Geographers,* Vol. 4, pp. 255-77.

Premi, M.K. (1976), Out-Migration Towns: A Study into the Nature, Causes and Consequences of Out-Migration, Report sponsored by *ICSSR,* New Delhi, pp. 1-10.

Premi, M.K.; and Mathur, M.D. (1995), "Emigration Dynamics: The Indian Context", *International Migration* Vol. 33, No. 3 & 4, pp. 627-63.

Pryor, R.J. (1969), "Laws of Migration: The Experience of Malaysia and Other Countries", *Goegraphica,* University of Malaysia Vol. 5 pp. 65-75.

Radhakrishana, R.; Rao, V.M. and Roy, Shoven (2004),"Beyond Quantification of Poverty: Emerging Issues in Poverty Reduction", *Indian Journal of Labour Economics,* Vol. 47, No. 2 April-June, pp. 342-45.

Raju, B.R.K. (1989), *Developmental Migration: A Proecessual Analysis of Inter-State Rural-to Rural Migration,* Concept Publishing Co., N. Delhi.

Rangi, P.S.; Sidhu, M.S.; and Singh, Harjit (2001), "Casualisation of Agricultural Labour in Punjab", *The Indian Journal of Labour Economics,* Vol. 44, No. 4, pp. 964-66.

Ravenstein, E.G.(1889), "The Laws of Migration", *Journal of the Royal Statistical Society,* Vol. 52, pp. 198-99 & 240-305.

Rahman, Anisur (1999), "Indian Labour Migration to West Asia", *Manpower Journal,* Vol. XXXV No. 2, July-September, pp. 87-99.

Rhoda, Richard E. (1979), Development *Activities and Rural-Urban Migration: Is it Possible to keep them down on the Farm?* Agency for International Development, Washington, p. 15.

Rodrigo, C.(1992), "Overseas Migration from Sri Lanka Magnitude, Patterns and Trends", Asian Regional Exchange for New Alternatives, *Asian Exchange* Vol. 8, No. 3 & 4,pp. 41-74.

Rogaly,B.;Biswas,J.; Coppard,D.; Rafique,A.; Rana,K.; and Gupta, S.A. (2001), "Seasonal Migration, Social Change and Migrants' Rights (Lesson from West Bengal)", *Economic and Political Weekly,* December 8, pp. 4547-57.

Rogers, A. (1966), "A Markovian Policy Model of Inter-regional Migration", *Papers of Regional Science Association,* Vol. 17, pp. 205-24.

Saxena, D.P. (1977), Rural-*Urban Migration in India,* Popular Prakashan, Bombay, pp. 50-54.

Shah, N.M. (1994), "An Overview of Present and Future Emigration Dynamics in South Asia", *International Migration* Vol. 32, No. 2, pp. 217-68.

Sharma, S.K. (1989), "Patterns of In-migration in Madhya Pradesh", *Geographical Review of India,* Vo1. 51, No. 3, September, pp. 62-75.

Sharma, A.N. (2005), "Agrarian Relations and Socio-economic Change in Bihar" *Economic and Political Weekly,* March, Vol. XL, No. 10, pp. 967-68.

Sharma, Manmohan (1982), "Impact of Migratory Labour on the Rural Economy of Punjab", *Man and Development*, Vol. IV, No. 3, pp. 66-111.

Siddiquii, T. (2003), "Migration as a Livelihood Strategy for the Poor—The Bangladesh Case", Refugee and Migrating Movements Research Unit (RMMRU), University of Dhaka, Bangladesh, Downloaded from the website: http/ www.eldis.org/static/doc 1683.htau.

Sidhu, M.S.; Rangi, P.S., and Singh, K. (1997), "A Study on the Migrant Agricultural Labour in Punjab, Department of Economics and Sociology, Punjab Agriculture University, Ludhiana, pp. 50-53.

Singh, H.K. Manmohan (1983), "Population Pressure and the Labour Absorbability in Agriculture", *Studies in Punjab Economy*, Punjab School of Economies, GNDU, Amritsar, pp. 402-03.

Singh, Kamaljit (1991), *Internal Migration in a Developing Economy*, National Book Organisation, New Delhi, p. 13.

Singh, Manjit (1995), *Uneven Development in Agriculture and Labour Migration: A Case of Bihar and Punjab*, Print Perfect, Mayapuri, Industrial Area, New Delhi, pp. 33-34.

Singh, Parminder; and Singh, Navsharan G. (1984), "Socio-economic Study of Migrant Farm Labour: A Case Study of Amritsar District in Punjab", P.S.E. *Economic Analyst*, Vol. V, Nos. 1 & 2, pp. 43-49.

Sinha, V.N.P. (1980), "Migration: An Interdisciplinary Topic", *Geographical Review of India*, Vol. 42, No. 2, June, pp. 103-19.

Sivakumar, M.N. (2001), "Selectivity in Rural-Urban Migration: Evidence From Tamil Nadu", *Man and Development*, March pp. 57-68.

Sjaastad, Larry A (1960), "The Costs and Returns of Human Migration", *Journal of Political Economy*, Vol. LXX, No. 5, pp. 80-93.

Skeldon, R. (1977), "The Evolution of Migration Patterns During Urbanisation in Peru", *Geographical Review*, Vol. 67, No. 4, pp. 396-411.

Skeldon, R. (2002), "Migration and Poverty", *Asia-Pacific Population Journal*, December, Vol. 17, No. 4, pp. 67-82.

Smith, T.Lynn (1960), *Fundamentals of Population Study*, Lippincott Co., New York, pp. 417-19.

Sovani, N.V. (1966), *Urbanisation and Urban India*, Asia Publishing House, New York p. 7.

Stouffer, S. (1960), "Intervening Opportunities and Competing Migrants", *Journal of Regional Sciences*, Vol. 2, pp. 1-26.

Stouffer, S. (1940), "Intervening Opportunities: A Theory Relating to Mobility and Distance", *American Sociological Review*, Vol. 5, pp. 845-67.

Subramanian K.P. and C.K. Balasubramaniam (2000), "Migration: Blessing or Burden? A Study of Tamil Nadu and Its Cities", *Urban India*, Vol. XX No. 2, pp. 91-119.

Sundari, S. (2005), "Migration as a Livelihood Strategy", *Economic and Political Weekly*, May-June, pp. 2295-2303.

Tarver, J.D. (1961), "Predicting Migration", *Social Forces*, Vol. 39, pp. 207-14.

Thomas, D.S. (1941), *Social and Economic Aspects of Swedish Population Movements*, McGraw-Hill Book Co. New York, p. 52.

Todaro, M.P. (1969), "A Model of Labour Migration and Urban Unemployment in Less Developed Countries", *American Economic Review*, Vol. 59, No. 1, March, pp. 138-48.

Todaro, M.P.; and Smith, S.C. (2004), *Economic Development*, Pearson Education (Singapore) Pvt. Ltd. India, Delhi, pp. 338-42.

Ward, Antony (1975), "European Capitalism's Reserve Army", *Monthly Review*, Vol. 27, No. 6, November pp. 30-31.

Wolpert, J. (1975), "Behavioural Aspects of the Decision to Migrate" in Emrys Jones (ed.), *Readings in Social Geography*, Oxford University Press, Oxford, pp. 191-99.

Yadava, K.N.S. (1996), *Rural-Urban Migration in India*, Independent Publishing Co., Delhi, pp. 113-15.

Zachariah, K.C.(1964), *A Historical Study of Internal Migration in the Indian Sub-continent, 1901-31*, Asia Publishing House, Mumbai, pp. 1-30 & 369-70.

Zachariah, K.C. (1968), *Migrants in Greater Bombay*, Asia Publishing House, Bombay, pp. 71-76.

Zachariah, K.C.(1969), "Bombay Migration Study—A Pilot Analysis of Migration of an Asian Metropolis", in G. Greese (ed.), *The City in Newly Developed Countries*, Prince Town University, pp. 367-70.

Zachariah, K.C.(1974), "A Note on Internal Migration in India, in Rural-Urban Differences in Southern Asia, Some Aspects and Methods of Analysis",UNESCO Research Centre, on Social and Economic Development in Southern India, Delhi, pp. 70-76.

Zachariah, K.C.; Mathew, E.T.; and. Rajan, S Irudaya (2003), *Dynamics of Migration in Kerala: Dimensions, Differentials and Consequences*, Orient Longman, New Delhi, pp. 20-25 & 460-70.

Zelinsky, Wilbur (1971), "The Hypothesis of the Mobility Transition", *Geographical Review*, Vol. 61, No. 2, pp. 219-50.

Zipf, G.K. (1946),"The $P_{1,}$ P_2/D Hypothesis: On the Intercity Movement of Persons", *American Sociological Review*, Vol. 11, No. 6, pp. 677-85.

Index